Kagaku Kyoshitsu

Memoirs of the Science Department, University of Tokio, Japan

Kagaku Kyoshitsu

Memoirs of the Science Department, University of Tokio, Japan

ISBN/EAN: 9783743362598

Hergestellt in Europa, USA, Kanada, Australien, Japan

Cover: Foto ©ninafisch / pixelio.de

Manufactured and distributed by brebook publishing software (www.brebook.com)

Kagaku Kyoshitsu

Memoirs of the Science Department, University of Tokio, Japan

OKADAIRA SHELL MOUND

AT

HITACHI,

BEING

AN APPENDIX

TO

MEMOIR VOL. I. PART I.

OF THE

SCIENCE DEPARTMENT,

TÔKIÔ DAIGAKU,

(UNIVERSITY OF TÔKIÓ.)

BY

I. IIJIMA, AND C. SASAKI,
STUDENTS OF BIOLOGY.

———•◆•———

PUBLISHED BY TÔKIÔ DAIGAKU,
TÔKIÔ.
2543 (1883).

OKADAIRA SHELL MOUND

AT

HITACHI,

BEING

AN APPENDIX

TO

MEMOIR VOL. I. PART I.

OF THE

SCIENCE DEPARTMENT,

TÔKIÔ DAIGAKU,

(UNIVERSITY OF TÔKIÔ.)

BY

I. IJIMA, AND C. SASAKI,
STUDENTS OF BIOLOGY.

PUBLISHED BY TÔKIO DAIGAKU,

TÔKIÔ.

2542 (1882).

PREFACE.

In the summer of 1879, I visited the province of *Hitachi* which is nearly 30 ri distant from Tokio, in order to collect mollusca in the lake of Kasumigaura. Along the coast, there exist numerous fossil remains of marine shells which show evidence that the lake had once been washed by the sea in past times. Bearing in mind this feature, I carefully examined the southern coast of this lake for shell heaps, and was finally rewarded by discovering three shell mounds on the top of a hill known as *Okadaira*; and afterwards found still other mounds at several places not far from the one previously mentioned, viz. one at *Kihara*, two at *Amimura*, one at *Shimadzu*; and on my return to Tokio, I again met with a single enormously large mound at *Kitakatamura* in *Shimōsa*.

In the winter of the same year in company with Mr. Iijima I again visited the same province in order to make still farther researches in regard to these mounds by the order of Mr. Kato President of Tokio Daigaku.

On this occasion, we found a number of other mounds in the same province already mentioned before, but only one was completely examined, and that was the Okadaira mound which was the largest and richest in ancient remains.

The contents of this paper are mainly confined to the contents of this mound, and one of our objects is to compare its features with those of the Omori Shell mounds, which have been well described and accurately figured by Prof. Edw. S. Morse in the first memoir of Tokio Daigaku.

Our thanks are particularly due to the never failing advice of Prof. Edw. S. Morse.

Our thanks are also due to Mr. M. Nishi for the determination of the nature of the stone implements and to Mr. H. Yoshida on chemical analysis, and lastly we are much indebted to our two sincere friends Mr. O. Taneda, and Mr. M. Kikuchi for their kind assistance in many ways.

To the artists Mr. J. Nomura, Mr. M. Indō, and Mr. K. Watanabe, our thanks are specially due for the fidelity with which they have made the illustrations.

I. IIJIMA.
C. SASAKI.

Tokio Japan
1st Sept. 2542 (1882).

OKADAIRA SHELL MOUND AT HITACHI.

BY

I. IIJIMA AND C. SASAKI.

GENERAL CHARACTERS OF THE OKADAIRA SHELL MOUND.

The Okadaira shell mound lies on the south western side of a hill called Okadaira, and the eastern and western sides of it are already cultivated for plantations. A white appearance due to broken shells which the ground possesses in the vicinity of this hill is due to the remains of former mounds which have been scattered and destroyed by the farmers.

The length of this mound is estimated about eighteen ken (about 33 m.) in length, and sixteen ken (about 29 m.) in width, and its surface is thickly covered with a number of huge trees. The soil covering the mound is about six inches in thickness. The height of this mound varies from a foot to seven feet. The thickness of the deposit which varies from six inches to three feet, is in its deepest parts about six feet.

The mound itself is nearly half a ri from the lake of Kasumigaura on the north-eastern side, and also half a ri distant from a branch of the same lake on the west. And furthermore it is distant about five ri (about 12.5 miles) from the shore of the sea of Kashima (Pacific ocean) of Hitachi.

The evidence that the lake was formerly washed by the ocean is shown by ancient historical records of Hitachi (Hitachi Fûdoki) and also from the presence of fossil remains of marine shells at various exposures along the coast.

SPECIAL CHARACTERS OF THE OKADAIRA DEPOSIT.

The Okadaira Mound does not show any remarkable difference in its features from those of the Omori mounds which are described by Prof. Edw. S. Morse in the first memoir of the science department of the University of Tokio in 2539 (1879). As a general rule, objects obtained from such a deposit in both the American and European Continents agree in their general aspect, but each deposit has its special characteristics.

Prof. Morse who is the first discoverer of a mound of this character in the Empire of Japan has pointed out the following characters in regard to the Omori deposit:—"The Omori deposits are also specialized. First: by the presence of enormous quantities of pottery of many different shapes, and of an almost infinite variety of ornamentation. Second: by great scarcity of stone implements, and the absence of arrow heads, spear points and other pointed implements of stone. Not a single arrow head, flake or chip has been found by the various parties who have been there in the interests of the University; and the combined time spent there, if represented by a single individual, would equal over eighty days work of seven hours each." These peculiarities exactly agree with the Okadaira deposit.

The objects thus far found in the Okadaira mound are enumerated as follows:—

POTTERY.

1. Cooking vessels.
2. Hand vessels.
3. Bowls.
4. Pots.
5. Cups.
6. Fragments of pottery possibly used for sinkers.

STONE.

1. Axes.
2. Celts.
3. Worked pumice.
4. Stone with circular pit-like depressions.

HORN.

1. Handle.
2. Prongs of deer's antlers.

BONE.

1. Os calcis of Deer.

POTTERY.

Many earthern vessels, and fragments of potteries were collected in the Okadaira deposit of Hitachi. The vessels are mainly composed of rough materials, and some of their shapes are extraordinarily curious. The pottery is generally thicker than that of the Omori deposit, and mostly ornamented with various designs, plain or unornamented pottery being comparatively rare.

Knobs are generally of large size, and of diversified form. The dimension of the largest one is 200 mm. in height. (Fig. 1, Pl. IV). This peculiarity in form has never been met with in other deposits, and in most cases, the knobs are large and thick, and perforated with from two to six holes which communicate internally. This remarkable conformation has not been met with in other parts of the empire, and seems to be peculiar to this deposit. In some the knob is simply a slight projection from the rim. In others it forms a twisted loop. In other it either projects outward, or internally from the inner surface of the rim. Still further, some rims are conical or notched or undulating.

The designs are various, but we may be able to classify them generally as follows:—as Prof. Morse has described in the Omori Deposit, "The designs are indifinitely varied; generally areas partially or wholly enclosed by curved lines, the area within or without the lines being cord marked, the other area being smooth" (Omori Mounds Memoir p. 8). In others, the entire outer surface is cord marked though in some an area near the margin is left which is destitute of the cord marks. Others have deep pits or grooves incised, and in others still the surface is entirely destitute of the cord impressions, and others have a little area near the margin which is separated from the cord-marked area below. The cord marks which are impressed on the entire surface of potteries extend as far as their margin. In some cases, potteries are entirely destitute of cord marks.

The margins of the potteries are generally smooth and even, but in some cases they are deeply incised forming a sort of knobbed or undulating appearance.

The common ornamentation is either in curved, spiral, or parallel impressions or lines. In many cases, lines cross each other regularly giving a reticulated appearance to the surface. The parallel lines are unevenly interrupted, or a number of parallel lines are interrupted by a zigzag line, or sometimes a number of zigzag lines are arranged one after the other in regular series.

The entire absence of legs or knobs for the support of the vessel shows in this respect a resemblance to the pottery of the Omori Deposits.

The inner surface of rims is, in some cases, marked with two or more parallel grooves. (Fig. 12, Pl. IX., Fig. 3, 9, Pl. VIII).

One hundred and eighty seven bases more or less broken were collected, of which four are marked with the matting impression, and six with irregular scratched lines, and the rest are smooth. The largest bottom thus far examined is about fourteen centimetres in diameter.

In a few vessels the base is slightly larger in diameter than the wall of the vessel arising from it.

Of thousands of specimens more or less broken, seventeen are sufficiently complete to recognize their entire shape. Some are bowl shaped, or cup-like or pot-like. Ten of the pots are bowl shaped of which one is marked with an exquisite ornamentation on the whole area of the body wall, leaving a smooth space near the bottom. The rim is provided with a single knob perforated near the centre. In this specimen evidences of repair are seen in two small holes which have been bored on the margins of a fracture. (Fig. 1, Pl. 1).

One of the bowls has a narrow bottom, the mouth is triangular in form, and three knobs marked with a circular impression stand respectively on each of its angles. The body wall is smooth, except the upper part of it where two cord marked bands run side by side. (Fig. 7, 8, Pl. I).

Two cup-shaped pots have thick walls, and both have smooth bases, and uneven rims. The one (Fig. 5, Pl. I) is ornamented with incised lines forming rude oval figures. The other (Fig. 1, Pl. II) is plain, and is somewhat cylindrical in form.

Two pots which have a smooth bottom bulge at the upper part of the body wall, and have flaring rims. (Fig. 6, Pl. I., Fig. 6, Pl. II).

The most curious vessel which is nearly complete, measures 300 mm. in height. The lower half of this vessel is cylindrical in form, while the upper half abruptly enlarges in size. The rim is provided with two knobs, and is marked with two grooves on the upper face. The unstable form of this pot leads us to believe that it might have been used for cooking, the narrower and lower portion being buried in the dirt or ashes, and the fire built about it. (Fig. 3, 4, Pl. I).

Of two pots, one (Fig. 2, Pl. II) is nearly round, its bottom is ill-defined, and its body walls are evenly ornamented with cord impressions. The other (Fig. 3, Pl. II) is similar in form and size, but has, besides a mouth, a single small hole, and that part which separates the mouth from this hole is slightly arched so as to form a sort of handle. Its body wall is rough and destitute of any impression. The material of this pot is reddish clay.

The largest vessel which we have already described (Fig. 9, Pl. II) has the lower half of the body wall ornamented with incised lines and its upper half entirely smooth; and on the boundary line between these two different regions, four small knobs occur leaving a similar space between them.

Bases:—Those with matting impressions are comparatively few, and their figures are more or less different in different vessels. (Fig. 5, 7, Pl. II). The majority of bases are smooth.

A single lump of reddish material was found associated with fragments of pots. This material which is determined as Ferric oxide ($Fe_2 O_3$) by our friend Mr. H. Yoshida, seems to have been used as a mixture with the clay of which the red colored pots were made.

A few pieces of pottery rectangular in shape have been rudely formed probably for the purposes of a sinker, the longer axis have each a single notch. (Fig. 3, 4, 5, Pl. X).

A single specimen of the same kind, has a roundish form and a circular hole near the centre. It is most probable that this fragment has also been used as sinkers of fishing nets.

The chief points which may be recognized under a careful examination of thousands of pots and fragments are briefly as follows:—

1st. The potteries are generally thicker than those obtained from other destricts of Japan, and their designs are mostly very ingenious.

2nd. The knobs are abundant in number, their forms exceedingly various, their sizes unusually large. The leading designs of the knobs are the opening of several holes in various styles, as shown in the figures.

3rd. Bottoms are rather numerous. Most of them are smooth though a few are ornamented with matting impressions.

4th. Some vessels are enormous in size, in one case measuring 320 mm. in diameter.

5th. All the pottery is rough and never painted with any sort of pigment.

STONE IMPLEMENTS.

The stone implements collected in the deposite were very few in number, and many were more or less broken, and showed evidences of wear in various ways. Those which are nearly perfect are four adzes and three others. The four entire adzes (Fig. 9, 12, 13, 14, Pl. X) have their edges worn showing that they had been much used. Another implement (Fig. 10, Pl. X) worked out of chlorite schist has both ends broken off, and shows an oval form in section. A specimen (Fig. 11, Pl. X) which is made of a sandstone is somewhat pointed at one end and round at the other. At the rounded end, two little notches are evidently chipped out for the purpose of fastening the stone tightly to a handle by means of a string.

Besides these implements, we have found two worked stones:—the one which is made of pumice nearly oblong in shape, well smoothed at their edges, is moderately flattened, and at a portion near the centre a single round hole occurs which was probably used to pass a string through in order to suspend it. (Fig. 15, Pl. X).

A single drilled stone which is exactly similar in character with that found in the Omori deposit was also found, and thirteen holes are counted on its surface. (Fig. 7, Pl. X).

No hammers, rollers, or mortars were met with such as Prof. Morse discovered lately in the Omori deposits.

It will be observed that as in the Omori and other mounds near Tokio the implements of stone are very rude and few in number.

WORKED HORN AND BONE.

The antlers of deer are abundantly found in the deposits. Most of them (Fig. 2, 3, 4) are roughly cut off, so that their points might be more conveniently used for implements. Another worked antler of deer (Fig. 1, Pl. XI), is well smoothed, the one end is somewhat pointed, and has, at its side three parallel incisions and a single projection below evidently worked out; and the other is much broader, and slightly curved. From this shape, we are inclined to suppose that it might have been used as a hook.

The os calces of deer were also found. They are, in most cases smoothed on their lateral face or at one or both ends. (Fig. 8, Pl. XI).

Three pieces of bone of some mammal not identified are well sharpened to a point. Besides these worked specimens, those found together with potteries are two bones of ox (one is a left humerus, and the other the coössified radius and ulna of the same leg), os calcis of deer, bird's bones, teeth and jaws of deer, a single human bone (left femur), cuttle-fish bones, and hundreds of pieces of the bones of various animals. The human femur is roughly broken off at either end, a comparison with the recent human femur shows no difference in proportions.

Among the deer's antlers, only three pieces have been charred. Among the great quantity of bones found only one bone belonging to man was met with. It is interesting to observe that this bone is rudely broken at both ends, and though it would be unsafe to draw any conclusion from a single example, yet its being broken in precisely the same way as the bones of other mammals might be taken as an indication of cannibalism. And this conclusion would be in accordance with the observations made by Prof. Wyman in the Florida and New England Shell Heaps and of those of Prof. Morse in the Omori and other deposits.

The presence of ox bones in the deposit, are evidently cases of intrusion unless we suppose the wild ox has existed in Japan.

ANCIENT MOLLUSCAN FAUNA OF OKADAIRA DEPOSIT.

Special efforts were made to collect sufficient material, so that a comparison might be made between the recent and ancient mollusks of this region. We failed to accomplish this object owing to the scarcity of the recent shells on the adjacent coast.

The following list enumerates the species of mollusks thus met with in the Okadaira deposit, and as special efforts were made to collect every species in the mound, the list will not probably be much increased by future additions.

The Lamellibranchiates thus far found in the deposit are:—

Arca inflata, Reeve.
Arca subcrenata, Lischke.
Arca granosa, Linné.
Lutraria Nuttali, Conrad.
Mactra veneriformis, Deshayes.
Dosinia Troscheli, Lischke.
Cytherea meretrix, Linné.
Ostrea denslamellosa, Lischke.
Ostrea sp.
Tapes sp.
Tapes sp.

Tellina sp.
Solen sp.
Anomia sp.

The Gasteropoda thus far present in the deposit are:
Eburna Japonica, Lischke.
Lampania multiformis, Lischke.
Potamides fluviatilis, P. et M.
Rapana bezoar, Linné
Turbo granulatus, Gmelin.
Natica Lamarckiana, Duclos.
Cyclina chinensis, Chem.
Purpura sp.
Cyclostoma sp.
Mya arenaria, Linné.

It is interesting to observe the great scarcity of Mya arenaria, a species extremely abundant in the Hokkaidō (Yeso) deposits as well as in the shell mounds of Omori and Tokio.

Only fourteen specimens of Arca granosa were found and these were much smaller in size than those existing in the southern portions of the empire. Among the twelve perfect specimens, the largest measures 33 mm. in height, 44 mm. in length, while the smallest measures respectively 17 mm. to 23 mm. The number of ribs were nineteen which is the average of the number of ribs seen in the Omori mound specimens. It is probable that this was its northern limit at that time.

The most abundant species found in the deposits are Arca inflata, Reeve, Arca subcrenata, Lischke, Mactra veneriformis, Deshayes, and Rapana bezoar, Linné, and the remaining species were few in number of individuals, and more or less broken.

No worked shells were met with. It is worthy of notice however that the specimens of Rapana bezoar, Linné, have almost always an irregular opening in their body whorl, as if it had been made for the more convenient extraction of the animal.

EXPLANATION OF PLATES.

PLATE I.

Fig. 1. 7 mm. thick, diameter across the mouth 205 mm., height 11 mm., bottom smooth. Color blended with black and red. ½ natural size.

Fig. 2. Thickness varies from 11 mm. to 5 mm., diameter across the mouth 160 mm., height 75 mm., bottom smooth. Color reddish with some black patches. ½ natural size.

Fig. 3. 15 mm. thick, diameter across the mouth 250 mm., height 300 mm., bottom (90 mm. in diam.) smooth, blackish above and below, midway reddish. ⅔ natural size.

Fig. 4. Top view of ditto. Margin 11 mm. thick. ⅔ natural size.

Fig. 5. 9 mm. thick, diameter across the mouth 80 mm., height 47 mm., bottom rough, reddish on one side, blackish on the other. ⅔ natural size.

Fig. 6. Thickness varies from 10 mm. to 16 mm., diameter across the mouth 180 mm., height 195 mm., bottom (65 mm. in diam.) reddish and rough; blackish in color, a few interwoven string marks above, and numerous longitudinal impressions below. ⅔ natural size.

Fig. 7. 6 mm. thick, mouth somewhat triangular in shape, height 135 mm., bottom (52 mm. in diam.) rough, blackish in color. Reddish above, blackish below. The upper part is decorated with two bands which are composed of oblique cord marks. ½ natural size.

Fig. 8. Top view of ditto. Margin marked with fine serrations, and a single triangular knob rests obliquely on each angle of the mouth. ½ natural size.

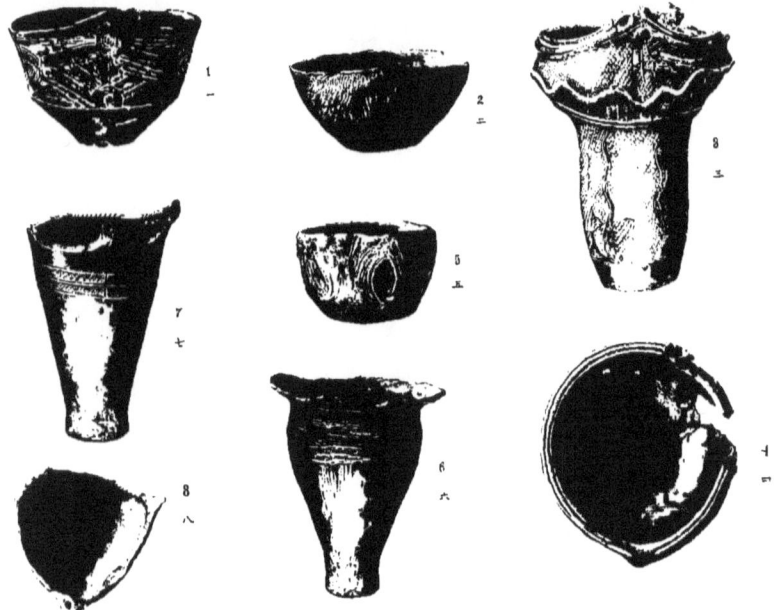

SHELL MOUND of OKADAIRA.

PLATE II.

Fig. 1. Thickness varies from 6 mm. to 8 mm., diameter across the mouth 45 mm., height 49 mm., bottom (48 mm. in diam.) rough and marked with a few deep scratches. Reddish grey. $\frac{2}{3}$ natural size.

Fig. 2. Thickness varies from 6 mm. to 8 mm., height 70 mm., bottom rounded, ornamented with cord impressions except near the margin which is smooth. $\frac{2}{3}$ natural size.

Fig. 3. Thickness varies from 4 mm. to 10 mm., height 70 mm., bottom (60 mm. in diam.) rough. Reddish in color. $\frac{2}{3}$ natural size.

Fig. 4. 9 mm. thick, height 80 mm., bottom smooth. Greyish. $\frac{2}{3}$ natural size.

Fig. 5. 7 mm. thick, bottom (70 mm. in diam.) with mat impressions. Reddish black. $\frac{1}{2}$ natural size.

Fig. 6. 6 to 8 mm. thick, smooth, bottom (70 mm. in diam.) with a few roughly scratched marks. $\frac{1}{2}$ natural size.

Fig. 7. 11 mm. thick, smooth, bottom (95 mm. in diam.) with mat impressions. $\frac{1}{2}$ natural size.

Fig. 8. 8 mm. thick, with cord marks above, and smooth below, bottom (80 mm. in diam.) smooth. $\frac{2}{3}$ natural size.

Fig. 9. 10 to 15 mm. thick, margin smooth, mouth 320 mm. in diameter. The upper portion smooth while the remaining portions are ornamented with lines. $\frac{1}{3}$ natural size.

Fig. 10. 10 to 13 mm. thick, margin smooth 7 mm. thick, height 90 mm., bottom (80 mm. in diam.) smooth. Color reddish black. $\frac{1}{2}$ natural size.

Fig. 11. 10 mm. thick, reddish. $\frac{1}{2}$ natural size.

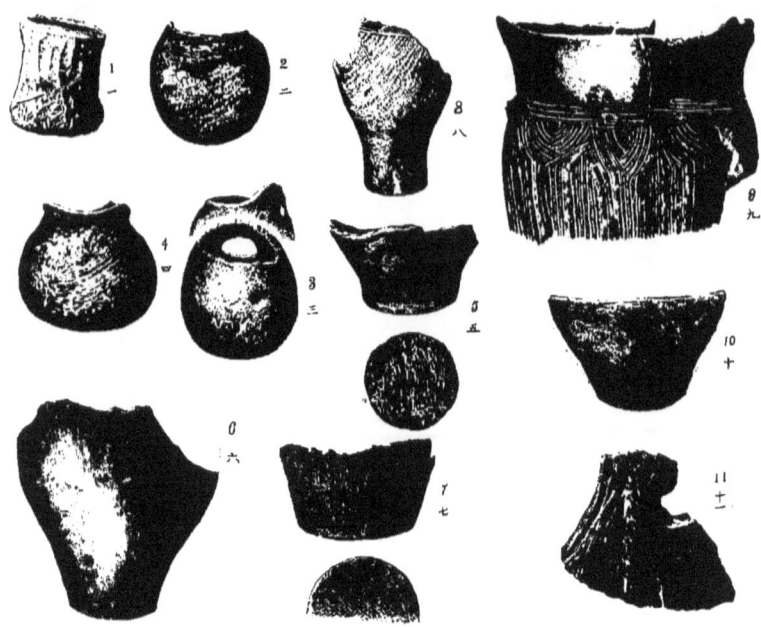

SHELL MOUND OF OKADAIRA.

PLATE III.

Fig. 1. 9 mm. thick, reddish above blackish below. $\frac{2}{3}$ natural size.
Fig. 2. Height 140 mm., breadth 95 mm. Brownish grey in color. $\frac{1}{2}$ natural size.
Fig. 3. Side view of ditto. $\frac{1}{2}$ natural size.
Fig. 4. Inside view of ditto. $\frac{1}{2}$ natural size.
Fig. 5. Height 105 mm. Reddish in color. $\frac{1}{2}$ natural size.
Fig. 6. Inside view of ditto. $\frac{1}{2}$ natural size.
Fig. 7. Reddish grey. $\frac{1}{2}$ natural size.
Fig. 8. Inside view of ditto. $\frac{1}{2}$ natural size.
Fig. 9. Reddish grey. $\frac{1}{2}$ natural size.
      a. inside view.
      b. side view.
Fig. 10. Having seventeen circular pits, (eight in front, three on either side, two behind.) $\frac{1}{2}$ natural size.
Fig. 11. Front view. Reddish black in color. $\frac{1}{2}$ natural size.
Fig. 12. Inside view of ditto. $\frac{1}{2}$ natural size.

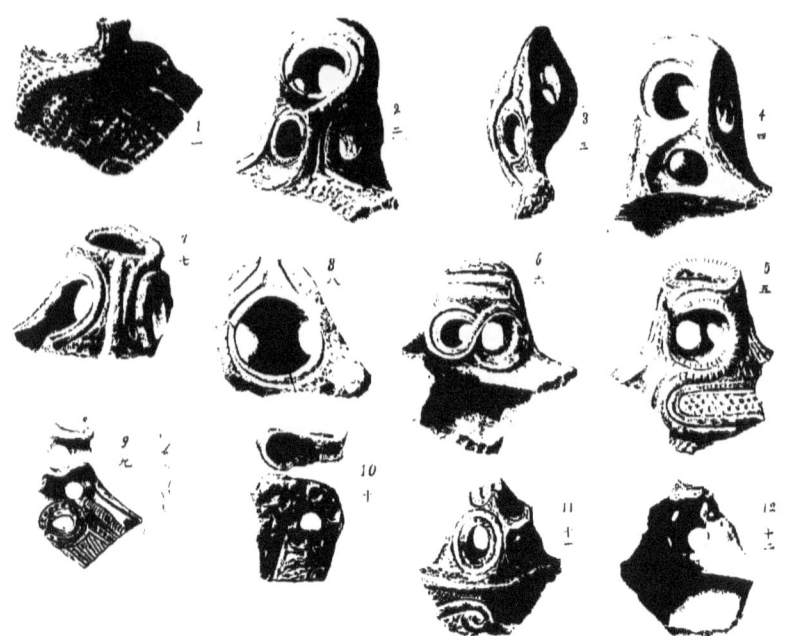

SHELL MOUND OF OKADAIRA.

PLATE IV.

Fig. 1.   Brownish red. ⅕ natural size.
Fig. 2.   Reddish. ½ natural size.
Fig. 3.   Reddish. ½ natural size.
Fig. 4.   Blackish. ¼ natural size.
Fig. 5.   Reddish. ½ natural size.
       a. front view.
       b. side view.
Fig. 6.   Body wall 11 mm. thick, blackish. ½ natural size.
Fig. 7.   Body wall 10 mm. thick, blackish. ½ natural size.
Fig. 8.   Body wall 13 mm. thick, reddish. ½ natural size.

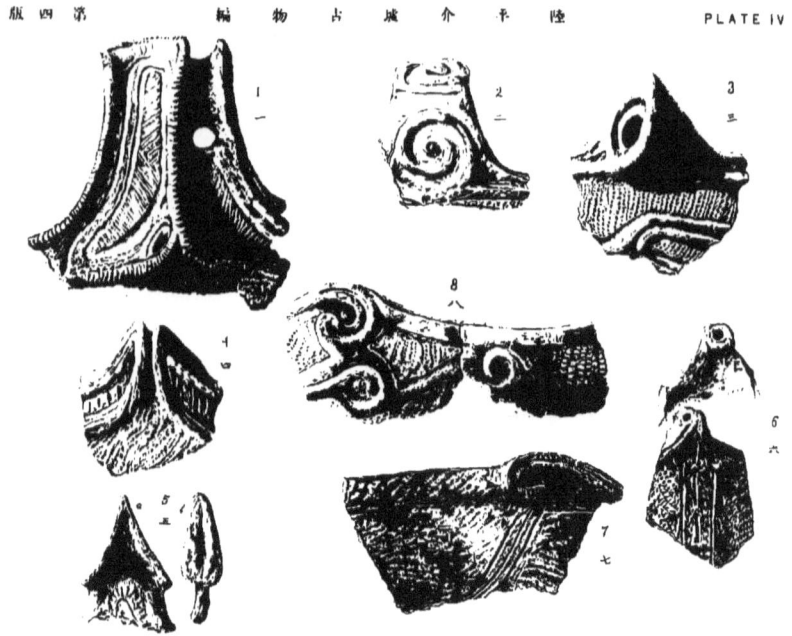

SHELL MOUND of OKADAIRA.

PLATE V.

Fig. 1. Body wall 10 mm. thick, blackish. $\frac{1}{2}$ natural size.
Fig. 2. Body wall 10 mm. thick, blackish above reddish below. $\frac{1}{2}$ natural size.
Fig. 3. Body wall 7 mm. thick, blackish. $\frac{1}{2}$ natural size.
Fig. 4. Body wall 11 mm. thick, blackish. $\frac{1}{2}$ natural size.
Fig. 5. Body wall 12 mm. thick, reddish. $\frac{1}{2}$ natural size.
Fig. 6. Body wall 9 mm. thick, reddish brown. $\frac{1}{2}$ natural size.
Fig. 7. Body wall 14 mm. thick, blackish. $\frac{1}{4}$ natural size.
Fig. 8. Body wall 10 mm. thick, reddish yellow. $\frac{2}{3}$ natural size.
Fig. 9. Body wall 8 mm. thick, reddish yellow. $\frac{2}{3}$ natural size.
Fig. 10. Body wall 7 mm. thick, reddish. $\frac{1}{2}$ natural size.
Fig. 11. Body wall 9 mm. thick, reddish. $\frac{1}{2}$ natural size.

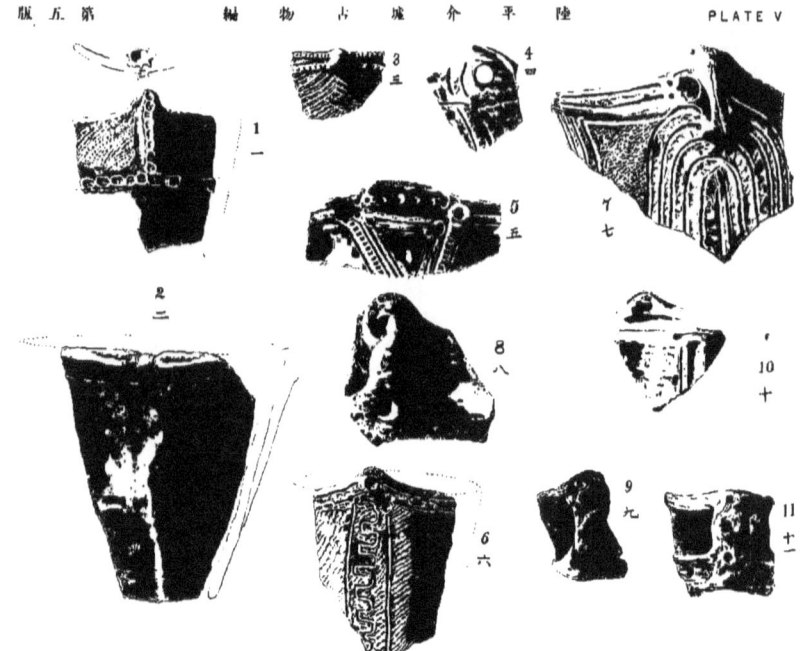

SHELL MOUND OF OKADAIRA.

ז

PLATE VI.

Fig. 1. Body wall 12 mm. thick, reddish with some black patches. $\frac{1}{3}$ natural size.
Fig. 2. Body wall 14 mm. thick, reddish above blackish below. $\frac{2}{3}$ natural size.
Fig. 3. Body wall 10 mm. thick, reddish. $\frac{1}{3}$ natural size.
Fig. 4. Body wall 9 mm. thick, blackish. $\frac{1}{2}$ natural size.
Fig. 5. Body wall 9 mm. thick, blackish. $\frac{1}{2}$ natural size.
Fig. 6. Body wall 8 mm. thick, blackish. $\frac{2}{3}$ natural size.
Fig. 7. Body wall 7 mm. thick, brownish red. $\frac{1}{2}$ natural size.
Fig. 8. Body wall 11 mm. thick, blackish. $\frac{1}{3}$ natural size.
Fig. 9. Body wall 10 mm. thick, reddish. $\frac{2}{3}$ natural size.
Fig. 10. Body wall 9 mm. thick, reddish above blackish below. $\frac{2}{3}$ natural size.
Fig. 11. Body wall 9 mm. thick, reddish. natural size.
Fig. 12. Body wall 10 mm. thick, reddish black. $\frac{2}{3}$ natural size.
Fig. 13. Body wall 13 mm. thick, reddish black. $\frac{1}{3}$ natural size.

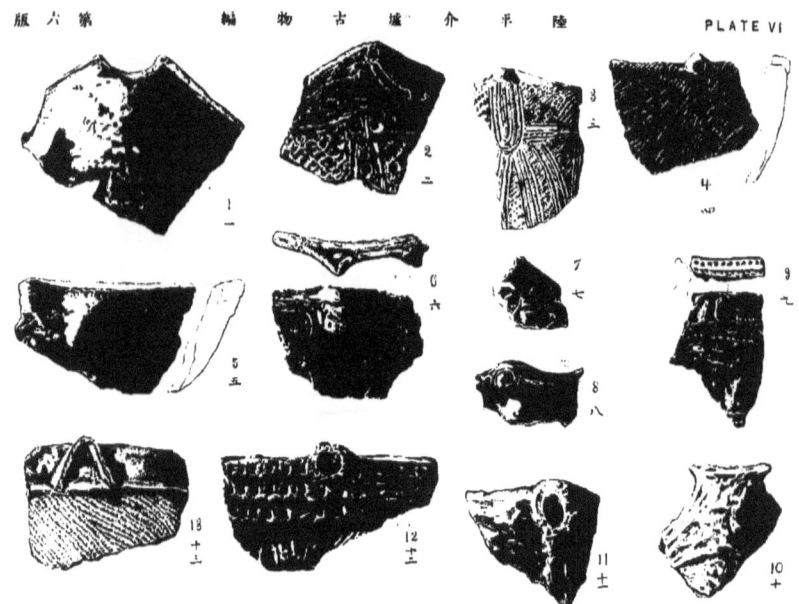

SHELL MOUND of OKADAIRA.

PLATE VII.

Fig. 1. Body wall 11 mm. thick, blackish. $\frac{2}{3}$ natural size.
Fig. 2. Body wall 9 mm. thick, reddish black. $\frac{1}{4}$ natural size.
Fig. 3. Body wall 9 mm. thick, reddish. $\frac{1}{2}$ natural size.
Fig. 4. Body wall 9 mm. thick, blackish. $\frac{1}{2}$ natural size.
Fig. 5. Body wall 11 mm. thick, yellowish grey. $\frac{1}{2}$ natural size.
Fig. 6. Body wall 12 mm. thick, blackish. $\frac{1}{2}$ natural size.
Fig. 7. Body wall 7 mm. thick, reddish. Margin wavy. $\frac{1}{2}$ natural size.
Fig. 8. Body wall 12 mm. thick, reddish. Ornamented with a series of dots. $\frac{1}{2}$ natural size.
Fig. 9. Body wall 10 mm. thick, reddish. $\frac{1}{2}$ natural size.
Fig. 10. Body 9 mm. thick, blackish. $\frac{1}{2}$ natural size.
Fig. 11. Body wall 11 mm. thick, reddish. $\frac{1}{2}$ natural size.
Fig. 12. Body wall 11 mm. thick, reddish black. $\frac{1}{2}$ natural size.
Fig. 13. Body wall 11 mm. thick, reddish yellow. $\frac{1}{2}$ natural size.
Fig. 14. Body wall 11 mm. thick, blackish. $\frac{1}{2}$ natural size.
Fig. 15. Body wall 11 mm. thick, blackish. $\frac{1}{3}$ natural size.
Fig. 16. Body wall 13 mm. thick, blackish. $\frac{1}{2}$ natural size.
Fig. 17. Body wall 8 mm. thick, brownish red. $\frac{1}{2}$ natural size.

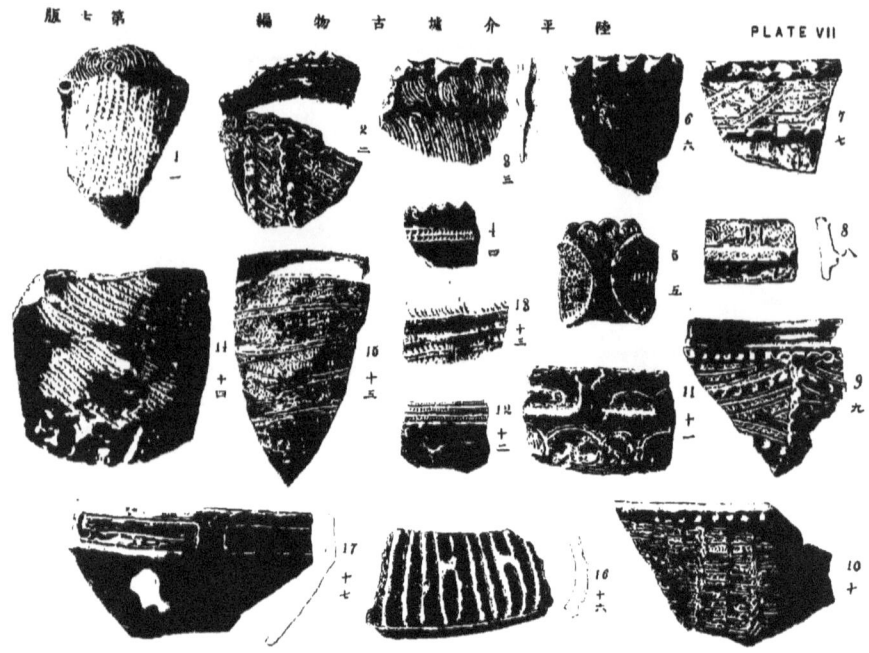

SHELL MOUND of OKADAIRA.

PLATE VIII.

Fig. 1. Body wall 11 mm. thick, blackish above reddish below. $\frac{1}{2}$ natural size.
Fig. 2. Body wall 12 mm. thick, reddish above blackish below. $\frac{1}{2}$ natural size.
Fig. 3. Body wall 9 mm. thick, blackish. $\frac{1}{2}$ natural size.
Fig. 4. Body wall 9 mm. thick, brownish red. $\frac{1}{2}$ natural size.
Fig. 5. Body wall 13 mm. thick, blackish above reddish below. $\frac{1}{2}$ natural size.
Fig. 6. Body wall 15 mm. thick, reddish. $\frac{1}{2}$ natural size.
Fig. 7. Body wall 13 mm. thick, brownish red. $\frac{1}{2}$ natural size.
Fig. 8. Body wall 15 mm. thick, reddish. $\frac{1}{2}$ natural size.
Fig. 9. Body wall 12 mm. thick, yellowish red. $\frac{1}{2}$ natural size.
Fig. 10. Body wall 9 mm. thick, reddish black. $\frac{1}{2}$ natural size.
Fig. 11. Body wall 10 mm. thick, reddish above, blackish below. $\frac{1}{2}$ natural size.

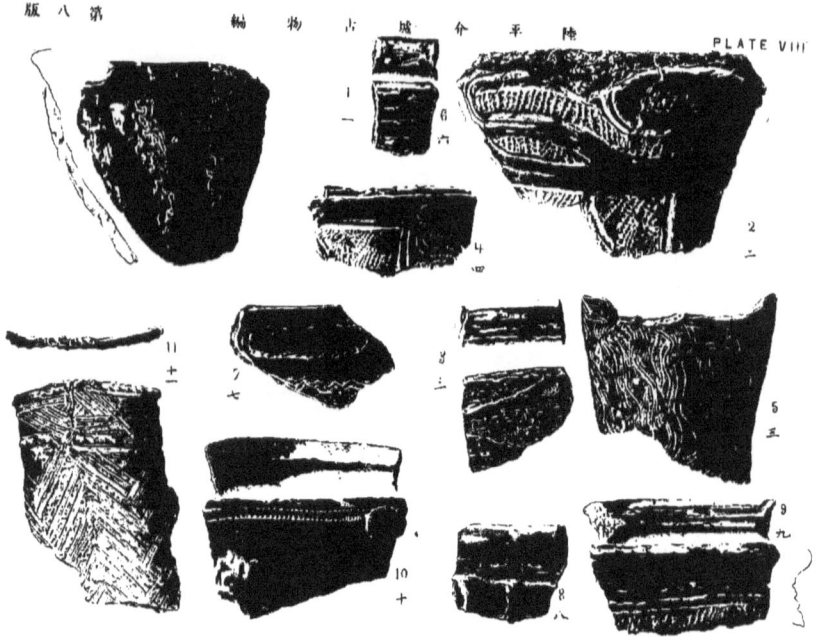

SHELL MOUND OF OKADAIRA.

PLATE IX.

Fig. 1. Body wall 9 mm. thick, brownish red. $\frac{2}{3}$ natural size.
Fig. 2. Body wall 13 mm. thick, light yellow. $\frac{1}{4}$ natural size.
Fig. 3. Body wall 7 mm. thick, blackish. $\frac{1}{2}$ natural size.
Fig. 4. Body wall 9 mm. thick, blackish above greyish below. $\frac{1}{3}$ natural size.
Fig. 5. Body wall 7 mm. thick, yellowish grey. $\frac{1}{2}$ natural size.
Fig. 6. Body wall 11 mm. thick, yellowish grey above reddish below. $\frac{1}{2}$ natural size.
Fig. 7. Body wall 6 mm. thick, brownish red. $\frac{1}{2}$ natural size.
Fig. 8. Body wall 9 mm. thick, blackish. $\frac{1}{2}$ natural size.
Fig. 9. Body wall 10 mm. thick, reddish. $\frac{1}{2}$ natural size.
Fig. 10. Body wall 13 mm. thick, blackish above reddish below. $\frac{1}{4}$ natural size.
Fig. 11. Body wall 10 mm. thick, reddish above blackish below. $\frac{1}{2}$ natural size.
Fig. 12. Inside surface of ditto showing eight parallel grooves, blackish. $\frac{1}{2}$ natural size.
Fig. 13. Body wall 9 mm. thick, brownish red. $\frac{1}{3}$ natural size.
Fig. 14. Body wall 11 mm. thick, reddish. $\frac{2}{3}$ natural size.
Fig. 15. Body wall 11 mm. thick, greyish. $\frac{1}{2}$ natural size.
Fig. 16. Body wall 9 mm. thick, reddish. $\frac{1}{2}$ natural size.
Fig. 17. Body wall 8 mm. thick, blackish. $\frac{1}{2}$ natural size.
Fig. 18. Body wall 7 mm. thick, blackish above, reddish below. $\frac{1}{2}$ natural size.
Fig. 19. Body wall 11 mm. thick, blackish. $\frac{1}{3}$ natural size.

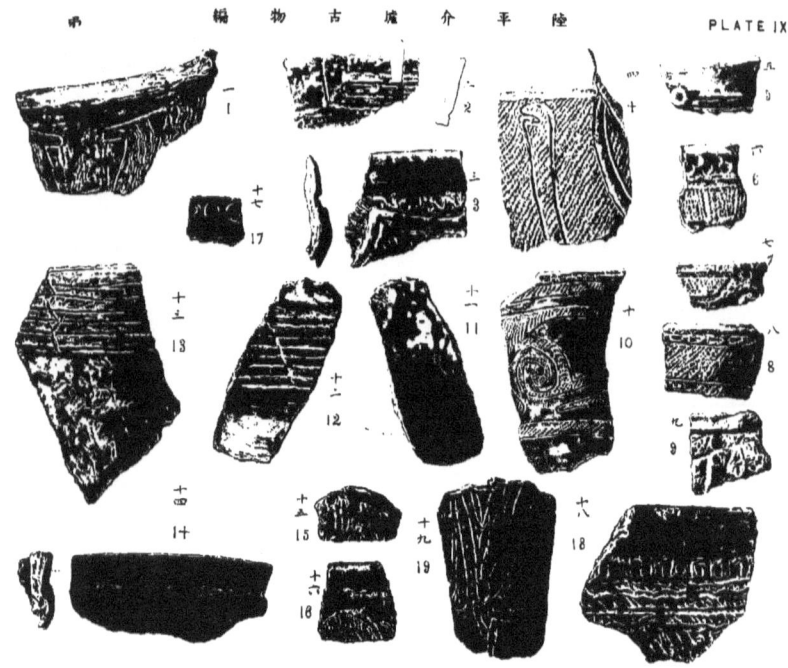

SHELL MOUND OF OKADAIRA.

MEMOIRS

OF THE

SCIENCE DEPARTMENT,

UNIVERSITY OF TOKIO, JAPAN.

VOLUME I. PART I.

SHELL MOUNDS OF OMORI.

BY

EDWARD S. MORSE.

Professor of Zoölogy, University of Tokio, Japan.

PUBLISHED BY THE UNIVERSITY.

TOKIO, JAPAN.

NISSHUSHA PRINTING OFFICE.

2539 (1879.)

U. S. NATIONAL MUSEUM.

The Rau Library of Archæology.
No. 1288

DR. CHARLES RAU was born in Belgium in 1826. He came to the United States in 1848, and was engaged as teacher at Belleville, Illinois, and in New York. In 1875 he accepted an invitation from the Smithsonian Institution to prepare an Ethnological Exhibit to be displayed at the Centennial Exhibition, and subsequently was appointed Curator of the department of Archæology in the National Museum, which position he held at the time of his death, July 25, 1887. He bequeathed his Archæologic collections and library to the U. S. National Museum.

SHELL MOUNDS OF OMORI NEAR TOKIO, JAPAN.

MEMOIRS

OF THE

SCIENCE DEPARTMENT,

UNIVERSITY OF TOKIO, JAPAN.

VOLUME I. PART I.

SHELL MOUNDS OF OMORI.

BY

EDWARD S. MORSE.

PROFESSOR OF ZOÖLOGY, UNIVERSITY OF TOKIO, JAPAN.

PUBLISHED BY THE UNIVERSITY.

TOKIO, JAPAN.

NISSHUSHA PRINTING OFFICE.

2539 (1879.)

PREFACE.

During the preparation of this Memoir on the Shell Mounds of Omori, I have examined, in company with others whose names are mentioned below, deposits of a similar nature at Otaru, on the western Coast of Yezo, Hakodate, a number within the city limits of Tokio, and one of enormous extent and depth in the Province of Higo, Island of Kinshiu.

From all these places large collections have been made, and are now in the Archæological Museum of the University of Tokio.

As the Omori Mounds have proved so rich in material, it was thought best to limit this first contribution to an exhaustive illustration of the various forms and ornamentations there occurring, thus making it the basis for future comparisons when the other deposits shall have been worked up. In Yamagata Ken, for example, as well as in the Tokio Deposits, fragments of pottery are met with, bearing so close a resemblance to the Omori forms that a reference to them may be made without further illustration, while only new forms need be figured and described. For these reasons, the attempt has been made to figure every typical form of shape and ornamentation. In many cases, also, the varietal modification in shape and design has been given, as with the rims on Plate VIII. and the knobs on Plates XI. and XII.

It may be stated that many of the other forms figured, are represented by a number of varieties which are contained in the Museum of the University.

Professional duties at the University, connected with instruction and the arranging of the Museum, prevented my giving that supervision over the plates necessary to secure the uniformity which they lack. When it is considered however, that the drawing (with the exception of the last plate) and lithographing have been done entirely by Japanese artists,— the art of drawing in foreign style, and the art of lithography being still new to them,—some allowances may be made for the imperfections they present.

On the other hand, it may be said with truth that all the outlines are correct, and that full reliance may be placed on the figures. The same excuse may be made with reference to the composition and press work, as these labors have been done in a Japanese office, the compositors not being able to speak a word of English. With some pride, it may be said that the paper on which the book has been printed is of Japanese manufacture, so that from composition to binding, the mechanical production is entirely Japanese. As a Japanese version has been issued, the plates have been lettered for that edition also.

To the intelligent and cordial interest displayed by Mr. Kato, the Director of the University, and Mr. Hamao, the Vice Director, archæologists are indebted for this contribution toward a knowledge of the prehistoric pottery of Japan.

It is not too much to say that there is no other country in the world where so great a number of gentlemen interested in archæology can be found as in Japan. A native Archæological Society holds its meetings regularly in Tokio, and many of the contributions are of great value.

In the preparation of this work I have been greatly aided by the sympathy and practical assistance of a large number of Japanese scholars.

My thanks are especially due to Mr. Kanda, Mr. Kato, Mr. Hamao, Mr. Hattori, Mr. Ninagawa, Mr. Takamine, Prof. Yokoyama, Prof. Yatabe and Prof. Toyama, for many favors. To my special students, Mr. Sasaki, Mr. Iijima, Mr. Iwakawa and Mr. Fujitani, I am under many obligations for various translations which they have made for me, and for other favors.

To my assistant Mr. Taneda who has copied all my manuscript for the printer, and who has assisted me in various ways, my thanks are also due.

To Prof. T. C. Mendenhall, of the University, my thanks are specially due for the reduction and averages of over a thousand measurements of Omori shells. I must also express my indebtedness to Prof. F. F. Jewett for a number of chemical analyses.

To Mr. E. H. House, Proprietor of the Tokio Times, for much assistance and advice I am also exceedingly grateful.

Acknowledgments are also due to Mr. Kimura the artist, Mr. Matsuda the lithographer, and the Nisshusha Printing Office, for the efforts they have made in securing accuracy in their respective lines of work.

The collecting of the material illustrated in this first part has been done mainly by Mr. Sasaki and the lamented Mr. Matsura.

Part II. will present the pottery of the Shell Mounds of Yezo, Tokio and Higo.

E. S. M.

Tokio, Japan.

July 16th, 1879.

CONTENTS.

Frontispiece. Shell Mounds of Omori, near Tokio.	Page.
Preface.	iii.
The Shell Mounds of Omori, Japan. Introductory.	1.
General character of the Omori Mounds.	4.
Special characteristics of the Omori Deposits.	5.
Pottery.	7.
Ornaments.	10.
Tablets.	11.
Implements of Horn and Bone.	13.
Implements of Stone.	15.
Remains of Animals.	16.
Cannibalism.	17.
Flattened Tibia.	19.
A comparison between the Ancient and Modern Molluscan Fauna of Omori.	23.
Explanation of Plates.	38.

THE SHELL MOUNDS OF OMORI, JAPAN.

BY EDWARD S. MORSE.

Since the appearance of Darwin's great work on the Origin of Species, and the subsequent revolution in the minds of thinking men regarding the origin of man and animals below him, a new impulse has been given to the investigations of man's early history; a new science, in fact, has sprang into activity, and Societies and Journals of Anthropology, Archæology and Ethnology are the results of this wonderful awakening.

With the idea so long dominant that man had been specially created at a certain time to be measured by years, only those documents and those evidences were scanned which came within the prescribed time limits. Thirty years ago it seemed as useless a task to study the evidences of man's existence before these dates, as it would be for one to study the evidences of the Spanish occupation of America before the year 1492.

In fact so apathetic were men's minds on this matter, or rather so throughly was incorporated the idea of man's recent origin, that many valuable evidences have been neglected, or lost through this lamentable condition of things. Observations on the high antiquity of man made by Dr. Schmerling, Mr. Mac Enery, Mr. Godwin Austen and others attracted but little attention. Indeed they were received with incredulity, and the memoir of Mr. Vivian read before the Geological Society was considered too improbable for publication.* Yet the labors and discoveries of these men have been repeatedly confirmed by subsequent investigations.

Difficult indeed is it to restore the past history of mankind from the fragmentary remains found buried in the earth. Their life history must be made up entirely from the imperishable objects which have been preserved in caves, burial places, the refuse piles of their villages, and similar places. They left no written record, no hieroglyphics to decipher, because they had none.

* Lubbock's Pre-historic Man.

It seems at first sight impossible to build up any idea of their habits and comparative states of savagery from the few objects which have survived the corroding influences of time.

Were we to apply the same methods to the study of civilized races to day, very little could be gathered of our life by an examination of the refuse piles of our dwellings. All the delicate works of art, wood carving, embroidery, books, models, etc. would disappear in the time that has elapsed since the earlier ages of man, and we should only have left the glass, porcelain, and stone fragments which would survive. From the refinement and delicacy of these objects, however, we would have a right to infer the progress and condition of the race, and would be justified in the assumption that in their perishable art the same refinement had been manifested.

It is true these deposits do not give us their textile fabrics, if they had any, or their wood work or more perishable art; but judging the ancient savage by the modern one, the sites of their villages, or contents of their refuse heaps, give us a very fair indication of what they possessed. The imprint of matting or cloth upon their pottery tells us at once the texture and kind of fabric used. An arrow head presupposes a wooden shaft. Knowing how scantily supplied with objects the hut of a low savage is to day, we have every reason to believe that the primitive savage was no better provided in these respects.

The importance of studying deposits of the nature of the Omori Mounds has been fully realized, since the investigations of the Danish shell mounds brought to light so many facts bearing on the habits of the primitive races of Denmark. Of such importance was an examination of the Danish deposits considered, that the Government appointed a commission consisting of three men highly eminent in science to make exhaustive explorations. And now so jealously does she guard her treasures that laws have been enacted prohibiting the exportation of archæological specimens or antiquities of any kind from the country. With the existence of an Archæological Society in Tokio, consisting exclusively of Japanese, who hold their meetings regularly, and the fact that there have already been a number of works published by native archæologists who have figured with more or less accuracy the stone implements, ancient vessels, inscriptions and the like, it seems proper and just that Government should follow the example of Greece, Italy and Denmark in passing laws to prevent these treasures from going on, of the country. May the Government not only prevent the exportation of specimens, but may it jealously guard its ancient temples, monuments, gate ways and idols. I can not refrain from quoting at this point the words of an accomplished English archæologist, Mr. Borlase, who expresses a hope "that the liberal views which have hitherto prompted the Mikado's Government in all that relates to science and art, may be extended to that *chef d'œuvre* of their country (which is indeed unmatched in the world) and that authors may yet have to record the graceful act, on the part of the present Administration, which has saved from destruction the most beautiful relic of 'Old Japan'—the tombs of the Shoguns." *

Besides the investigations of Steenstrup in Denmark, we have the valuable memoirs of Wyman on the shell mounds of Florida and New England. Deposits of a similar nature have been recorded or described as occurring in England, Scotland, Ireland, France, the Eastern coast of the United States, the valley of the Mississippi, on the west coast from California to Behring Strait, Brazil, the Gulf of Guayaquil, Australia, Tasmania, and the Malay Archipelago ; and doubtless they will be found scattered all over the world.

That these deposits are not all of the same age is certain ; for just as the stone age exists in certain parts of the world to-day, so these deposits are in process of formation both among savage and civilized people. While the shell heaps of New England have the same essential features as those of Denmark, it can not be safely assumed they were made long before the advent of the European : for the natives were then living in the stone age, as it were, and were still forming deposits of shell in precisely the same way. It is true that many of these deposits when first observed by the earliest settlers were covered with a heavy growth of forest trees, and the presence of a molar tooth of the polar bear, and the abundance of the remains of the great auk now supposed to be extinct, lead us to believe that the New England deposits have some antiquity.

In Japan, however, the case is quite different ; for with its ancient civilization and history, running back for fifteen hundred and perhaps two thousand years, and the fidelity of its records, we have as it were a longer time measurement by which to estimate the age of the shell deposits here. For this reason a much greater importance attaches to the minute and faithful exploration of such deposits in Japan.

Having for years studied these deposits in Maine and Massachusetts in company with Prof. Jeffries Wyman and Prof. F. W. Putnam, I felt prepared to undertake a similar investigation in this country and therefore at the outset kept a sharp look out for evidences of their occurrence. A few days after my arrival in the country I fortunately discovered a large and extensive shell mound on the immediate line of the railway a few miles from Tokio. A series of explorations was made in company with my special students, Mr. Matsura and Mr. Sasaki, and, in the first excavations Prof. Yatabe, Prof. Toyama, Mr. Matsumura, Mr. Fukuyo, Dr. David Murray, and Prof. Parson participated. The collections from Omori are now arranged in the Archæological Museum of the Tokio Daigaku. Most of the specimens have been collected by Mr. Sasaki and the lamented Mr. Matsura, who were indefatigable in their efforts to make the series as complete as possible.

* Niphon and its Antiquities.

GENERAL CHARACTERS OF THE OMORI MOUNDS.

The Omori Shell Mounds lie on the western side of the Imperial railway between Yokohama and Tokio, at a distance of nearly six miles from Tokio. They may be seen from the car windows just after leaving Omori Station in going toward Tokio.

The railway has indeed passed through a large portion of the mounds, as in the field beyond the track the ground is strewn with the fragments of pottery and the shells formerly composing the deposit. The length of the deposit along the embankment is about eighty-nine meters. Its depth in the thickest part is four meters. Another exposure of considerable thickness is seen, back from the track at a distance of ninety-five meters, but whether it is a continuation of the first deposit I have not been able to determine.

The fields to the south show that in their cultivation another deposit has been removed.

The mounds are nearly half a mile from the shores of the Bay of Yedo.

As deposits of this nature are always made along the immediate shore, whether they be upon the banks of a river, or on the coast, the occurrence of these deposits inland may be looked upon as an evidence that the land has been elevated since they were made. And when they occur inland, geological, and often historical evidences are not wanting to support this view.

The shell mounds along the Baltic are in many cases far removed from the coast line. They also contain species of shells not found in the Baltic, in consequence of the freshening of the water resulting from the geological changes that have taken place in that water basin.

Along the eastern coast of the United States, the ocean has been encroaching upon the land, and shell mounds in Casco Bay, Maine, are in process of being washed away by the waves.

Rev. James Fowler, in the Smithsonian Report for 1870, comments upon the absence of these deposits along the New Brunswick coast, and offers this as one of the evidences that the sea is encroaching upon the land, and calls attention to the fact that buildings which stood at some distance from the shore, fifty years ago, have since been washed away.

Geological evidences show that marked changes have taken place in the shore line of the Bay of Yedo. A portion of these changes are recorded historically on ancient maps of Yedo.

Shell mounds discovered by Mr. Kanda and Prof. Yatabe in the Botanical Garden, and others discovered by Prof. Chaplin and Mr. Ishikawa in Oji, show a recedence of the waters of the Bay of Yedo of from five to seven miles.

In every case these mounds are on ground slightly elevated above the surrounding country, and in indicating their various positions on a map of Tokio, the coincidence between the shaded line of an embankment, and the position of the deposit is at once seen.

SPECIAL CHARACTERISTICS OF THE OMORI DEPOSITS.

The shell mounds, or deposits, in various parts of the world have many features in common. They also have their distinguishing peculiarities. Their similarity arises from the fact that they are the refuse piles of savage races who came to the shore at certain times of the year, or who occupied the shore permanently and there availed themselves of the food so easily secured from the water, in the shape of mollusks and fishes. That they were hunters as well as fishermen is attested by the presence of the bones of wild animals, such as the deer, bear, and wild boar, as well as the bones of certain birds. The bones being in nearly every case broken into fragments, show that they did this to secure the marrow, or to more conveniently get them into their cooking pots. That they cooked their food in clay vessels, is evident from the carbonized remains of the food found on certain fragments of pottery. In all these deposits various primitive implements are found, fabricated out of either bone, horn, stone or shell.

The horn, bone and shell implements are generally in the shape of gouges, bodkins, needles and other pointed instruments. The stone implements are usually of the rudest kind, and consist of hammers, celts, axes, arrows, and spear points. The pottery is rude, and in all parts of the world bears the impression of the well known cord mark. Beside this ornamentation, if indeed it was intended for that purpose, there are often rude designs, (rarely, if ever imitative of natural objects) made by incised lines in the soft clay, or impressed upon the clay by stamps. While these features are common in deposits of this nature, even in those most widely removed, the deposits of each country and region seem to have their distinguishing peculiarities, so that one familiar with the description of them might tell with considerable accuracy the place of each deposit by an examination of a mass of material from it. The Danish deposits contain a great many flint chips and rude flint implements. The pottery does not appear to be common, and is of the simplest description. No evidences of cannibalism have been noticed. The New England deposits resemble greatly the Danish deposits in the character of the animal remains. The stone implements are very much fewer however, and the pottery is not common.

Simple horn and bone implements occur in both. In the New England deposits, Prof. Wyman found a few evidences of cannibalism. In the Florida mounds, as studied by Prof. Wyman, the pottery is again very rude, and besides the cord mark and incised lines, presents an ornamentation produced by stamps with definite designs upon them. Rude arrow heads and spear points were met with, and more rarely bone implements. These are made from the bones of the deer, and Wyman observes that the bones are broken, rather than split, as is the case with the old world deposits. Beside the stamped pottery, another marked peculiarity of the Florida mounds consists in the presence of gouges, chisels and other implements worked out of shell, generally the columella or axis of the large Strombus and Fasciolaria being used. Widely distributed evidences of cannibalism also occur.

The Omori deposits are also specialized. First: by the presence of enormous quantities of pottery, of many different shapes, and of an almost infinite variety of ornamentation. Second: by the great scarcity of stone implements, and the absence of arrow heads, spear points and other pointed implements of stone. Not a single arrow head, flake or chip has been found by the various parties who have been there in the interests of the University; and the combined time spent there, if represented by a single individual, would equal over eighty days work of seven hours each. The men of the Omori period were also cannibals, the evidences of which will be presented further on. Peculiar clay tablets or amulets, to be described elsewhere in this memoir are also unique. The Omori deposits are not only peculiar for what they possess, but for what they do not possess.

The following list presents the objects thus far found at Omori, and in another column is also given a list of objects characteristic of shell mounds generally, not yet found there.

OBJECTS FOUND AT OMORI.

EARTHEN.

Cooking vessels.
Hand vessels.
Ornamental jars.
Ornamental bead.
Tablets.
Spindle whorl —(?)
Disk, shaped from fragment of pottery.

STONE.

Hammers.
Celts.
Rollers.
Skin dresser —(?)

Stone mortar.

HORN.

Awls.
Handle.
Prongs of deers' antlers.
Other implements — (use unknown.)

BONE.

Fish spine needles.
Bird bone with two holes in side.
Cube from metatarsal of deer.
Os calcis of deer probably used as handle.

MISCELLANEOUS.

Arrow point from boars, canine.
Shells used as paint cups.

OBJECTS NOT FOUND AT OMORI.

Flint or obsidian implements.
Arrow heads.
Spear points.
Scrapers.
Skinning knives.
Mortars or pestles—(?)
Drilling stones.
Ornamental stones.
Stone net sinkers.
Pipes.
Worked shell.
Wampum.
Stone beads.

POTTERY.

A great many earthen vessels, more or less perfect, and thousands of fragments, were collected in the Omori deposits.

The material of which the vessels is composed is coarse, and the vessels are in many cases, unevenly baked.

The pottery with few exceptions is quite thin, averaging 6 mm. in thickness; the surfaces are in many cases smooth. The rims of the vessels are either straight, undulating, notched, or projecting at intervals into points, or into variously formed knobs.

In some cases loops take the place of knobs. The borders of the vessels are often ribbed within, and sometimes marked with one or more parallel lines outside, the lines often enclosing a row of rude dots.

The lines marking the surfaces of the vessels are either roughly incised in wet clay, or smoothed out of wet clay, or carved in dry clay before baking.

The designs are infinitely varied; generally areas partially or wholly enclosed by curved lines, the area within or without the lines being cord marked, the other area being smooth. Deep pits or grooves often join the areas, and these may be repeated in regular succession round the vessel.

A common mode of ornamentation is a band of oblique lines running in one direction round the vessel, followed by a band of oblique lines running in an opposite direction. Somtimes these lines cross each other.

In many cases wreaths of clay, pinched into scallops by the fingers, border the vessel in one or more bands, either straight or undulating. These wreaths frequently separate from the vessel, showing that they were put on after the vessel was made.

Dr. Wilson in his work on Pre-Historic Man has mentioned the absence of imitative figures in the pre-historic pottery of Europe. He says; " In no single case is any attempt made to imitate leaf or flower, bird, beast or any natural object." His words would apply with equal truth to the Omori pottery for in no case can any form or design be construed into representing any natural object.

More curious still is the absence of legs or knobs of any description for the support of the vessel from below. A feature so common in the ancient pottery of Peru and Central America, is entirely absent in the ancient pottery of Omori. On the contrary the Omori pottery presents knobs and loops of an infinity of form projecting from the rim of the vessel. In this respect the Omori pottery resembles the pre-historic pottery from Brazil and Porto Rico, though these forms often represent the heads of animals.

Some of the knobs from the shell mounds of the Amazon discovered by Prof. Hartt bear a remarkable resemblance to the commonest types of knobs from Omori.

The earthen vessels may be grouped as follows :—

Cooking vessels answering to pots, stewpans, etc. Hand vessels such as bowls and cups. Vessels with constricted necks, used as water bottles, possibly, and a few vessels of various forms which may be designated as ornamental jars and bowls.

The cooking vessels are of the following kinds: Deep vessels with slightly bulging sides and flaring rims, ornamented, walls thin. Plain deep vessels with bulging sides and slightly flaring rims, bottoms smooth, or marked with matting impressions. These are the most common forms of all. Straight sided deep vessels, thick walls, roughly made. Large shallow bowl shaped vessels. The hand vessels present the following varieties. Shallow bowl shaped vessels with incurved rims; generally ornamented. Shallow saucer shaped vessels, plain. Very shallow bowl shaped vessels with flaring rims, plainly ornamented.

The vessels with constricted necks are very imperfect, the necks and portions of the bodies only being found. Most of these are dry carved before baking.

The ornamental jars and vessels are figured on plate I. with accompanying descriptions in the explanation of the plate. Two of the larger ones are gracefully formed, though they may have been used for cooking.

One has four handles united above, the knobs on the handles perforated for the passage of a cord, the handles deeply grooved in a line with the perforations. Another one has a widely flaring margin projecting in four lobes with thickened border.

The most extraordinary one of all has two apertures, and recalls some of the unique features seen in the ancient Peruvian pottery.

Of fifty vessels more or less complete, five are bowl-shaped cups, three are large bowls, seven are cups with flaring rims, two are shallow saucer-shaped vessels, two are ornamental bowls with flaring rims, five are deep sided pots with slightly bulging sides, the bottoms of which generally have matting impressions, ten are cooking pots, eight have constricted necks, and eight are diversified in form and ornamentation. Among these vessels, thirty-seven are ornamented as follows: twenty-four have smoothed depressed lines, one has wide shallow lines, four have rough incised lines, two have dry carved lines, one has uneven rough lines, and four are plain.

Of the thirty-seven, also, twenty have the cord marked impressions, eighs have the surface smooth, and the remainder have rough surfaces.

Of the same number, nineteen have straight rims, and the remaining onet have the rims knobbed, or notched in various ways.

Several of the vessels are painted with mercury sulphide, but in no case is an attempt made to produce designs or patterns, except that in some instances the color is applied to interspaces between lines, or areas already marked upon the vessel. Reference is made to these in the explanation of plates.

Many of the vessels at first sight appear remarkable for their symmetry, and yet measurements show that they vary in their diameters, and the walls of the vessels vary greatly in their thickness. No trace of lathe work is found.

The economy of the makers of this pottery may be seen by the careful way in which they bored holes in the fractured edges of their vessels for the purpose of mending them. In some cases the hole was commenced too near the edge and the edge breaking away, a new hole was made, further removed from the edge.

The holes are always bored from the two sides, being smaller in diameter in the centre, showing that the boring instrument was rude, and probably consisted of a fragment of rock or bone.

Many fragments were finally matched and joined, by bringing together all fragments having perforations in them.

The economy of these people is again illustrated by the broken base of a vessel which has had its fractured margin smoothly ground down. That such an article as the broken bottom of one of the commonest forms of pots should be treated in this way, is an indication of the difficulty experienced in making these objects.

The pottery is found in such great abundance, and with such an infinite variety of form and ornamentation, that one would think that here at least was the site of some ancient manufacture ; but thus far no unfinished vessels, or masses of potters clay have been met with. The shell mounds of Tokio show an equal abundance of pottery, and in many cases forms and designs similar to those found at Omori.

ORNAMENTS.

In the remains of the work of pre-historic races in various parts of the world, there are commonly found objects of stone, shell, bone and horn, which were evidently intended for personal adornment.

The entire absence of objects of this nature in the Omori remains, with one exception, may be looked upon as somewhat extraordinary. Considering also the highly ornamental and extremely diversified character of the pottery, the absence of these objects must be regarded with interest.

In various parts of Japan there are found many kinds of stone beads known under the name of Cha-usu-ishi, Mikawa-kuda-kara, Juto-tama, Ruri-tama, etc.—some long and cylindrical, others globular, and the Ruri-tama shaped more like the shell beads of the United States. The well known Maga-tama also, must have been an object of personal ornament. These various ornaments, as well as many others, are associated with the polished stone age, which seems well marked in Japan. Old accounts of the Ainos represent their wearing beads and ornaments of various kinds, and whenever these are found, they are regarded by the Japanese as personal ornaments. In fact the Japanese antiquarian regards objects of this nature as of the highest antiquity.

Nothing of the kind, however, so far as I am aware, has been met with in the Omori shell mounds, nor in the shell mounds in Tokio. In fact I have examined many shell heaps from the west coast of Yezo to the southern portions of Kiushiu, without meeting with a single example of those objects above mentioned.

It may be suggested that the clay tablets, to be described further on, were objects of this nature, but I am inclined to believe that they were not intended for this purpose.

The clay bead which is figured, natural size, on plate XV., is made of coarse slate-colored clay. It is dead black on the outside, and has a surface resembling many of the ornamented vessels.

The markings, consisting of curved lines and deep incisions and punctures, are arranged in graceful designs which are repeated three times round the circumference. The hole is eight and a half millimeters in diameter, is straight, and of the same diameter throughout. Within the hole, light spiral lines are plainly seen, indicating that the bead was fashioned and wrought on a round stick, and that the stick was afterward withdrawn, and twisted several times in the act of withdrawing,—this act being performed while the clay was yet soft.

Mr. Taneda has found at Omori, too late for illustration, a fragment of pottery which has been broken into an irregular oval shape and the rough edges partially ground or worn down. Its longest diameter is 75 mm. with a width of 65 mm. and a thickness of 9 mm. In a line with the longest diameter the edges are deeply and smoothly notched. A narrow and deeper channel at the base of the notches suggests the idea that the object has been tied, or bound by a cord which passed through these notches.

The fragment is much worn. It is impossible to suggest its use, though it is described under this head for want of a more appropriate place.

TABLETS.

I have designated these curious clay objects as Tablets, for want of a better name. Five tablets have thus far been found; four of them have the same general proportions, as will be seen by reference to plate XV., where they are all figured, natural size. The fifth one is smaller than the others, though nearly as thick.

The designs are widely different in each one, though a surface of one of the larger specimens is similar in design to that made on the smaller specimen. Two of them have designs in relief with depressed areas. The designs on the others are produced by the figures being cut out on a flat surface, and one, fig. 1, has a hole through one of its corners.

While differing so much in design, they possess some characters in common. They are all made of the finest clay, the material being much finer than that used in most of the vessels. They are all light colored, two of them being a light brick red. There is no blackening upon the surface, neither is there a trace of the red paint.

The designs are all carved, or wrought out of dry clay before baking, in the same manner as a certain class of pottery found with them. With the exception of the largest one, they all appear to be more or less worn. One of them has the design almost wholly effaced.

For such solid and well made objects, it is curious that they are all broken.

It is difficult to conjecture their use. The fact that they are ornamented on both sides, some of the figures being in high relief, and in some instances the design being carried over the margins, excludes the idea that they were used as stamps to impress designs upon cloth, if the fabricators possessed such material. It is impossible that they could have been used for weapons, or implements of any kind.

That they were considered choice, is evident from the fine material of which they are made, and the care and skill bestowed on their ornamentation.

That they were used as personal ornaments seems out of the question, because, excepting in one instance there seems to be no arrangement for suspending them about the person. Their pottery so often presents knobs, loops or holes, for the purpose of suspending their vessels, that such conveniences might be looked for in the tablets if they had been designed for personal ornaments.

That they were household idols, or objects of veneration, seems an equally untenable supposition, for they are much worn ; and this would not be the case if they had been at all protected, or cared for in their huts.

We can hardly conceive of their being weights, because the weighing of things in traffic is an advance we should hardly expect in a people of so primitive a character as these appear to have been. They certainly were not objects to be buried with their dead, from the fact that they appear to have been much used.

It is hardly possible that they represent substitutes for coin, for we should expect to find more variation in their size ; and judging these people by other primitive races, we might suppose that wampum, or some other small objects would have been adopted for such a currency.

We may hazard some conjectures regarding their use. *First :* they might have been used in some game, like quoit, in which the object is pitched, or thrown at a mark ; their being worn, and broken, and the convenient size the larger ones have for grasping, and tossing, suggest this idea. *Second :* they may represent insignia of authority in which case they would be carried about the person. *Third :* they may represent amulets, or the charms, possibly, of some medicine man, in either case to be carried, or worn about the person.

So far as we know, they are unique. We can only compare them to the famous Cincinnati Tablet, to which they bear some resemblance, in the incurving sides and general proportions.

The Cicinnati Tablet † was found in a mound at Cicinnati, Ohio, in the year 1841. This tablet "is made of a fine grained compact limestone of a light brown color. It measures five inches in length, three in breadth, and two and six tenths inches in the middle, and is about half an inch in thickness." One side is wrought into curious figures in low relief, quite symmetrically disposed on each side of a median line. The figures are in the shape of scrolls, and curves, not unlike the conventional designs of leaves on wall paper.

The obverse side of the tablets is flat, having three longitudinal diverging grooves. Mr. Squier was inclined to believe that this tablet resembled peculiar stamps made of burnt clay, which occur in the Mississipi mounds, and in Mexico. These stamps, have fanciful or imitative figures upon them in low relief, and were used to imprint ornamental figures upon the cloth, or prepared skins, of the people. Dr. Daniel Wilson in his "Prehistoric Man," questions Squier's interpretation of its use, and suggests its being some standard of measurement, from the occurrence of two series of lines, bordering each end of the tablet.

It does not seem that Dr. Wilson is justified in this opinion, for the larger lines vary in their distance from each other, and the smaller spaces vary even more than the larger ones in proportion. A workman capable of duplicating so closely, in bilateral symmetry, the difficult and odd shaped designs upon the tablet would have found it the simplest thing to have made equidistant spaces.

IMPLEMENTS OF HORN AND BONE.

While the shell heaps of Denmark, Florida, and New England, present a number of implements made of bone, and a few made of horn, those of the Omori mounds are mostly made of horn, —or more correctly, the antlers of the deer. Wyman figures, in his article on the shell heaps of New England twelve implements made of bone, and one made of horn. Three of these are awl shaped implements; the others are variously notched or barbed at the ends. One has a notched edge like a saw, another has a blunt pointed extremity with seven notches on one side and eight on the other. Another one has two notches on one side and three on the other. One is barbed on one side, others are bluntly pointed, and one looks like an ivory tooth-pick. A tooth is also represented, ground down on one side to a cutting edge. The implements of horn are chisel, or gouge shaped, and rude.

The Florida mounds also yielded implements of bone, every one of them pointed. One is in the shape of a long slender bodkin; another one is worked from a longitudinal fragment of bone. Not one of these show a notch, or con-

† In 1872 Col. Charles Whittlesey pronounced this a forgery. Robert Clarke Esq., of Cincinnati, has completely vindicated its genuineness in a pamphlet published in 1876, entitled "Prehistoric Remains of Cincinnati, Ohio."

striction, or barb at the point. Of twelve bone implements figured by Wyman from the New England shell heaps, five only are similar to the Florida specimens.

Of ten horn implements figured from Omori only two may be considered as identical with the Florida forms, and these are bodkins. These two also bear a slight resemblance to one or two figured from New England. The remaining ones are quite unlike the Florida, or the New England specimens. This marked difference in implements of so primitive a nature is worthy of attention, and particularly so, since the relation these are supposed to bear to the Aino ought also in turn resemble the New England specimens, which bear such a resemblance to the horn and bone implements in use among the Esquimaux and Aleutians. The implements of this nature in the Omori Mounds are, with few exceptions, made of fragments of deer's antlers. The common use of this material is shown by the frequency with which fragments of deers antlers cut at one or both ends, were met with. These fragments were cut off by making a circular groove round the antler, and then breaking the piece away. No examples of diagonal cutting from each side, were met with, such as Wyman figures from the New England mounds, though the circular groove method of cutting occurs in the New England and Florida mounds. The natural prongs, much worn by use, are common.

The incisor teeth of the deer, and the canine teeth of the wild boar, are met with in comparative abundance, and they all show marks of use. A very characteristic horn handle is figured on Plate XVI Fig. 4. This was deeply and smoothly perforated at one end, and a deer's incisor so nicely fitted into the cavity, that the kind of tool held by this handle was evident enough. An exquisitely wrought arrow point or fish lance point was found, made from a boar's canine. The natural layer of enamel forming one face of it. Its shape is peculiar, one side appearing to be broken away, making the outline unsymmetrical, but as this face is polished it is evidently intentional. In the museum of the Kaitakushi, there is a silicious specimen of almost precisely the shape is the one above described, and that it was intended for a similar purpose is unquestionable. Dr. A. O. C. Geerts in his valuable work entitled " *Les Produits de la Nature Japonaise et Chinoise* " figures it on plate VIII., fig 3.

The bone cube made from the end of a deer's metatarsal is an odd shaped piece; the surfaces have been evenly ground down, and its use may possibly be surmised by associating it with some game.

A well defined hook made from a deer's antler is unique. A bird's bone having two perforations is another object of interest. An irregular fragment of bone has one end ground down to a cutting edge. A great many fish spines were collected, which in many cases bear marks of considerable use. They probably served as needles. The *so calcis* of the deer occur in great numbers and nearly all of them show indications of wear.

Wyman found the *olecranon* of the deer, used as an implement of some kind by the builders of the Florida mounds. It is difficult to conjecture the use that was made of the *os calcis*, unless it answered for a handle, — its irregular articular faces perhaps offering certain facilities for binding an instrument to it.

With the presence of so many shells of massive size, with thick and dense columellas, such as Rapana, it seems a little singular that not a single worked shell, either as an implement, utensil, or ornament has yet been found; particularly so, as objects useful and ornamental made from shell are frequently met with in the Florida mounds, and other parts of the Southern States and Mississipi Valley. Similar articles are also found in remains of this nature along the coast of California. Of the characteristic wampum,—that is little beads made of shell, so common in the American deposits, no trace was found in the Omori mounds.

IMPLEMENTS OF STONE.

It seems remarkable that a people capable of fabricating vessels of such symmetry in form, such variety in shape, and displaying such varied methods in ornamentation, should have left the few primitive, and ill-shapen implements, that have thus far been discovered in the Omori mounds. While thousands of fragments of pottery, a remarkable set of tablets, a bead of curious workmanship, and other objects have been found, only the few rude implements figured on Plate XVII. have thus far been met with ; and the few among these approaching to any symmetry in outline are made of soft stone, and easily worked.

The stone implements thus far discovered are as follows : three chisel like implements made of soft lava rock ; fragments of two rollers, one made from clay slate, and the other of some schistose rock, the latter bearing the marks of fire.

A portion of one, composed of talcose rock, is the best finished of the lot. It has two grooves transversely marking the blunt and smooth ends of one extremity. Two large and ill shapened implements have been worked out of jasper pebbles. One face is broken away, the other face shows the natural surface of the pebble. The constrictions have been chipped out, to accommodate a wooden handle, probably of twisted thorn. The evidence of wear is apparent in both. In the larger one, the rough edges are worn down in those places where the handle would naturally rub against them. The smaller one shows small surfaces in the same region, highly polished, and one of the worn surfaces shines like glass. I have supposed these to be hammers, from the manner in which one end is broken, as if by repeated blows. It is hardly probable that they were intended for net sinkers.

As so many finished stone implements of various kinds are found widely distributed in Japan, the absence in the Omori mounds of many groups of implements, and of common forms too, is remarkable, and lends additional evidence to the antiquity of the deposits.

Beside the stone implements, there were found many stones of irregular shape, but showing no marks of an artificial character. There were also found a few flat pieces of rock, having conical shaped holes bored into the flat sides. There was no evidence of design in the way the holes were arranged on the rock, nor did it appear that any attempt had been made to bore through the rock. These holes were 18 to 20 mm. in diameter, and 9 to 11 mm. deep. A fragment of a stone bowl with a heavy rim, 70 mm. thick in its widest part, and having a comparatively thin bottom was found in the deposits. The marks of wear on the inner surface, show that the fragment probably formed part of a mortar.

Two very symmetrically rounded stones were also found, but it was difficult to determine whether they had been rounded artificially, or not.

Large fragments of pumice were not uncommon in the mounds.

Implements of precisely the same character have been found in a number of the Tokio deposits.

REMAINS OF ANIMALS.

A great many bones of wild animals were found, mixed with the shells composing the deposits. These were all broken or split irregularly, and in this fragmentary condition it is difficult to identify them.

The remains of the following animals have thus far been recognized. :—Man, Monkey, Deer, Wild Boar, Wolf and Dog.

The bones of the Deer and Wild Boar are most numerous.

A few fragments of the vertebræ of a large cetacean, and also fragments of the ribs of a large Tortoise were found.

A few bones of the smaller mammals and birds, and many bones of fishes also occur, but their species have not yet been identified.

The antlers of the Deer are remarkable for their proportions, and the skulls of the Wild Boar indicate creatures of the largest size.

In ancient deposits in other parts of the world, the same difference in size and solidity of the bones, as compared to similar bones of recent species, have been noticed.

Beside the remains of the Japanese monkey, Macacus, I have detected the right lower jaw of what may prove to be a large baboon-like ape. It is certainly unlike anything found in Japan to-day. It may possibly be Cynopithicus, a species of which is found in the Philippine Islands and Celebes.

That this species existed in Japan during the historical period is not improbable, as the Japanese have long been familiar with accounts of monstrous apes, though the more intelligent among them have regarded these stories as mythical.

Mr. Ninagawa, the distinguished antiquarian, informs me that seven hundred years ago it was reported that a curious monster, supposed to be a large monkey, was seen near the Emperor's Palace at Kioto. Mr. Fujitani, a student in the Imperial University, has kindly collected a number of references in regard to this animal, and while many impossible things are told about it, yet some of the figures and descriptions recall an ape of large size, with long muzzle and protruding lips—features that ought well to accord with Cynopithicus.

Without specimens of the recent species to compare, it is of course impossible to state with certainty the character of the animal from the single fragment found at Omori.

CANNIBALISM.*

One of the most interesting discoveries connected with the Omori Mound is the evidence of cannibalism which it affords, this being the first indication of a race of anthropophagi in Japan. The human bones were found mixed with bones of the wild boar, deer and other animals. They were all fractured in a similar manner, either with the object of extracting the marrow or for convenience of cooking in vessels of too small dimensions to admit them at length. When discovered, they were entirely unrelated to each other. Some hopes were entertained that the place might have been used for purposes of burial, and special search was made for a continuous series of bones; but no proof was obtained in support of this supposition, and this is in accordance with the experience of those who have examined similar deposits in other parts of the world. The bones were mixed indiscriminately with other remains of feasts. Some of them are strongly marked with scratches and cuts, especially in those areas of muscular attachment where the muscles are separated from the bones with difficulty. The very mode of fracture in some cases is conspicuously artificial, and the surfaces for the attachment of muscles are strongly incised. These testimonials of cannibalism are of precisely the same nature as those educed by Professor Wyman in his memoir on the shell mounds of Florida. The accompanying passage is extracted from that memoir, page 68.

"The reasons derived from our own observations for believing that the ancient inhabitants of the St. John's were cannibals may be stated as follows:

1.—The bones, an account of which we have given, were not deposited in the shell heap at an ordinary burial of a dead body. In this case, after the decay of the flesh, there would have remained a certain order in the position of the parts of the skeleton, especially in the pelvis, the long bones of the limbs, the vertebral column and the head. The bones would be entire, as in other burials. In the cases here described, they were, on the contrary, scattered in a disorder-

* Read before the Biological Society of the Imperial University, Tokio, Jan. 5, 1879, and originally published in the Tokio Times Jan. 18, 1879.

ly manner, broken into many fragments, and often some important portions were missing, as the head, at one of the mounds near Blue Spring, the bones of an arm and leg at another, and in other mounds a still larger number of bones. The fractures, as well as the disorder in which the bones were found, evidently existed at the time they were covered up, as is shown by the condition of the broken ends, which had the same discoloration as the natural surfaces.

2.—The bones were broken, as in the case of those of edible animals, as the deer, alligator, etc. This would be necessary to reduce the parts to a size corresponding with the vessels in which they were cooked, or suitable for roasting, or even for eating raw.

3.—The breaking up of the bones had a certain amount of method; the heads of the humerus and femur were detached, as if to avoid the trouble, or from ignorance as to the way of disarticulating the joints. The shafts of these bones, as also those of the fore arm and leg, were regularly broken through the middle. The olecranon process of the ulna was in some cases detached in the same manner as the corresponding part of the deer."

Had this description referred especially to the Omori Mounds, there could not have been a more perfect accordance with the facts as they stand.

The evidence of cannibalism in the New England and Florida heaps was to have been expected, as history shows us that many tribes of North American Indians were eaters of human flesh, and tribes exist to-day, both in North and South America, who retain the habit. The evidence of cannibalism in Japan, however, has a different significance, because the minute and painstaking chronicles of her historians, running back with considerable accuracy for fifteen hundred years or more, give no trace of so monstrous a practice. Not only were the Japanese not cannibals, but there is no account of the tribes they encountered being addicted to tastes of this character, and so remarkable a trait would have found some acknowledgment in their records. The early historians speak of the Ainos as being of so mild and gentle a disposition that the art of murder was unknown among them. The failure of an adequate supply of food invariably drives even the highest of civilized races to this extremity, but no such necessity forced the people of the Omori period to so shocking an alternative. In this connection it would be interesting to know whether there are any records of the Japanese having been compelled by great exigency to subsist upon human flesh. There are many accounts of drifting Japanese junks given by Mr. Charles Walcott Brooks in the proceedings of the California Academy of Sciences. In these instances the survivors had prepared for burial those of their number who had perished from exposure and starvation.

The following is a list of the human bones thus far met with in the Omori Mounds:—

Right humerus; lenth of fragment, 195 man.; proximal end gone.

Left humerus; length of fragment, 215 mm.; both ends gone.
Left humerus; length of fragment, 160 mm.; both ends gone.
Right ulna; length of fragment, 200 mm.; distal end gone.
Right ulna; length of fragment, 180 mm.; both ends gone.
Right radius; length of fragment, 80 mm.; upper portion only.
Right femur; length of fragment, 150 mm.; proximal end and portion of shaft only.
Right femur; length of fragment, 270 mm.; both ends gone.
Right femur; length of fragment, 230 mm.; both ends gone.
Right femur; length of fragment, 197 mm.; upper portion of shaft.
Right femur; length of fragment, 304 mm.; articular surfaces broken; child.
Left femur; length of fragment, 160 mm.; shaft only.
Left femur; length of fragment, 270 mm; great trochanter and head and distal end gone; child.
Left femur; length of fragment, 85 mm.; lower portion only; articular surface gone; child.
Right tibia; length of fragment, 135 mm.; upper portion of shaft.
Right fibula; length of fragment, 205 mm; both ends broken.
Fifth right metatarsal; length, 65 mm.; distal articular surface partially gone.
Left lower maxillary.
Left parietal.

Of sixteen long bones of the arm and leg, nine are destitute of both extremities; and of the remaining seven, three are destitute of the lower extremity, two of the upper extremity, and in two, the articular surfaces of both ends are gone. Nothing more clearly illustrates the indiscriminate way in which the bones were scattered about, than the fact that the eight femora found represented at least seven different individuals, four being adults and three either women or children. None of the human bones show marks of having been wrought, but this we should not expect, since most of the implements discovered are made of horn.

A recent examination of Shell Mounds in the southern portion of the Empire has disclosed the most abundant and unquestionable evidences of cannibalism.

FLATTENED TIBIA.

A special search was made for fragments of the human tibia, on account of the remarkable deviation the tibia of ancient man presents, in comparison with that of recent man.

This deviation consists in a lateral flattening of the shaft of the bone. So wide spread is this variation in primitive man that it has given rise to a new name in science, and tibia possessing this lateral flattening are known as Platyenemic tibia.

It has frequently been met with in ancient mounds and Cave explorations in Europe, and Prof. Wyman has observed platycnemic tibia in ancient mounds in Kentucky, Tennesee, California, Florida, Labrador and other places. Mr. Henry Gillman discovered, in mounds in Michigan, tibia that possessed a remarkable lateral flattening.

According to Prof. Wyman's observations, the flattening of the tibia is not a race character, but seems to be of common occurrence in all prehistoric races.

Our labors at Omori were fortunately rewarded by the discovery of a portion of the shaft of a tibia, associated with other human bones.

From the variation this bone presents in man, the single example here mentioned can have but little significance. It may be of interest, however, to give its proportionate measurements in contrast with corresponding measurements given by Wyman in his Florida mounds memoir.

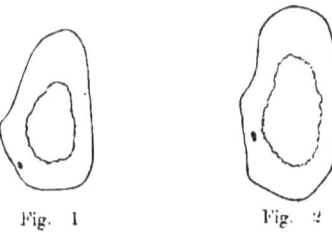

Fig. 1.   Fig. 2.

Transverse sections of Platycnemic Tibia.
Fig 1. Omori, Musashi.   Fig. 2. Onomura, Higo.

The antero-posterior diameter being taken as 100, the transverse diameter in
Twelve, white race (recent), was 0.70;
Twelve, from the Florida Mounds, 0.64;
Seven, from the Kentucky Mounds, 0.63;
One, from the Omori Mound, 0.62.

There were others from the Florida mounds as low as 0.59, and Mr. Gillman discovered one in a mound on Rouge River, Michigan, with the excessive lateral flattening of 0.48. This latter tibia far exceeds the famous Cro Magnon tibia of Broca, which gave an index of 0.60. The Omori specimen, with its index of 0.62, may be looked upon as a fair platycnemic tibia. It has a remarkable lateral flattening in contrast with nine recent Japanese tibia, which were measured at random and which gave an index of 0.74;—the lowest index in the lot being 68.4.

This flattening of the tibia is peculiar to the higher apes also, but as Prof. Wyman properly remarks, it is not so much the lateral flattening, as the rounding of the angles, and the bending of the shaft forward, which gives to it a distinct ape like character. The Omori tibia possesses this character in a marked degree.

This peculiarity associated with its lateral flattening, gives greater importance to the bone, and may be looked upon as an evidence of considerable antiquity of the remains found associated with it.

Since writing the above, I have examined a shell mound of immense size in the province of Higo.

The bones of mammals were not numerous yet of forty fragments found, more than half were those of man. They were all broken, and were scattered promiscuously through the deposit. Fortunately, fragments of a number of tibia were found, and these were all platycnemic. One showed an excessive lateral flattening, giving an index of 50.2, this being one of the lowest ever recorded.

the human bones were remarkable for the roughness and prominence of the bony ridges for muscular attachments.

A description of this mound with its pottery, etc. will be given in a future memoir.

A COMPARISON BETWEEN THE ANCIENT AND MODERN MOLLUSCAN FAUNA OF OMORI.

Some interesting facts are revealed in studying the remains of the animals which form the bulk of these deposits in Denmark, New England, Florida and Omori.

These facts show the following:

First: that a change has taken place in the relative abundance of individuals of certain species.

Second: that a change has taken place in the relative size of certain species.

Third: that a change has taken place in the relative proportions of the shells of certain species.

Fourth: that a change has taken place in the extinction of certain species.

The modification in the relative size and proportions of certain species is profound, and would seem to indicate, either that species vary in a much shorter time than had been supposed, or else that deposits presenting these peculiarities have a much higher antiquity than had before been accorded them.

We quote the following from Lubbock's "Prehistoric Times" page 231, as bearing upon this subject. In the Danish Mounds the four most abundant species of mollusks are:

> The oyster,................... *Ostrea edulis L.*
> The cockle,................... *Cardium edule L.*
> The mussel,................... *Mytilus edulis L.*
> The periwinkle,............... *Litorina litorea L.*

All four of which are still used as food for man. Other species occur more rarely, namely,—

> *Nassa reticulata L.*
> *Buccinum undatum L.*
> *Venus pullastra, Mont.*

And six other species of mollusks which he enumerates. He then says, "It is remarkable that the specimens of the first seven species are well developed, and decidedly larger than any now found in the neighborhood. This is especially the case with the *Cardium edule*, and *Litorina litorea*, while the oyster has entirely disappeared, and, even in the Kattegat, occurs only in a few places; a result which may, perhaps, be partly owing to the quantities caught by fishermen." And he concludes that "on the whole their disappearance, especially when taken in connection with the dwarfed size of other species, is evidently attributable in a great measure to the smaller proportion of salt in the water."

Among the birds occuring in the Danish shell heaps, is *Tetrao urogallus*, which feeds principally on the buds of the pine, showing that at the time the deposits were made, extensive pine forests once covered the region, a fact previously established by a study of the peat beds. Bones of the great auk, *Alca impennis*, also occur in the same deposits, and this bird is now probably extinct.

The shell mounds along the coast of Maine also indicate a marked change in the distribution of certain species. A number of species of mollusks occur in them, which are not found at present north of Cape Cod. Some of them present a remarkable solidity of form in comparison with recent specimens.

The bones of the great auk are likewise met with in many of the deposits, in such numbers as to show that it was then a common bird, and furnished an article of food. More curious still is the occurence of a molar tooth discovered by me in one of the deposits on the coast of Maine, which Prof. Wyman beieved to be the molar tooth of the polar bear, a species which is now confined to the Arctic regions.

In a paper published fifteen years ago on the occurrence of land snails in ancient deposits on one of the islands in Casco Bay, Maine,* I showed that at the time of their existence, a hard wood growth must have abounded. The island has been covered since the earliest memory of man with a dense spruce growth.

I have in preparation a paper on the changes in the character of certain species of Mollusca from the deposits in Massachusetts. In those I have measured and drawn, the differences between present existing species and their ancestors are constant.

Prof. Wyman observed similar changes in the mollusks of the Florida deposits. He says, in his memoir on the Florida Mounds, that the Ampullariæ, and Paludinæ, are much larger than their living representatives. "The average size of the aperture in twenty large Ampullariæ from the mounds was, breadth 34.4 mm, and length 53.9 mm; while in the largest living shells we have found, the aperture did not exceed 30 mm. in breadth and 48 mm. in length, which would seem to indicate a greater vital activity in former days."

* On the occurence of rare Helices in ancient shell heaps. Proceedings Portland Soc. Nat. Hist. Vol. 1 1863.

With these facts before me, I was impelled to examine the various species of shells found in the Omori Mounds, in comparison with similar species now living along the immediate shores of the Bay. The followings descriptions and measurements will show that changes more or less great have taken place since the ancestors of those now living along the shore formed the food of the savages who made the deposits.

As a preparation for these comparisons, a number of visits were made to the shores of Omori village, in which I was accompanied by a class of special students and others who had collected with me in Yezo.

A most searching exploration was made along the coast for a considerable distance, and many specimens of every species bearing upon the subject were obtained. A special search was made for those forms common in the Mounds. A similar number of visits was made to the Mounds, accompanied by the same corps of assistants, with directions to collect every species found there. In this way an immense amount of material was brought together, and from this material only mature and perfect specimens were selected for comparison. Besides this material, I had a large number of species collected at Yenoshima, year before last, as well as a large amount of material collected by the University Expedition at Otaru and Hakodate, in Yezo, Sendai Bay, and on the west coast at Funagawa, and Niigata. Use was also made of valuable collections made at Kishiu this winter by Prof. Yatabe and Mr. Sasaki. All of these collections were of use in showing the degree of variation between Northern and Southern forms of the same species. Collections of the edible mollusks in the Tokio markets, and at Shinagawa, were also considered in these comparisons. Measurelments were made in millimeters, and the tables of figures were submitted to Prof. T. C. Mendenhall, of the Tokio Daigaku, who kindly offered to compute the averages and proportions for me.

Every precaution has been taken to insure accuracy, and the results will certainly be of interest to those who recognize a change in species, coincident with change in time, and environment.

Area suberenata Lischke.

Specimens of this species were not uncommon in the Mounds, and were also found scattered along the shores of the Bay. Lischke gives the number of ribs as from 31 to 33. Twelve recent specimens from the shores of Omori averaged $33\frac{1}{4}$ ribs, while 15 specimens from the Mounds averaged $30\frac{1}{2}$ ribs. The hinge, or umbonal area in the recent specimens,—measuring the area of one valve transversely, gave an average of 5.7 mm., while in the mound specimens the same area averaged 5.9 mm.

The following figures show that the ancient specimens are not only larger, but that the proportions of the shell are also different:—the shell having increased in length, in proportion to its hight.

		Length.	Hight.
Average dimensions of ten largest specimens,	Recent,	61.8	50.4
	Mound,	65.7	52.
Assuming length to be 100, hight in,	30 Recent.	81.2	
	28 Mound.	79.1	
Dimensions of largest specimen,	Recent,	69.5	54.
	Mound,	80.5	69

These differences, though slight, appear to be constant, and indicate a change in the character of the shell, as to its relative size, number of ribs, size of hinge area, and proportionate diameters.

Arca inflata Reeve. PLATE XVIII. FIG. 5.

This species is comparatively rare in the Mounds though of common occurrence along the shores. It is a common edible mollusk in the markets of Tokio. The average number of ribs in the recent specimens from Omori is 41.2 Reeve gives 40 as the number in his description of the species, though Schrenck states that they average 42 to 43.

In the few specimens found in the Mounds the ribs averaged 39.6 This average, drawn from so few specimens, is of but little value, yet, taken in connection with the other species of Arca, wherein the ancient specimens exhibited a less number of ribs, it is of some interest.

In the dimensions of the hinge area, however, the most remarkable change is seen between the ancient and recent forms. The average width in nine recent specimens, measuring one valve, was 6.4, while in five ancient specimens it was 15. These dimensions in the recent specimens ranged as follows : 8, 5, 4, 7, 6, 6, 5, 6, 11 ; and in the ancient specimens, 17, 16, 13, 17, 12.

Arca granosa Linné.

This is one of the most abundant shells in the Mounds. I have never met with it in my collections made at Yenoshima, Yedo Bay, or Yezo. Takamine did not obtain it in his dredgings and shore collecting at Funagawa and Niigata, on the west coast. Sasaki did not find it at Sendai Bay. Prof. Yatabe and party made exhaustive collections by dredging, and shore collecting, at various points along the coast at Kishiu, yet failed to secure a single specimen.

Lischke in his great work, *Japanische Meeres Conchylien*, records examples from Nagasaki only. He gives the following localities: Tochi-fu, North China and Cochin China, *Debeaux*; Philippine Islands, *Reeve*; Ceram and Celebes, *Rumphius*; Tranquebar and Nikobaren, *Chemnitz*. R. E. C. Stearns Esq. of the University of California says that the Mound specimens have a less number of ribs;—the species at present having from 23 to 26 ribs, while the Mound specimens range in number of ribs from 18 to 20.

Mr. Stearns further remarks that the Mound specimens differ from the present form in being less equilateral, and in having the umbones less produced. He says it is at present a southern form, and belongs to a widely separated geographical province.

In the digging of wells in Tokio it is often brought up in a semi-fossil condition from considerable depths. I have also found it in great numbers in an ancient mound in Tokio proper, associated with pottery and rude stone implements, and Mr. Ishikawa has found it associated with cord marked pottery beyond Oji. From these evidences it must have been a common shell in past times, but has now become extinct in this and neighboring waters.

Lischke gives the following measurements of two specimens from Nagasaki, and one from Singapore.

	Length.	Hight.
Nagasaki,	54	40
"	44	31
Singapore,	32	28
Largest specimen from the Mound	57	42
Average of ten largest specimens from the Mound,	52.9	41.1

It is interesting to observe that the two other species of *Arca* from the Mound possess a less number of ribs than the present species. In other words the three species of *Arca* at the present time differ in possessing a larger number of ribs than their ancestors, beside the other differences already recorded, as follows:

Number of ribs in,	Mound.	Recent.
Arca sub-crenata,	30.5	33.3
" *inflata*,	39.6	41.2
" *granosa*,	18 to 20	23 to 26

Cyclina Chinensis Chemnitz. Plate XVIII, Fig. 1.

This species is not common along the shores at Omori. Lischke records a single example from the Bay of Yedo, and thirteen from Nagasaki. I have a number of specimens from Omori village.

It is by no means an uncommon shell in the Mounds, and the larger size as compared with the recent form is seen at a glance.

	Length.	Hight.
Average dimensions of { Recent,	47.5	51.4
ten largest specimens, { Mound,	52.4	55.4

Assuming length to be 100, hight in { 27 Recent specimens 105.7 / 69 Mound „ 104.2

	Length.	Hight.
Largest specimen, { Recent,	50.5	54.
{ Mound,	57.5	62.5

Tapes sp. PLATE XVIII, FIG. 2.

This species is one of the most abundant forms in the Mounds, as well as one of the most common shells along the shore. It is a common edible mollusk in the markets. Not being able to refer to a description or figure of the species, I cannot give its specific name. It is sufficient to say that the living specimens collected for comparison are of the same species as those found in the Mounds.

The proportions of the shell have scarcely changed, though curiously enough the recent ones are somewhat longer than the ancient ones, and the umbones are more eroded.

	Length.	Hight.
Average dimensions of { Recent,	54.2	39.4
ten largest specimens, { Mound,	49.2	35.8

Assuming length to be 100, hight in { 49 Recent, 72.3 / „ Mound, 72.

	Length.	Hight.
Dimensions of largest specimen, { Recent,	58.	42.
{ Mound,	50.5	35.

Dosinia Japonica Dunker. PLATE XVIII. FIG. 6.

This species is not common, either in the Mounds, or along the shores of the Bay. A comparison of the measurements shows a change in proportions, and indicates also that the ancient specimens were larger than the recent.

	Length.	Hight.
Average dimensions of { Recent,	65.6	61.5
ten largest specimens, { Mound,	69.8	65.7

Assuming length to be 100, hight in { 10 specimens, Recent, 93.4
                                      9   ,,   Mound, 95.2

	Length.	Hight.
Dimensions of largest specimen, Recent,	68.	63.
Mound,	77.5	73.

Mactra veneriformis Deshayes.   PLATE XVIII. FIG. 3.

This species is very common in the Mounds, and along the shores of the Bay. It is also common in the markets of Tokio. Lischke gives the average size of the species as follows : length 38, hight 34.

He also gives the dimensions of a specimen from Kishiu as follows : length 48, hight 44.

The following are the dimensions of the Mound specimens in comparison with the recent at Omori.

	Length.	Hight.
Average dimensions of Recent,	43.4	38.1
ten largest specimens, Mound,	50.6	49.1

Assuming length to be 100, hight in { 21 Recent, 88.3
                                      15 Mound, 86.6

	Length.	Hight.
Dimensions of largest specimen, Recent,	48.5	43.5
Mound,	59.	51.5

It will be seen by the above figures that the average hight of the Mound shell exceeds the length of recent specimens as given by Lischke, and is much longer than the shell as it exists to day at Omori. Its proportions have moreover changed.

Cytherea meretrix Linné.   PLATE XVIII. FIG. 7.

Under this name Lischke probably refers to the species to be considered. It is one of the principal shells in the Mounds and appears equally common along the Omori shores.

The proportionate diameters vary but little, but the difference in size is noticeable at once, the Mound specimens being larger.

	Length,	Hight,
Average dimensions of Recent,	85.8	66.1
ten largest specimens, Mound,	97.3	75.1

Assuming length to be 100, hight in { 18 Recent. 77.2
{ 18 Mound, 78.5

		Length.	Hight.
Dimensions of largest specimen	Recent,	95.	73.
	Mound,	106.5	81.5

Mya arenaria Linné. PLATE XVIII. FIG. 4.

Not an abundant shell in the Mounds nor common along the coast. It is often seen in the markets at Tokio, brought from Shinagawa.

It will be seen by the figures that the proportions have changed slightly, though the size remains nearly the same.

		Length.	Hight.
Average dimensions of	Recent,	98.5	62.1
ten largest specimens,	Mound,	98.2	59.9

Assuming length to be 100, hight in { 17 Recent, 62.5
{ 17 Mound, 61.1

		Length.	Hight.
Dimensions of largest specimen,	Recent,	105.	62.5
	Mound,	112.	66.

The following species of Lamellibranchiates are present in the Deposits.

Arca subcrenata Lischke.
" *inflata* Reeve.
" *granosa* Linné.
Dosinia Troschelii Lischke.
Cyclina Chinensis Chemnitz.
Mactra veneriformis Deshayes.
Mya arenaria Linné.
Cytherea meretrix Linné.
Tapes sp.
Solen strictus Gould.
Lutraria Nuttalli Conrad.
Ostrea denslamellosa Lischke.
" *sp.*

Those species whose dimensions have been given were represented by a sufficient number of specimens for the purposes of measurements and comparisons. Of the others, with the exception of *Ostrea*, only a few specimens were found, not enough to justify comparisons.

It will be seen by the foregoing measurements that the following species from the mounds are larger than their living representatives from the same locality:

Arca subcrenata, *Cyclina Chinensis*, *Cytherea meretrix*, *Mactra veneriformis* and *Dosinia Troscheli*. *Arca granosa* is much larger than any dimension given by Lischke.

Among the few gasteropods which occur in sufficient numbers for comparison, the differences in proportions between the Mound specimens and the recent ones are quite as conspicuous.

Eburna Japonica Lischke. Plate XVIII. Fig. 9.

This is a very common shell in the deposits, and is also found scattered along the shores. It is very common further south in the Bay.

The differences between the ancient and recent shells are easily recognized without the aid of measurements.

The recent shell, though larger than the ancient one, is not so broad compared to its length, as in the ancient form. While both have the same average breadth, the recent form is nearly six millimeters longer. This gives the recent shell a more acute spire, while the ancient shell appears more robust.

A large number of recent and ancient specimens were brought together, and from these, the perfect and mature ones, for the purposes of measurement were selected.

The angle of the spire was measured in fifty specimens of the Mound and fifty specimens of the recent, and the difference is shown in the following diagram.

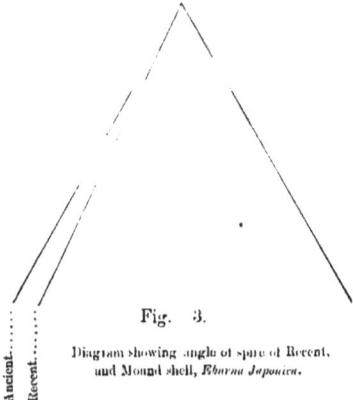

Fig. 3.

Diagram showing angle of spire of Recent, and Mound shell, *Eburna Japonica*.

The mean angle for the recent was 57°45′, and for the Mound, was 61°45′.

The following measurements will show the differences in the proportions between the recent and the Mound specimens.

	Breadth.	Length.
Average dimensions of { Recent,	41.8	67.9
ten largest specimens, { Mound,	40.7	63.1
Assuming length to be 100, breadth in { Recent was 63.		
{ Mound ,, 66.		
Dimensions of largest specimen, { Recent, 47.	75.	
{ Mound, 45.	67.5	

Purpura luteostoma Chemnitz.

The specimens referred to of this species from the Omori Mounds are so much larger than any Purpura found today in the Bay of Yedo that it is quite difficult to determine their affinities. At present, the species described under the names of *luteostoma* and *clavigera* can be pretty easily determined. In the Omori days the forms were not so well defined. The nearest resemblance to the Omori Purpura is the *Purpura luteostoma* from the west coast of Japan at Funagawa. *Purpura luteostoma* from Yenosima resembles somewhat *P. Bronni* Dunker as it occurs at Kishiu, while the *P. clavigera* Kuster from Kishiu resembles the variety described by Reeve under the name of *P. tumulosa*.

We searched in vain for an example of *Purpura* along the Omori shores.

The specimens from Yenosima are so small as to be worthless for comparison.

It is easy to believe that not long ago the various species of Purpura were once varieties of a single species, and that *P. Bronni, luteostoma, clavigera, tumulosa* and many others are modifications of a single form. Indeed I can recall as great a variation among examples of *Purpura lapillus* along the eastern coast of the United States as one sees among these so called species.

Lischke mentions the length of his largest specimen from Hakodate as 40 mm. The largest specimen from Omori measures 53 mm.

The following are the dimensions of the Omori specimens in comparison with those of Hakodate.

	Breadth.	Length.
10 largest specimens from Omori Mounds,	27.8	47.4
,, ,, ,, ,, Hakodate,	23.9	35.4
Assuming length to be 100, breadth in { Omori shell is 58.		
{ Hakodate, 67.		

Natica Lamarckiana Duclos. PLATE XVIII. FIG. 8.

This is another common shell in the Omori Deposits, and is also one of the most common shells along the Omori shores.

The differences between the Mound specimens and the recent ones are so profound, that it may be recognized as a marked variety. The elevated spire, the heavy callosity almost concealing the umbilicus, and the marked differences in the proportions of the shell are noticeable at once, and distinguish it from its iving representative.

The Omori Mound variety approaches nearer the form which occurs much further north at Hakodate.

The differences between this species and *Natica duplicata* Say, which occurs along the eastern coast of the United States, are very slight.

	Hight.	Breadth.
Average dimensions of ten largest specimens, Recent,	60.2	68.4
Mound,	62.	65.8

Assuming breadth to be 100, hight in { 10 largest Recent, 88.1
{ 10 largest Mound, 94.2

	Hight.	Breadth.
Dimensions of largest specimen, Recent,	68.	76.
Mound,	66.	71.5

Turbo granulatus Chemnitz.

This is one of the most abundant shells in the Omori deposits, but the shores of Omori have been repeatedly searched without bringing to light a single specimen. Lischke records forty specimens from Nagasaki only. It is a common species at Hongkong and further south. Prof. Yatabe and Mr. Sasaki collected a very large and marked variety at the Bonin Islands, and also the ordinary form from Kishiu. Mr. Takamine met with it in abundance at Funagawa some distance north of Niigata, on the west Coast, and I have collected small specimens at Yenoshima.

In past times it must have been one of the most common shells along the shores at Omori, judging from the number that occur in the Mounds. It must have had a more northern range in past times, but like *Arca granosa* has retreated south.

The following measurements are given from ten largest specimens from the Omori Mounds, Kishiu, and Funagawa.

Average dimensions of ten largest specimens.

	Breadth.	Hight.	Proportion of hight to breadth.
Omori Mounds.	25.4	23.	90.5
Kishiu,	24.6	21.8	84.3
Funagawa,	23.2	22.1	95.2

Lischke's largest specimen from Nagasaki measured 25 millimeters in diameter.

As this species varies greatly with each locality, it would be unfair to make any comparisons between the Omori Mound specimens and those from Kishiu and Niigata. It will be observed however, that the average diameter of the Omori specimens, exceeds the largest diameter as given by Lischke, as well as those from Kishiu and Niigata.

Of the other species of mollusks found in the Mounds, no special comparisons have been made, owing either to the lack of a sufficient number of mature and perfect specimens, or of recent specimens with which to compare.

The following is a list of the gasteropods thus far found in the deposits.

Fusus inconstans Lischke.
Rapana bezoar Linné.
Hemifusus tuba Gmelin.
Purpura luteostoma Chemnitz.
Eburna Japonica Lischke.
Nassa sp.
Potamides sp.
Lampania sp.
Natica Lamarckiana Duclos.
Turbo granulatus Gmelin.
Rotella globosa Gould.

The few specimens of *Fusus inconstans* appears to be more robust than the species as it exists to day in the vicinity, and resembles the typical form as figured by Lischke, while the recent ones along the shore resembles his small varieties.

Rapana bezoar is exceedingly abundant, of large size, with massive shell. Many of the specimens have a portion of the body wall broken through, as if for the purpose of more conveniently extracting the flesh.

The Mound specimens of *Hemifusus tuba* were large, light, and the tubercles were prominent and acute. The recent specimens along the shore were about half the size, quite solid, with the tubercles obtuse.

The species of *Nassa* and *Lampania* were too small for edible mollusks, and were probably accidently introduced with the larger species. Only a few specimens of each species were collected, and those were too much eroded for comparison.

The following species were more or less common along the shores of Omori village, but have not yet been found in the Mounds.

> *Mactra*, possibly *sulcataria*.
> *Cancellaria Spengleriana* Lischke.
> *Soletellina olivacea* Jay.
> *Liocardium* sp.
> *Pecten* sp.
> *Natica janthostoma* Deshayes.

With the exception of the last species, these are all edible mollusks, and the *Mactra* is one of the most common mollusks in the Tokio markets. Their absence from the Deposits certainly indicates a change in the fauna.

In this respect the absence of *Haliotis* and *Pinna* from the Mounds is certainly of great interest, for it shows, either the lack of proper means for water transport, or a disinclination on the part of the people to go far from their abiding place in quest of food.

On the opposite side of the Bay, and also south of Yokohama, the *Haliotis* may be found, and large numbers of the shells are brought to Tokio for the pearl they afford. No trace of the large species, *Haliotis gigantea* or of the smaller species, *Haliotis Gruneri*, has as yet been met with in the Mounds.

A race of fishermen accustomed to venture far in their boats would certainly have left some trace of these species in their refuse piles.

In conclusion it may be said that a pronounced change has taken place in the molluscan fauna of the Bay of Yedo since the Omori deposits were made. The extinction of certain forms within comparatively recent times might be accounted for in considering the upheaval of the water basin, and the consequent narrowing of the Bay and shoaling of the waters, but the profound changes which have taken place in the size and contour of certain species demands time.

There are but few units of time that can be used to measure the interval required to effect such changes. One of two hundred and thirty years has presented itself to me in the removal of a portion of the Suruga-dai canal embankment. This canal was dug through Suruga-dai two hundred and thirty years ago. The earth was piled up in immense embankments on each side of the canal.

Recently at Misaki Cho, near the Suido Bashi, a portion of this embankment was removed in the construction of a new street. In the removal of this earth, a deposit of shells was exposed presumably as old as the embankment, which rested upon it.

The deposit was composed of the following species. *Placuanomia* sp, *Ostrea denslamellosa*, *Ostrea* sp., *Cytherea meretrix*, *Cyclina Chinensis*, *Mactra veneri-*

formis, *Arca subcrenata*, *Tapes* sp. *Rapana bezoar*, *Turbo spinosus*, *Turbo granulatus*, and *Lampania multiformis*.

The shells bore the marks of age, having that peculiar yellowish and chalky color and characteristic appearance of the nacreous portion, generally seen in shells long buried in the ground.

Not a single fragment of ancient pottery was found. On the contrary, fragments of tiles and a few pieces of glazed pottery and porcelain of Owari and Kioto, were met with.

The two species of *Ostrea* formed the bulk of the deposit.

Specimens of *Cyclina Chinensis* were very large. A single small specimen only of *Turbo granulatus* was met with. Special search, however, was made for *Purpura luteostoma* and particularly for *Arca granosa*, but no trace of either was found. *Arca inflata* had the same narrow hinge area that the species presents to-day. In fact no appreciable change has taken place between the species living two hundred and thirty years ago, and their descendants which live at the present time.

Another deposit of shells, somewhat old, judging from the appearance of the shells, was examined near Kameido, and no trace of *Arca granosa* was found nor trace of pottery.

The occurrence of *Arca granosa*, in this region at least, may be looked upon as an evidence of the presence of ancient cord marked pottery.

EXPLANATION OF PLATES.

PLATE I.

Note. All figures drawn half size unless otherwise mentioned.

Fig. 1. 5 to 7 mm. in thickness, hight 242 mm., diameter across mouth 268 mm. Black above, reddish below, bottom with matting impression. 1ª top view of rim, natural size. 1ᵇ section of rim, natural size. 1ᶜ front view of rim, natural size.

Fig. 2. Margin 12 mm. thick, side 7 mm. thick, diameter of mouth, 100 mm. Black, bottom slightly concave and smooth. Design repeated four times. Inside of vessel stained with *ferric oxide*.

Fig. 3. 8 mm. thick Below, 5 mm. thick near rim, hight 200 mm., largest diameter 177 mm. Blackish, mouth triangular in shape. 3ª top view of rim, natural size.

Fig. 4. Wall 5 mm. thick, diameter of rim 150 mm. Black.

Fig. 5. Body 9 mm. thick, bottom 12 mm. thick, handle 10 mm. thick. Hight from bottom to top of handle 147 mm. Light Brick red. Handles grooved, and loops perforated for passage of cord. Clay nearly dry before ornamenting.

Fig. 6. 7 mm. thick at margin, 4 mm. below, diameter 120 mm. Black, bottom flat.

Fig. 7. 5 mm. thick, diameter 140 mm., bottom depressed, smooth areas depressed. Above first band of cord marks painted with *mercury sulphide*. Cord marked areas black, bottom smooth, olive brown color. Inside of vessel rough clay washed. Length 150 mm., hight 125 mm., breadth 71 mm.

Fig. 8. Varying from 5 to 13 mm. in thickness, black outside, bottom massive, greatly depressed, very roughly and coarsely made.

Fig. 9. Rim 6 mm. thick, body 5 mm. thick, mouth 144 mm. in diameter. Reddish, with signs of use over fire. Many rims of vessels similar to this were found, one fragment showing a diameter of the perfect vessel of 354 mm.

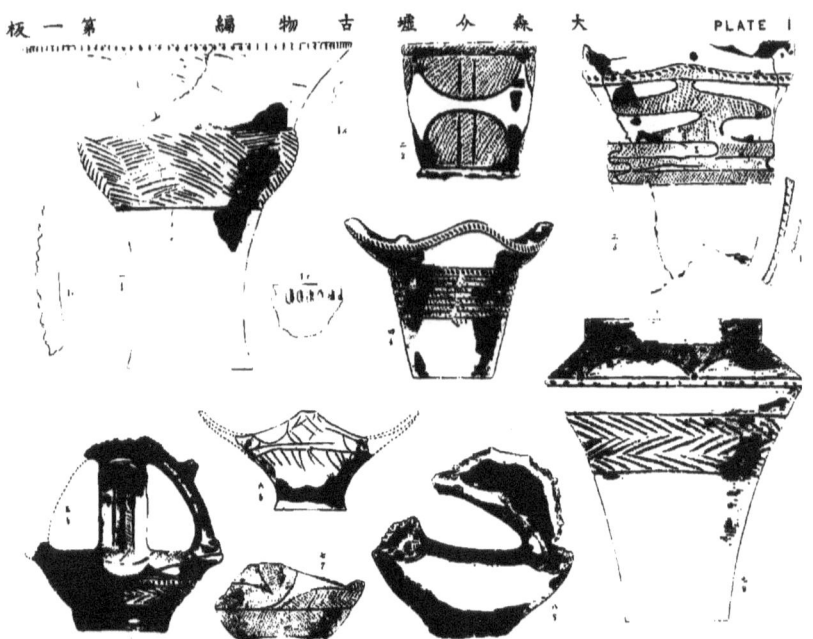

PLATE II.

Note. All figures drawn half size unless otherwise mentioned.

Fig. 1. Bottom 4 to 7 mm. thick, bulge 3 to 4 mm., rim 7 mm. Black, rudely made.

Fig. 2. Restored from large fragment, bottom 10 mm., rim 4 mm., diameter 165 mm. Blackish.

Fig. 3. Bottom 7 mm. thick, margin 4 to 5 mm., diameter 120 mm. Clay colored, made of fine clay and very light.

Fig. 4. *One quarter natural size*, rim 9 mm., below 5 mm. Black.

Fig. 5. 5 mm. thick, diameter 60 mm. Light brick red, bottom with mat impression. Very nicely made.

Fig. 6. 6 mm. thick, red with black stains.

Fig. 7. Rim 5 mm. thick, body 7 mm., black. Bottom with mat impression. Incrusted within, like paint.

Fig. 8. Rim 4 mm. thick, bottom 10 mm. Black.

Fig. 9. 5 mm. thick, black with traces of red.

Fig. 10. 8 mm. thick, diameter 124 mm. Black, smooth, bottom with mat impression. The bottom has not been accurately represented by the lithographer.

Fig. 11. 6 mm. thick, diameter 190 mm. Dark colored bisquit, black within and without. Shining. This is the finest made vessel in the whole collection. It will be observed that the design on the bottom is repeated four times, while the rim has five undulations. A similar feature will be seen in the vessel figured on this plate, Fig. 1.

Fig. 12. Wall 5 mm. thick, bottom 8 mm., diameter 260 mm., red below, black above, smooth within.

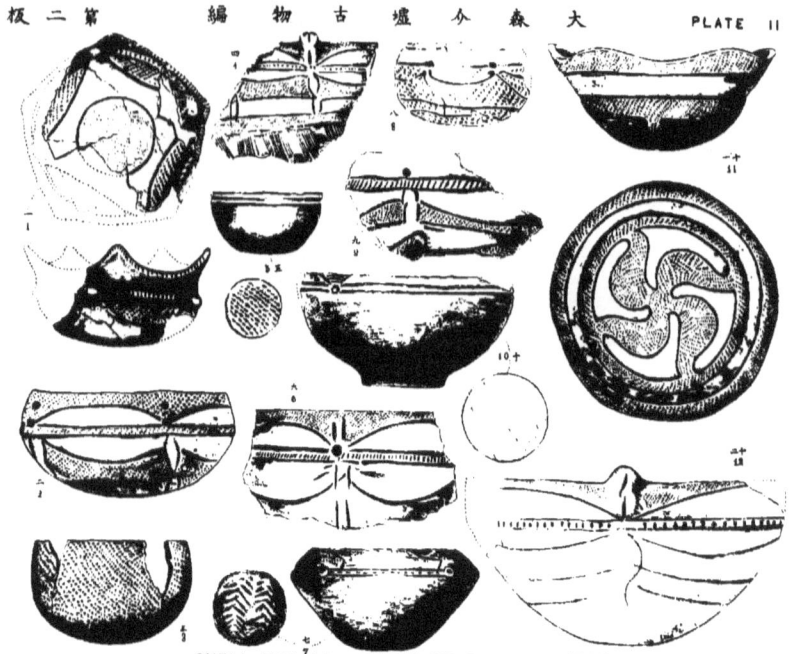

SHELL MOUNDS of OMORI NEAR TOKIO, JAPAN.

PLATE III.

Note. All figures drawn half size unless otherwise mentioned.

Fig. 1. 5 mm. thick, diameter 160 mm., nearly black, smooth inside.
Fig. 2. 4 mm. thick, blackish, dry scratched.
Fig. 3. Margin 7 mm. thick, black, flat bottom, rough finish inside.
Fig. 4. Bottom 7 mm. thick, diameter 114 mm. thick, black.
Fig. 5. Upper edge 7 mm. thick, very coarse clay, roughly made, thickly painted with *mercury sulphide*. Dotted lines indicate contours of inside and bottom.
Fig. 6. 5 mm. thick, black. Restored from large fragment.
Fig 7. 5 mm. thick, diameters across mouth 137 and 150 mm. Black, bottom flat, groove on inside of rim, faint mat impression on bottom, very uneven in shape.
Fig. 8. 4 mm. thick on side, light reddish, smooth finish within.
Fig. 9. 10 mm. thick, black, smooth inside.
Fig. 10. Lower edge 5 mm., thick, blackish.
Fig. 11. 7 to 10 mm. thick, clay colored.
Fig. 12. 6 mm. thick, diameter 160 mm.
Fig. 13. 6 to 8 mm. thick, slate color.
Fig. 14. 5 mm. thick near rim, diameter 177 mm., black, bottom rough.
Fig. 15. 5 mm. thick, light reddish colored, hight 77 mm., upper margin roughly rounded, lower rim broken, bottom flat.
Fig. 16. 8 mm. thick, diameter 154 mm., clay colored, unevenly made. Dotted lines indicate contours of inside and base.

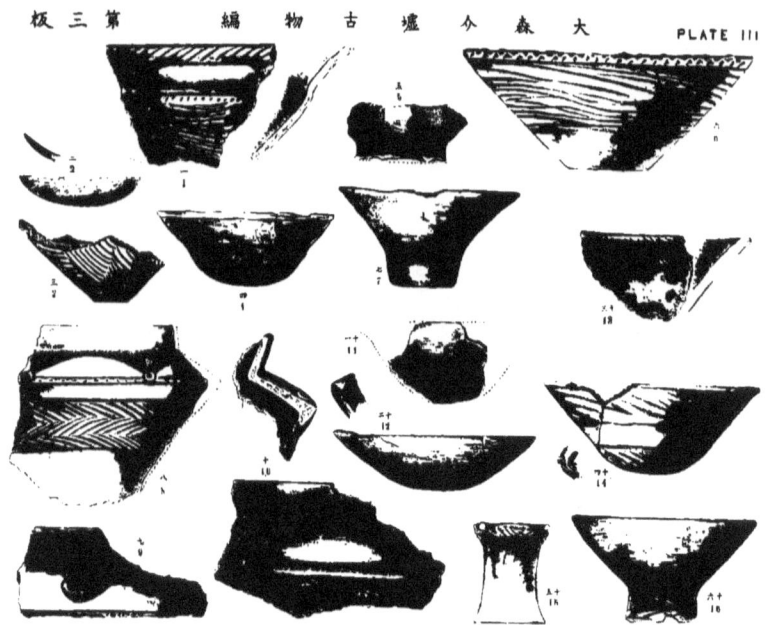

SHELL MOUNDS of OMORI NEAR TOKIO, JAPAN.

PLATE IV.

Note. All figures drawn half size unless otherwise mentioned.

Fig. 1. 7 mm. thick, black with reddish tinge, bands finger squeezed and put on after pot was shaped.
Fig. 2. 4 mm. thick, nearly black, smooth inside.
Fig. 3. 5 mm. thick, rim thicker, reddish.
Fig. 4. 6 mm. thick, reddish.
Fig. 5. *One quarter natural size.* 7 mm. thick, black. Inside are fine parallel lines, two to a millimeter; these are partially obliterated by a vertical smoothing motion of some implement.
Fig. 6. 7 mm. thick, dark red, smooth.
Fig. 7. *One quarter natural size.* 6 mm. thick, clay colored.
Fig. 8. 5 mm. thick, margin thicker and grooved above. Diameter of vessel about 190 mm. Central design repeated eight times round, reddish, smooth. Numbers of fragments of this vessel were found.
Fig. 9. 6 mm. thick, reddish, diameter about 200 mm.
Fig. 10. *One quarter natural size.* 8 mm. thick, diameter of vessel 245 m.m. Black, coarsely made.

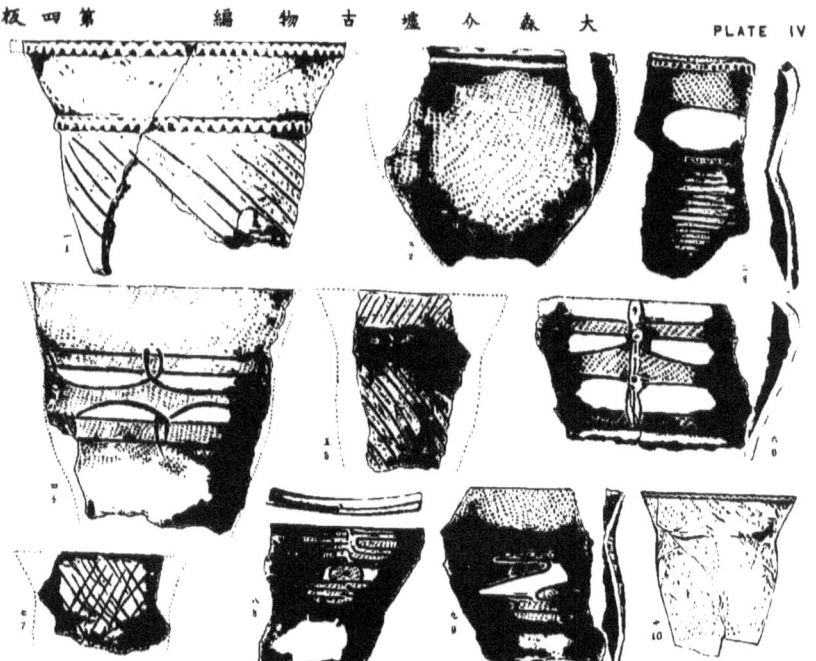

SHELL MOUNDS OF OMORI NEAR TOKIO, JAPAN.

PLATE V.

Note. All figures drawn half size unless otherwise mentioned.

Fig. 1. The broken portions of pots of this nature are the most common forms in the mounds. Varying from 5 to 10 mm. in thickness. Nearly half show the mat impression, and these impressions show a variety in the mode of braiding the mat. The color of the fragments are generally reddish.

Fig. 2. 3 mm. thick, black, very delicate walls and very fine mat impression.

Fig. 3. 10 mm. thick, light reddish. This specimen has had its fractured edge ground down, probably for the purpose of utilizing it as a cup.

Fig. 4. 7 mm. thick, black, with areas of brick red, bowl shaped bottom within.

Fig. 5. 6 mm. thick, black with areas of brick red, smooth bottom, rough inside.

Fig. 6. Light clay colored.

Fig. 7. 7 mm. thick, black.

Fig. 8. 6 mm. thick, black.

Fig. 9. Above 10 mm. thick, below 7 mm. thick, black. One groove inside twenty millimeters below rim and parallel to it.

Fig. 10. Rim 10 mm. thick, lower edge of fragment 5 mm. thick, reddish colored, rough surface.

Fig. 11. 8 mm. thick, hight 140 mm. thick, rim with five rude knobs around periphery; roughly made. A few rounded pebbles mixed with bisquit; burnt mud color.

Fig. 12. 5 to 6 mm. thick, light brick red, well made.

Fig. 13. *One quarter natural size.* 5 mm. thick, black.

Fig. 14. 4 to 5 mm. thick, 155 mm. in diameter, light brick red.

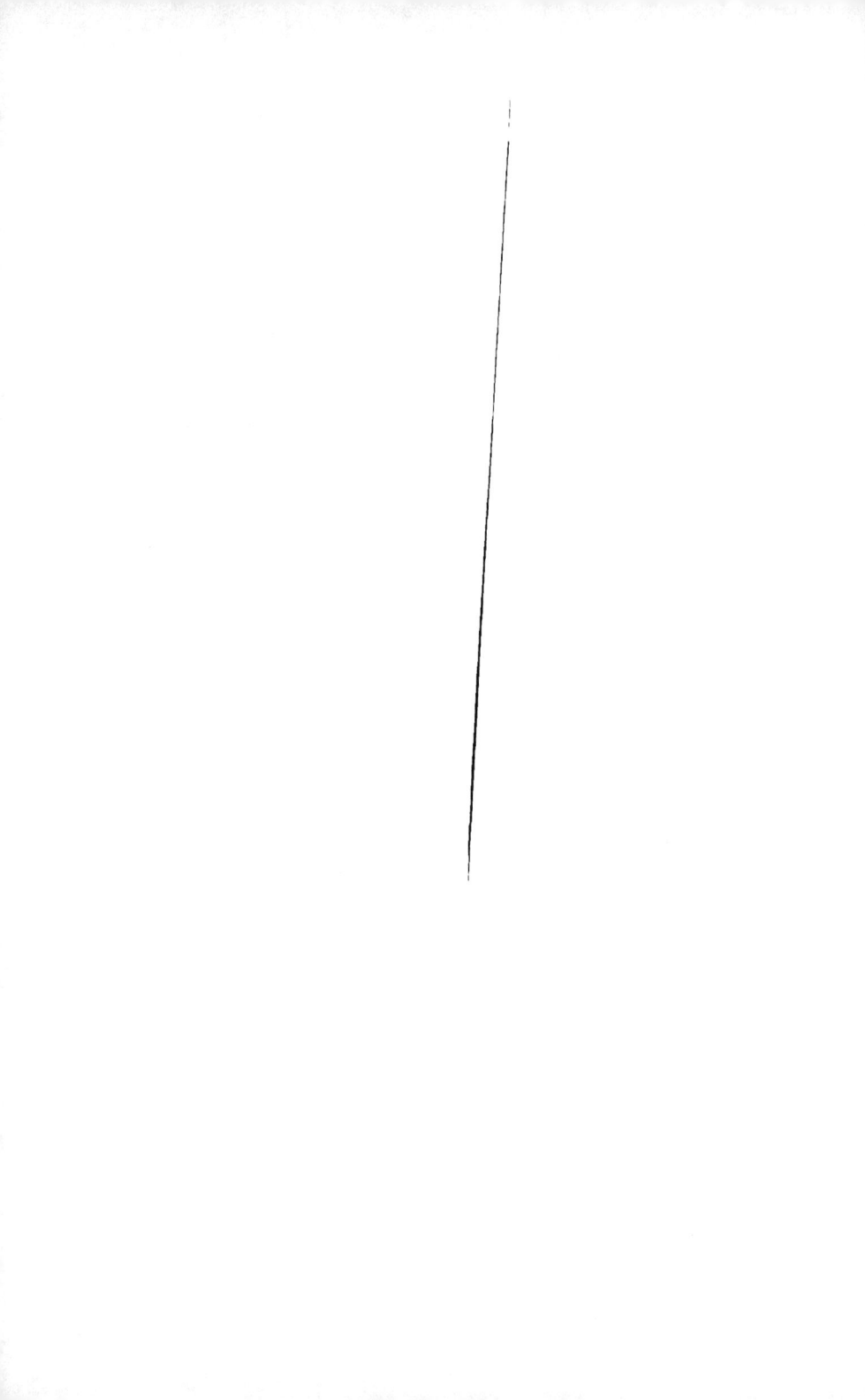

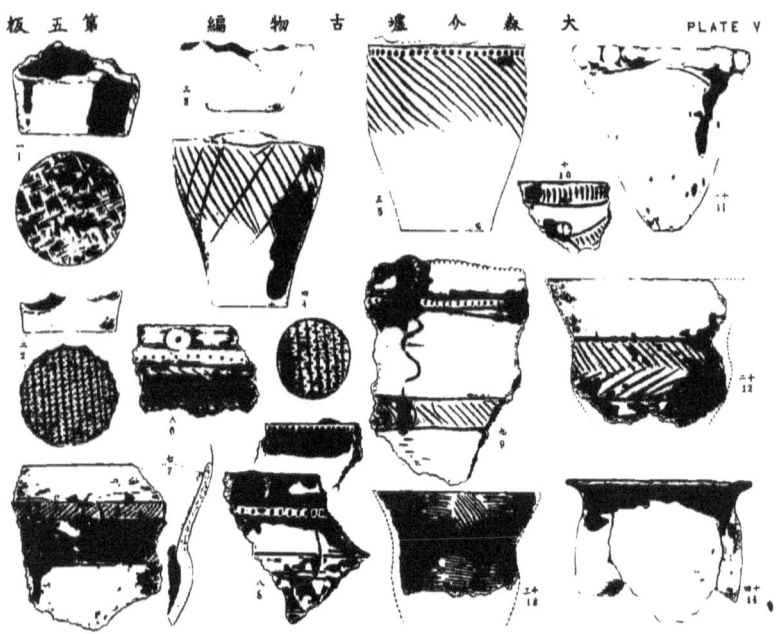

SHELL MOUNDS of OMORI NEAR TOKIO, JAPAN.

PLATE VI.

Note. All figures drawn half size unless otherwise mentioned.

Fig. 1. *Natural size.* 4 to 5 mm. thick, black, outside polished, inside rough.
Fig. 2. 6 mm. thick, light brick red, neck joined to body in making.
Fig. 3. *Natural size.* 8 mm. thick, black.
Fig. 4. 7 mm. thick, reddish black. Rim put on spirally, and very roughly joined inside.
Fig. 5. 3 mm. thick near margin, 8 mm. thick below, black, with here and there spots of *mercury sulphide*; rough inside.
Fig. 6. 5 mm. thick, blackish red, smooth inside.
Fig. 7. Rim 9 mm. thick, body 7 mm. thick, light reddish, neck nearly at right angle with body, dry carving.
Fig. 8. *Natural size.* 5 mm. thick, red clay, black surface with spots of *mercury sulphide*; dry carving.
Fig. 9. 5 mm. thick, light brick red, rough within, dry carving.
Fig. 10. Body 6 mm. thick, broad rim thickened, black.
Fig. 11. Rim 11 mm. thick, body 7 mm. thick, light brick red, dry carving. Evidently not used.
Fig. 12. *Natural size.* 8 mm. thick, thickly painted with *mercury sulphide* outside, and inside to bottom of rim, neck put on separately, and roughly joined; dotted line shows where loop had been.
Fig. 13. Rim 8 mm. thick, body 6 mm. thick, clay colored, red inside, dry carving.
Fig. 14. 6 mm. thick, light clay colored and blackish in spots, dry carving.
Fig. 15. 6 to 7 mm. thick, very light clay colored, dry carving.

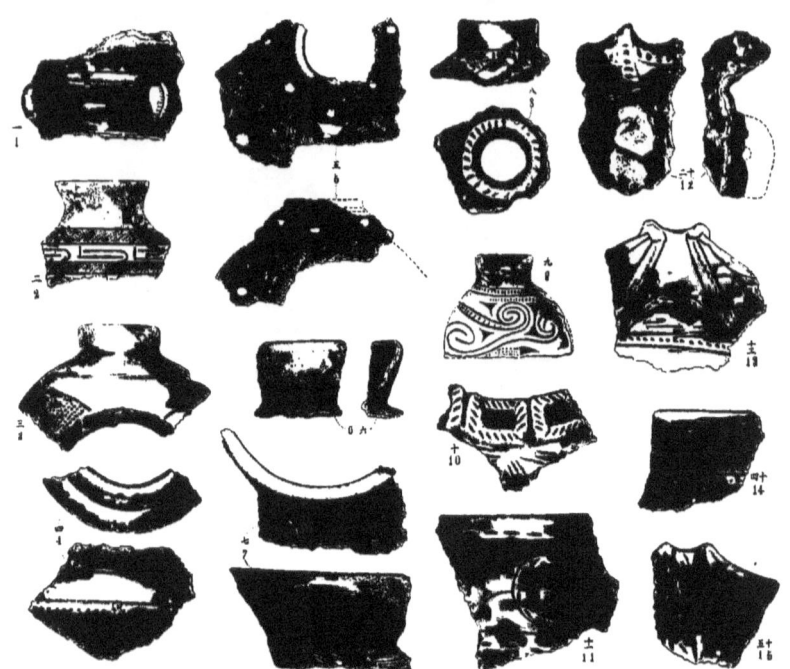

SHELL MOUNDS OF OMORI NEAR TOKIO, JAPAN.

PLATE VII.

Note. All figures drawn half size unless otherwise mentioned.

All the specimens figured on this plate have wreaths of clay put on in bands, and ornamented with finger squeezings, the impression of finger nails and papillæ of the flesh being plainly visible.

Fig. 1. 9 mm. thick, reddish, lines made with groove pointed stick, or possibly the end of a hollow reed or bone. Hole at side made for mending, the hole being commenced in two places.
Fig. 2. 7 mm. thick, black.
Fig. 3. 8 mm. thick, nail marks plainly seen.
Fig. 4. 9 mm. thick, groove within just below rim, very coarsely made.
Fig. 5. 6 mm. thick, reddish, deep groove within, below rim.
Fig. 6. 10 mm. thick, very coarsely made, rough inside.
Fig. 7. 7 mm. thick, reddish.
Fig. 8. 8 mm. thick, light clay color, deep groove within, below rim.
Fig. 9. 9 mm. thick, reddish.
Fig. 10. 7 mm. thick, reddish.
Fig. 11. *One quarter natural size.* 6 mm. thick, reddish, rough.

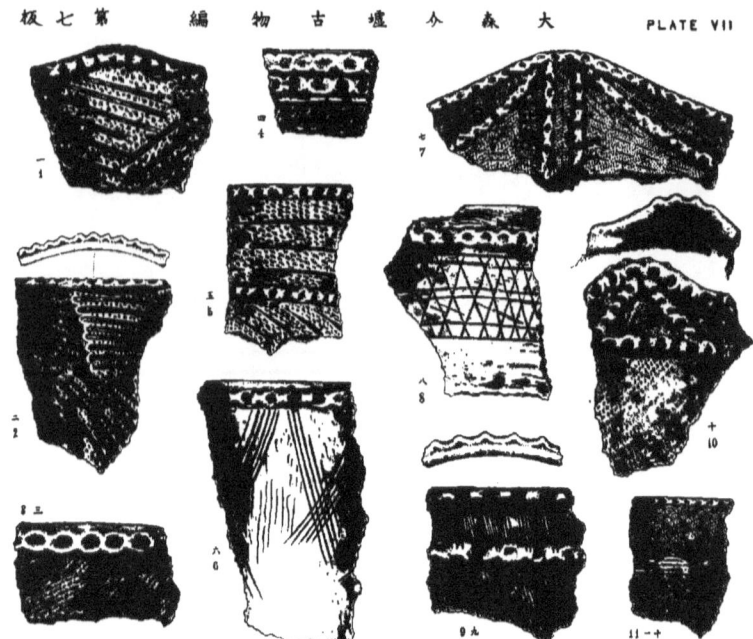

SHELL MOUNDS of OMORI NEAR TOKIO, JAPAN.

PLATE VIII.

Note. All figures drawn half size unless otherwise mentioned.

Fig. 1. 5 mm. thick, black.
Fig. 2. 5 mm. thick, reddish black, groove within 28 mm. below margin.
Fig. 3. 4 mm. thick, black.
Fig. 4. 6 mm. thick, black, notches in rim pressed down while clay was yet soft.
Fig. 5. 7 mm. thick, black.
Fig. 6. 7 mm. thick, black, notches cut while clay was soft and then rounded down.
Fig. 7. 6 mm. thick, black.
Fig. 8. 6 mm. thick, groove within below rim.
Fig. 9. 6 to 7 mm. thick, reddish, rough.
Fig. 10. 6 mm. thick, black.
Fig. 11. 6 mm. thick, black.
Fig. 12. 6 mm. thick, reddish, grooves and punctures inside as shown in upper figure.
Fig. 13. 5 mm. thick, black within, reddish.
Fig. 14. *Natural size.* 5 mm. thick, reddish.
Fig. 15. 8 mm. thick, reddish. Figs. 13, 14 and 15 have the inner surface ornamented. Fragments of this nature were of rare occurrence in the deposits. The fragments indicated shallow bowls or plates of smooth and delicate finish. Fig. 15 was rough on the outside but the finish within was of extreme delicacy.

It will be observed that in Figures 12 and 15 the upper figures represent the inner surface, while in Figures 13 and 14 the lower figures represent the inner surface.

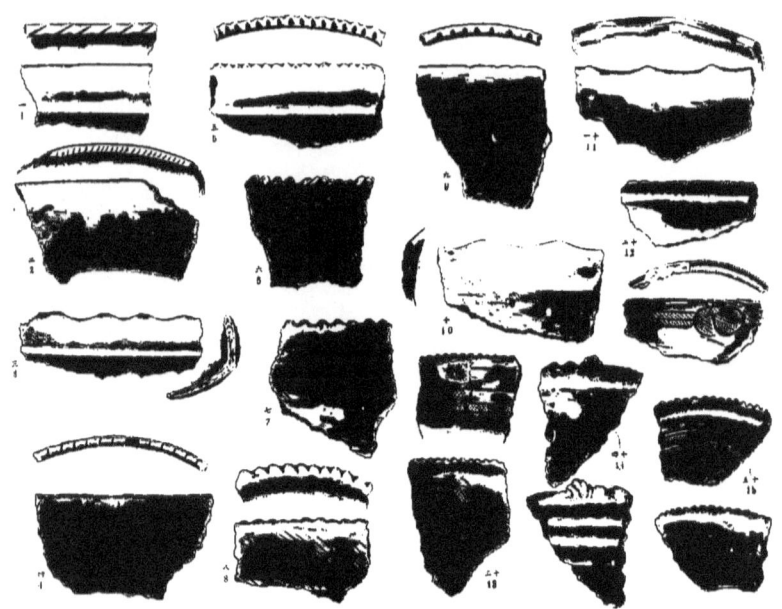

SHELL MOUNDS OF OMORI NEAR TOKIO, JAPAN.

PLATE IX.

Note. All figures drawn half size unless otherwise mentioned.

Fig. 1. 7 mm. thick, black, rim flaring.
Fig. 2. 7 mm. thick above, 5 mm. below, black.
Fig. 3. 8 mm. thick, black.
Fig. 4. 6 mm. thick, black.
Fig. 5. 6 mm. thick, black, flaring rim, cooking vessel.
Fig. 6. 5 mm. thick, red, flaring rim.
Fig. 7. *One quarter natural size.* 6 mm. thick, flaring rim outside, bright red with black discolorations from uneven baking. Inside bright red. Never used.
Fig. 8. *One quarter natural size.* Rim 7 mm. thick, body 6 mm. thick, reddish, smooth within.
Fig. 9. 4 to 5 mm. thick, black throughout.
Fig. 10. 6 mm. thick, black. Cooking vessel.
Fig. 11. 8 mm. thick, dark clay. Evidently fragment of shallow flat bottomed basin.
Fig. 12. 7 mm. thick, black, deep groove within below rim.
Fig. 13. 6 mm. thick, black.
Fig. 14. 4 mm. thick, rim thicker, black, roughly made. Cooking vessel.
Fig. 15. 7 mm. thick, black. Most if not all of these are cooking vessels. Those designated as such, have charred remains of food encrusted within.

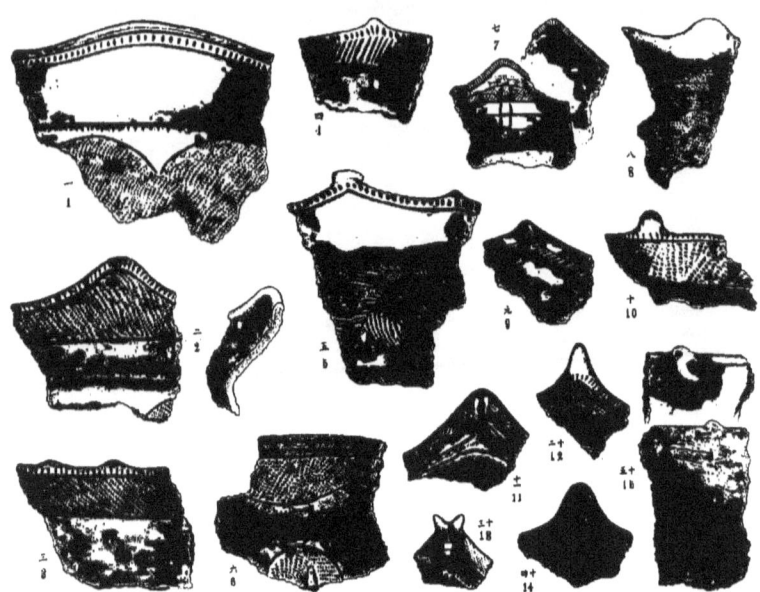

SHELL MOUNDS OF OMORI NEAR TOKIO, JAPAN.

PLATE X.

Note. All figures drawn half size unless otherwise mentioned.

Fig. 1. 5. mm. thick, black, outside rough, inside smooth. A series of grooves within.
Fig. 2. 10 mm. thick above, 8 mm. thick below, reddish, very coarsely made.
Fig. 3. 3 mm. thick, black.
Fig. 4. 10 mm. thick, black, very coarsely made.
Fig. 5. 7 mm. thick, reddish black, very smooth. This vessel is unlike anything else found in the deposits, and may be of a different age.
Fig. 6. Thinner portion 10 mm. thick. Possibly the base, or else a projecting knob from the side of some vessel. Clay color, very rough, finger marks within.
Fig. 7. 4 to 6 mm. thick, black, lines deeply and sharply incised.
Fig. 8. 6 mm. thick, clay colored, very irregular in shape.
Fig. 9. 6 to 7 mm. thick, black.
Fig. 10. 5 to 6 mm. thick, reddish, dry carved.
Fig. 11. 4 mm. thick, black throughout.
Fig. 12. *Natural size.* 5 mm. thick, black, painted with *mercury sulphide*, hole in nozzle straight, 7 mm. in diameter throughout.
Fig. 13. 8 mm. thick, black, hole in nozzle 7 mm. in diameter at tip, dilating toward vessel, where it is 14 mm. in diameter.
Fig. 14. *Natural size.* 8 mm. thick, black. Hole 12 mm. in diameter at both ends and perfectly straight. Within are seen oblique spiral lines, showing that the nozzle was made round a stick and the stick was afterwards withdrawn with a spiral motion.
Fig. 15. 5 to 6 mm. in diameter, red, hole 11 mm. in diameter, irregular in size, nozzle rudely made.
Fig. 16. Coarse reddish baked clay, roughly made. Probably a spindle whorl.

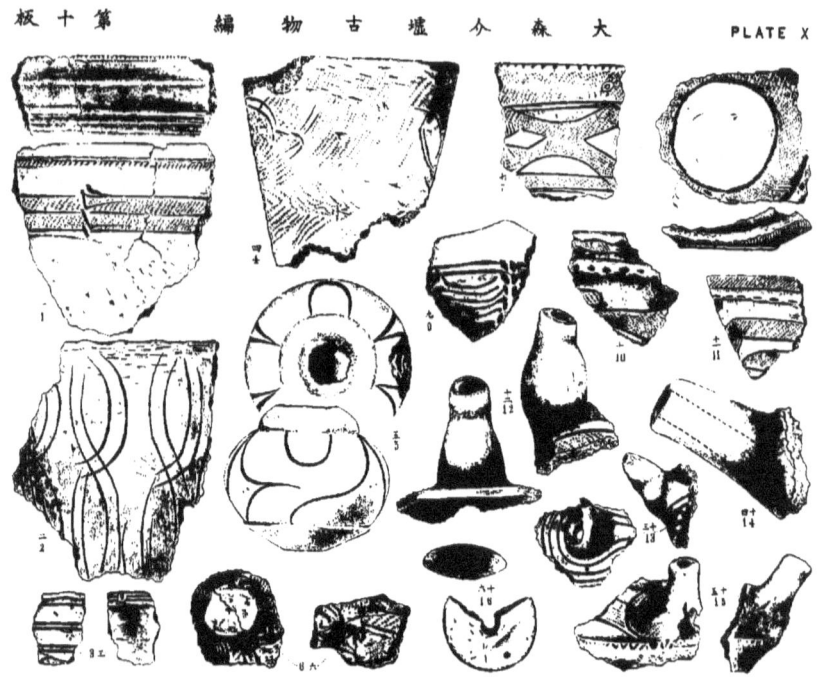

SHELL MOUNDS OF OMORI NEAR TOKIO, JAPAN.

PLATE XI.

Note. All figures drawn half size unless otherwise mentioned.

The following measurements refer to the body wall and not to the thickened knob.

Fig. 1. 7 mm. thick, black, rim thin.
Fig. 2. 6 mm. thick, black, rough.
Fig. 3. 10 mm. thick, brick red, three grooves diverging within.
Fig. 4. 8 mm. thick, black, rim sharp, incurving.
Fig. 5. 5 mm. thick, black. Two semilunar grooves within.
Fig. 6. 6 mm. thick, brick red, delicately made.
Fig. 7. 5 mm. thick, blackish.
Fig. 8. 5 mm. thick, black, corresponding circular depression within.
Fig. 9. 5 mm. thick, black. Broad flat rim, incurving edge.
Fig. 10. 5 mm. thick, black, deep circular depression within, incurving rim.
Fig. 11. 7 mm. thick, light brick red.
Fig. 12. 5 mm. thick, black.
Fig. 13. 7 mm. thick, blackish red, incurving rim.
Fig. 14. 9 mm. thick, bright red inside, dull red without, incurving rim.
Fig. 15. 6 mm. thick, black, incurving rim.
Fig. 16. 6 mm. thick, black, double groove within, rim thin.
Fig. 17. 7 mm. thick, black, vertical depression within, smaller one near tip.
Fig. 18. 5 mm. thick, reddish and clay color, knob perforated.
Fig. 19. 7 mm. thick, red outside, black within, round depression within.
Fig. 20. 6 mm. thick, black, groove within.
Fig. 21. 8 mm. thick, brick red, knob projecting.
Fig. 22. 6 mm. thick, reddish, incurving rim.
Fig. 23. 4 mm. thick, black, knob perforated; thimble shaped depression above, 21 mm. deep, and 22 mm. in diameter.
Fig. 24. 7 mm. thick, black, rim incurving.
Fig. 25. 7 mm. thick, black, reddish within, knob perforated, incurving rim.
Fig. 26. 5 mm. thick, black, roughly wrought.
Fig. 27. 8 mm. thick, black.
Fig. 28. 6 mm. thick, reddish black, deep groove within, knob perforated.

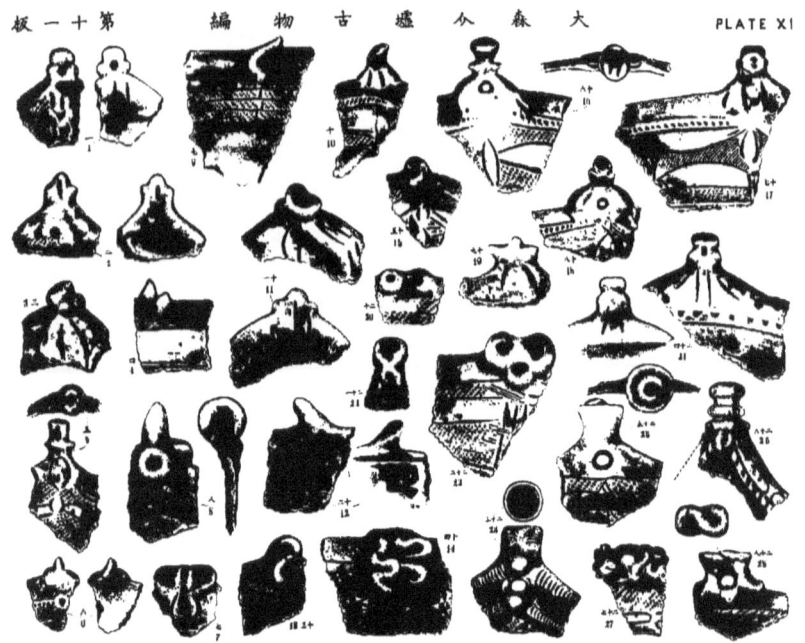

SHELL MOUNDS of OMORI NEAR TOKIO, JAPAN.

PLATE. XII.

Note. All figures drawn half size unless otherwise mentioned.

Fig. 1. Reddish black, rough and irregular.
Fig. 2. 7 mm. thick, reddish black.
Fig. 3. 7 mm. thick, black.
Fig. 4. 6 mm. thick, black.
Fig. 5. 5 mm. thick, black, deep depression within, corresponding to one outside.
Fig. 6. 7 mm. thick, black, rough.
Fig. 7. 7 mm. thick, black, flaring with rim incurving, double groove within.
Fig. 8. 7 mm. thick, clay black, rough.
Fig. 9. Black, ridged inside, deep circular depression within with border slightly raised.
Fig. 10. 5 to 8 mm. thick, black.
Fig. 11. 5 to 8 mm. thick.
Fig. 12. 5 mm. thick, black, reddish within.
Fig. 13. 7 mm. thick, reddish black, very rough inside.
Fig. 14. 7 mm. thick, black, very rough inside, perforated ear.
Fig. 15. 5 mm. thick, black.
Fig. 16. 4 mm. thick, light brick red, soft clay, minute perforation passing into loop from below at place marked o. Figures 4 to 12 are the most common forms in the deposits. Figures 13 to 16 are unique.

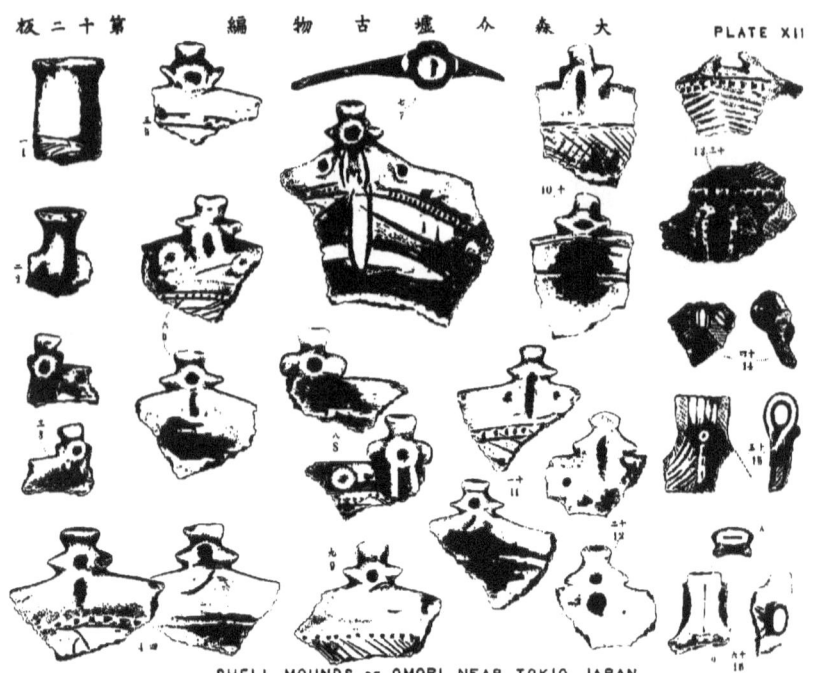

SHELL MOUNDS OF OMORI NEAR TOKIO, JAPAN.

PLATE XIII.

Note. All figures drawn half size unless otherwise mentioned.

Fig. 1. *Natural size.* 2 mm thick, handle moulded from wall, bent over and welded.
Fig. 2. 7 mm. thick, reddish black, rim slightly flaring, hole made in wall while clay was yet soft.
Fig. 3. 6 mm. thick near rim, 4 mm. thick below, brick red.
Fig. 4. 8 mm. thick, pale red, double groove within 20 mm. below rim.
Fig. 5. 8 mm. thick, dark clay.
Fig. 6. 8 mm. thick, black, smooth within.
Fig. 7. *Natural size.* Black grooves and smooth areas heavily painted with *mercury sulphide.*
Fig. 8. 7 mm. thick, reddish.
Fig. 9. 5 mm. thick, reddish.
Fig. 10. 5 to 7 mm. thick, black, carbonized remains of food encrusted within.
Fig. 11. 5 mm. thick, black.
Fig. 12. 4 mm. thick, black.
Fig. 13. 5 mm. thick, rim 8 mm. thick, black.
Fig. 14. 6 mm. thick, black, rim rounded and thicker.
Fig. 15. 6 mm. thick, nearly black.
Fig. 16. 7 mm. thick, reddish.
Fig. 17. 9 mm. thick, black. Ears projecting from side of vessel.
Fig. 18. 6 mm. thick, dark reddish.
Fig. 19. 4 mm. thick, rim 8 mm. thick, reddish.
Fig. 20. 5 mm. thick, very light clay. The hole is countersunk from both sides. A first attempt was made too near the fractured edge.

SHELL MOUNDS OF OMORI NEAR TOKIO, JAPAN.

PLATE XIV.

Note. All figures drawn half size unless otherwise mentioned.

Fig. 1. 8 mm. thick, black, knob thick and massive.
Fig. 2. 5 mm. thick, black
Fig. 3. 7 mm. thick, black.
Fig. 4. 7 mm. thick, red; nicely and squarely finished on rim.
Fig. 5. 6 mm. thick, black.
Fig. 6. 7 mm. thick, black, end of knob continued up, and bent down in making.
Fig. 7. 7 mm. thick, black, nicely finished.
Fig. 8. *One quarter natural size.* 8 mm. thick, black, massive, symetrically finished.
Fig. 9. 6 mm. thick, black, rim flat, 13 mm. in width, very smooth.
Fig. 10. 6 mm. thick, nearly black.
Fig. 11. 12 mm. thick in middle, black and smooth.
Fig. 12. *Natural size.* Fine reddish clay, bottom depressed.
Fig. 13. 8 mm. thick, reddish.
Fig. 14. *Natural size.* Light brick red, very roughly made. On three sides grooved in a similar way. Evidently a handle.
Fig. 15. *Natural size.* 8 mm. thick, reddish inside, black outside. This may be a rim knob of a vessel.
Fig. 16. *Natural size.* 10 mm. thick, black, inside rough. Evidently a handle.
Fig. 17. Light brick red, very coarse. Possibly a rim knob.
It is difficult to suggest the use of the objects represented by Figs. 10, 11, 12 and 15.

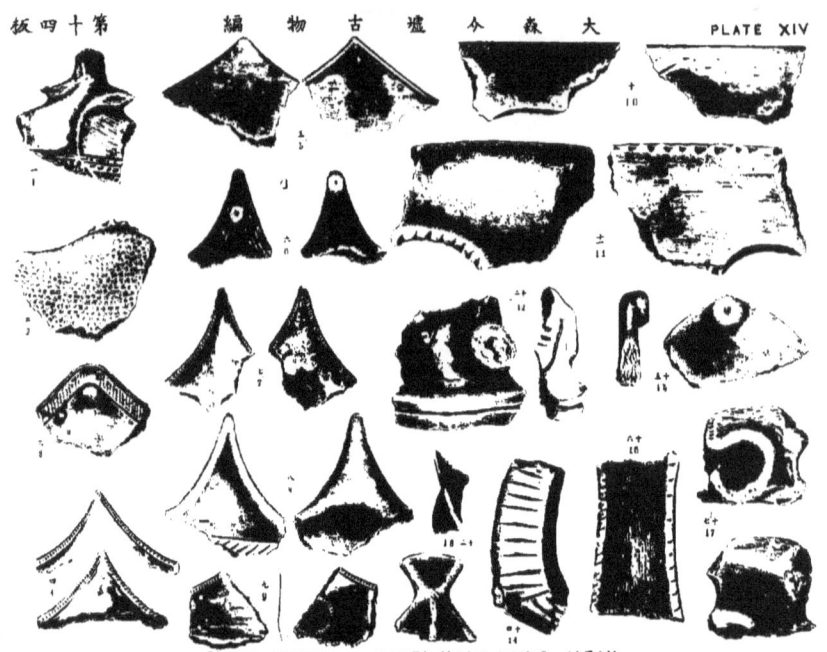

SHELL MOUNDS of OMORI NEAR TOKIO, JAPAN.

PLATE XV.

Note. All figures on this plate are drawn natural size.

Fig. 1. Center 18 mm. thick, clay color with a pale reddish tinge. The dark spot in one corner represents a hole which passes through the tablet.
Fig. 2. Light clay color, much worn.
Fig. 3. Bright brick red.
Fig. 4. Clay color, light reddish tinge.
Fig. 5. Light brick red, very much worn.
Fig. 6. Black outside, within clay colored. Central design repeated three times round circumference. Hole straight. $8\frac{1}{2}$ mm. in diameter. Light spiral lines are seen on the walls of the hole showing that it was made on a round stick, and the stick was twisted in the act of withdrawing.

The tablets are made of the finest clay. They are all deeply wrought and this was done after the clay was dry and before baking.

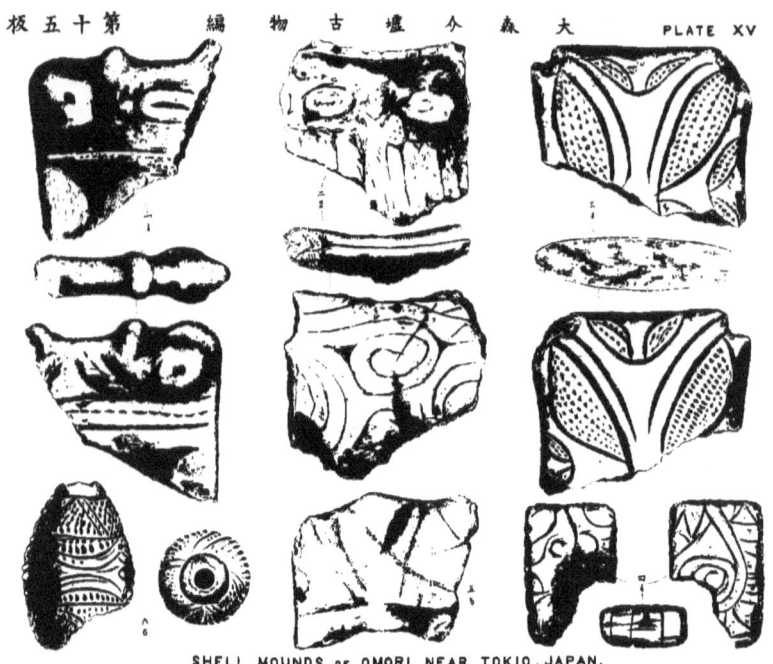

SHELL MOUNDS of OMORI NEAR TOKIO, JAPAN.

PLATE XVI.

Note. All figures on this plate are drawn natural size.

Fig. 1. Prong of deer's antler, much worn by use. The detached prongs bearing evidences of much use, are common in the Deposits.
Fig. 2. Portion of deer's antler showing rude cutting.
Fig. 3. Similar to Fig. 1.
Fig. 4. Handle made out of deer's antler. The incisor tooth of a deer is figured as the probable tool for which the handle was intended.
Fig. 5. Fragment of deer's antler cut at both ends.
Fig. 6. Hook made of deer's antler.
Fig. 7 and 8. Bodkins made of deer's antler.
Fig. 9. Fragment of bone with lower edge ground down.
Fig. 10. Arrow point made from the canine tooth of a boar.
Fig. 11. Bird's bone with two perforations.
Fig. 12. Cube made from metatarsal bone of deer.
Fig. 13. Dorsal spine of fish used as a needle.
Fig. 14. Mammalian claw, with lower surface cut away.
Fig. 15. 16, 17, 18, 19 and 20 are implements of various and unknown use, worked from deer's antlers.
Fig. 21, 22, and 23. Dorsal spines of fish used as needles.

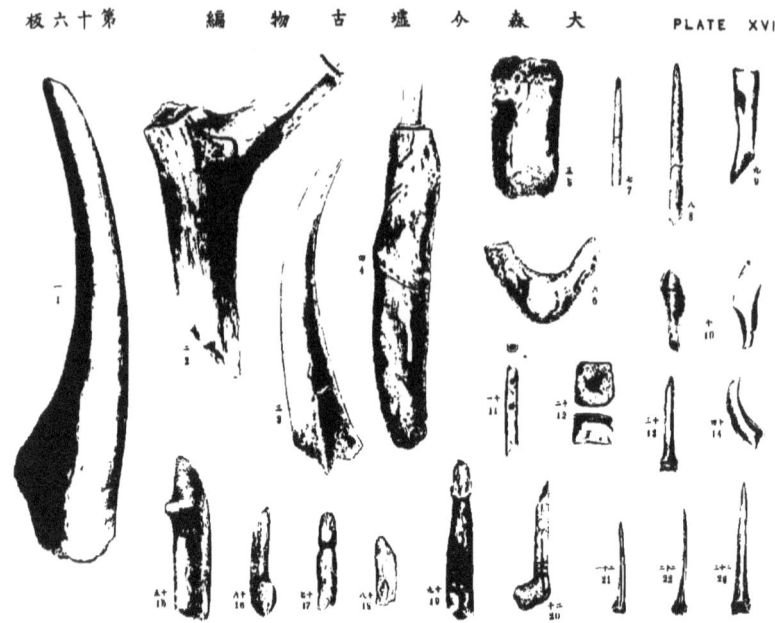

SHELL MOUNDS of OMORI NEAR TOKIO, JAPAN.

PLATE XVII.

Note. All figures in this plate are drawn natural size.

Fig. 1. Jasper pebble, one side clipped away.
Fig. 2. Jasper pebble, one side clipped away.
Fig. 3. Shistose rock, burnt.
Fig. 4. Clay slate.
Fig. 5. Lava rock.
Fig. 6. Lava rock.
Fig. 7. Talcose slate.
Fig. 8. Lava rock.
Fig. 9. ?

The first two implements are probably hammers, as the lower ends are fractured as if from use. Figs. 3 and 4 are rollers. Figs. 5, 6 and 8 are rude adzes. Fig. 7 represents a portion only of some implement. Fig. 9 is a of a mortar.

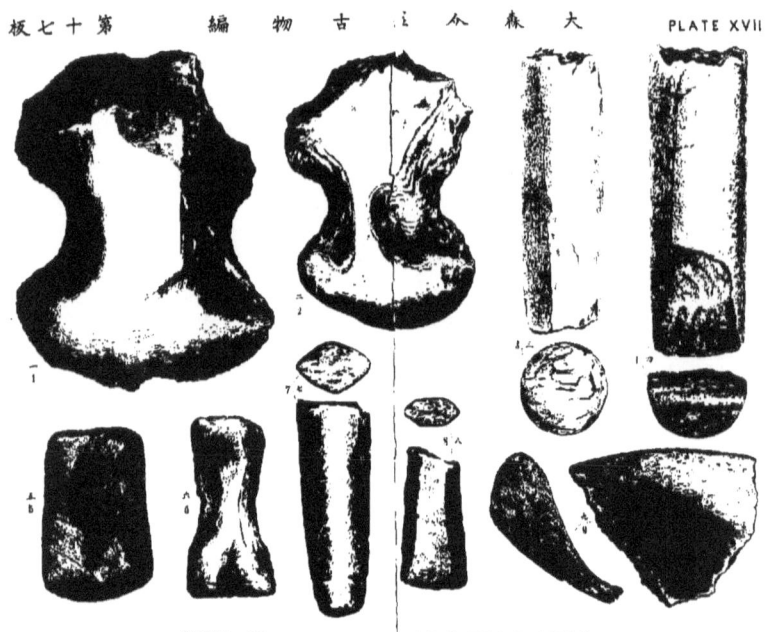

PLATE XVII

SHELL MOUNDS of OMORI NEAR TOKIO, JAPAN.

PLATE XVIII.

Note. All figures on this plate are drawn natural size.

When two figures occur side by side, the left hand figure represents the ancient form from the Omori Mounds. The right hand figure represents the recent form from the Omori shore.

When an outline and a dotted line occur together, the dotted line represents the ancient form. The figures marked by a cross also indicate the ancient form.

Fig. 1. Cyclina Chinensis Chemnitz.
Fig. 2. Tapes sp.
Fig. 3. Mactra venerformis Deshay.
Fig. 4. Mya arenaria Linné.
Fig. 5. Arca inflata Reeve.
Fig. 6. Dosinia Japonica Lischke.
Fig. 7. Cytherea meretrix Linné.
Fig. 8. Natica Lamarckiana Duclos.
Fig. 9. Eburna Japonica Lischke.

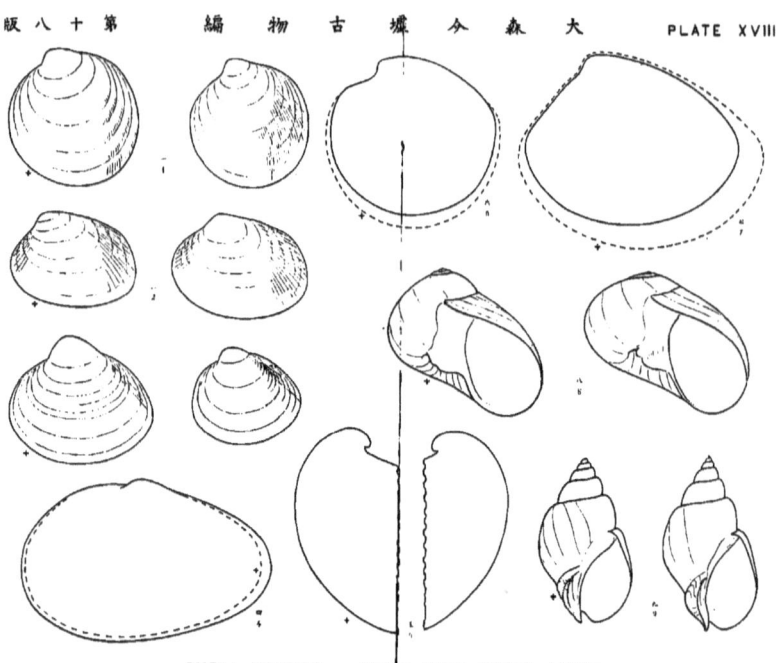

SHELL MOUNDS of OMORI NEAR TOKIO, JAPAN.

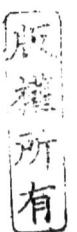

MEMOIRS

OF THE

SCIENCE DEPARTMENT.

UNIVERSITY OF TOKIO, JAPAN

VOLUME II.

ON MINING AND MINES IN JAPAN.

BY

C. NETTO, M. E.

PROFESSOR OF MINING AND METALLURGY, UNIVERSITY OF TOKIO, JAPAN.

PUBLISHED BY THE UNIVERSITY.

TOKIO, JAPAN.

NISSHUSHA PRINTING OFFICE.

2539. (1879.)

東京大學文理學部印行

MEMOIRS

OF THE

SCIENCE DEPARTMENT.

UNIVERSITY OF TOKIO, JAPAN.

VOLUME II.
ON MINING AND MINES IN JAPAN.

BY

C. NETTO, M. E.

Professor of Mining and Metallurgy, University of Tokio, Japan.

PUBLISHED BY THE UNIVERSITY.
TOKIO, JAPAN.

NISSHUSHA PRINTING OFFICE.
2539. (1879.)

PREFACE.

When in the present memoir I attempted a brief sketch of mining in Japan in its technical, statistical and administrative aspects, I was fully aware, that much was still wanting for a *complete* picture of the same. Although I have now been for several years in the country, part of which time I have been occupied in the technical supervision of mines and reduction-works, and although I when travelling, whether on service or as private individual, have as far as possible improved the opportunity for collecting information, it is yet only a fraction of the large number of mines of various kinds, which I have learnt to know from personal observation, while with regard to the remainder I have had to be guided by communications from others.

In my efforts as far as lay in my power to discover and suggest the means for advancing the mining industry in Japan, it became my duty clearly to expose the still existing defects, and I trust, that the frankness, with which this has been done in the sole interest of the problem to be solved, will on all sides be appreciated in that sense.

The lecture was originally delivered in the *Deutsche Gesellschaft für Natur- und Völker-Kunde Ostasiens*. As the transactions of the said society, on account of the language in which they are published are here accessible to only a narrow circle of readers, an English edition was decided upon by the Honourable Board of Directors Mr. H. Kato and Mr. A. Hamao, of the Tokio Daigaku Sangakubu, to whom I here publicly tender my hearty thanks for the courtesy, with which they have met every wish of mine with regard to the execution of the work. For the translation of the original, which, owing to the great number of technical terms, offered especial difficulties, I am indebted to Mr. A, Rosenstand.

My thanks are further due to Mr. W. Watanabe for his valuable assistance in various directions.

As in Vol. I of the *Memoirs*, so also in this volume, is the entire mechanical part of the pamphlet—drawings, lithographs, printing and paper—of Japanese origin, and I wish to record my thankful acknowledgement to Mr. Yamaoka the artist, Mr. Otta the draughtsman, to the lithographic establishment of Gengen-do and to that of the Tokio Daigaku under Mr. Kobayashi and finally to the Nisshusha Printing Office for their painstaking cooperation in their respective departments.

Tokio, December 1879.

C. N.

INDEX.

Introduction	pag.	1.
Occurence of Minerals.	,,	5.
Method of Attack.	,,	6.
Methods of Breaking Ground.	,,	7.
Productive Work.	,,	7.
Paying for the Ore.	,,	7.
Timbering.	,,	8.
Haulage.	,,	8.
Drainage.	,,	9.
Ventilation.	,,	10.
Illumination.	,,	11.
Equipment of the Miner.	,,	11.
Coal Mining.	,,	11.
Improvements suggested for Mining.	,,	11.
Dressing.	,,	13.
Washing of Gold-Ores.	,,	14.
Improvements suggested for Dressing.	,,	14.
Metallurgy.	,,	15.
Roasting.	,,	15.
Smelting.	,,	16.
The Charge.	,,	17.
Defects in the old Smelting Process	,,	17.
Improvements suggested for Smelting.	,,	18.
Assaying.	,,	19.
Surveying.	,,	20.
Officers and Workmen.	,,	20.
Mining Law.	,,	22.

General improvements suggested	pag.	24.
Model-Works	,,	27.
Formation of Private Companies	,,	27.
Central Reduction-Works	,,	27.
Engineering Office	,,	28.
Geological Survey	,,	29.
Enumeration of those Mines which already are worked on modern system	,,	29.
Table I: Total Productions of Government and Private Mines	,,	32.
Table II: Comparison of average outturn and outturn in 1877/78	,,	33.
Table III: Comparison between production of Government and Private Mines	,,	34.
Production of Iron	,,	37.
Table IV: Import of Iron and Steel	,,	38.
Production and Export of Coal	,,	40.
Table V: Coal-Export and-Import	,,	41.
Juxtaposition of the Mineral Production of Japan with that of other countries	,,	42.
Table VI: Export of Mining Products	,,	47.
Total Export of Copper	,,	48.
Export of Bullion	,,	48.
Table VII: Export and Import of Bullion	,,	49.
Total value of exported and imported goods	,,	50.
Comparison of the Production and the Export of Bullion	,,	51.
Probable future Mineral Production	,,	52.
Explanation of the Plates	,,	53.

ON
MINING AND MINES IN JAPAN,

BY

C. NETTO.

When Japan was thrown open for intercourse with the outer world, the belief was general, that the mineral treasures of the country would in a prominent degree become the subject of commercial enterprise. In the first place, the reports of Marco Polo and Kaempfer spoke of the country's inexhaustible wealth in gold ; then the large quantities of bullion (estimated at 500 millions of dollars), which the Portuguese and the Dutchmen, notwithstanding that their intercourse with the natives had always remained of a limited nature, had been able to export in the course of little more than a century (1550-1671), were proof, that a considerable quantity at all events had existed. Add to this, that originally the rate of exchange between the two precious metals was to the European mind an abnormous one, as gold was only six times as much worth as silver. People were only too apt to attribute this fact to a superfluity of gold, instead of ascribing it to the at all events truer cause, a relative scarcity of silver.

Also with regard to copper, the public were, immediately after the opening of the country, enticed into an over-estimate of the power of production, as they judged the same by the exports ; but the latter included a large portion of metal, that had already been manufactured, which the Japanese threw on the market in the shape of old gate-mountings, temple-ornaments, idols &c., either directly or after having re-melted them. Nor was it surprising, if the foreigners relished the hope, that they here, as in other countries, which had been suddenly opened to their invasion, might be able to discover hitherto unknown deposits, and by the application of rational methods raise the production to its utmost capacity. If to this we add the mystic nimbus, which surrounded the country, and which made everything appear in the most favorable lights, then there is nothing strange in a notion of Japan's mineral treasures having at that time prevailed, which was far from corresponding with the actual facts.

In the course of the succeeding years, the truth had, although reluctantly, to be admitted, that the expectation in Japan to have found a second Eldorado, was without any actual foundation. Those happy times have unfortunately gone by, when a large amount of gold could be obtained with a comparatively small amount of labor, through the working of *placers* that is, spots where nature through thousands of years has worked for man by disintegration of rocks, by floating away a portion of the worthless, and by leaving behind a sediment, that had become enriched by natural washings; the few still remaining alluvia are so poor, that it does not pay to work them. In the same manner as the miners in the far more important goldfields of California, Australia &c., were very soon compelled to leave off mere washing of the alluvium and to commence real mining, so they have also here already long ago had to hunt for the gold in its original hiding places, the veins. And even in those, it mostly occurs in only small quantities, and the extent and volume of the veins themselves are so inconsiderable, that in many cases even the most improved working system gives no promise of a favorable pecuniary result. I hereby by no means intend to deny the existence of gold-mines, which either already now are worked with profit, or at all events, if properly worked, might yield a surplus; I merely intend to lay stress on the fact, that the gold-mining is not of such a nature as to justify extraordinary hopes for the future. In the same manner as the gold-production, which in 1877 amounted to only about 11,000 English ounces, so the production of silver, which in the same year aggregated about 350,000 ounces, must also be pronounced low.

Further disappointments followed with regard to copper, the export of which quickly fell off as soon as the old stock had been exhausted. (The quantity of copper annually exported—manufactured, in ore and in slabs—, which in the years 1868-73 had risen from a value of about $33,000 to $1,330,000, fell from then down to $236,000 in 1875, and has only since that time again gradually risen, so that it in 1878 amounted to about $750,000.) It moreover became evident, that the Japanese had much more throughly, than had been anticipated, searched the soil for mineral treasures: in many districts the mountains were literally honeycombed with old explorations and workings. A further proof of the zeal, with which the natives had carried on mining, was afforded by the existence of a rather comprehensive mining literature, and by the care, with which reports on mines have been drawn up and preserved.

Formerly the hopes had been too sanguine; now, as the same were not realized, there was a reaction in the opposite direction and a bias to entertain most pessimistic views in respect to the future of mining in Japan. These views could not but gain strength from the circumstance, that the mines, which the government had commenced to work by modern methods, did not yield such surplus as had been anticipated. The principal reason thereof is this, that it is only in later years, that the government has become possessed of really good mines, and that it formerly, if it at all wanted to set private industry a good example, and to create something new, had to devote its attention to mines of inferior importance.

If the development of *private* mining and metallurgical industry has not kept pace with other industries of similar moment, several circumstances are the cause of this. In the first place, even the best mine will always require a considerable outlay of capital, if it is to be organized on modern system. That capital either did not exist, because the mines mostly belong to single individuals, and association into companies is only in its infancy, while foreign capital is by law strictly excluded from the mines or where it perhaps might have been raised, capitalists were afraid of the risk, the more so as the not very brilliant results obtained by the government were not of a nature to encourage imitation. It was therefore preferred to go on in the old fashion, which although defective requires only a small outlay of capital, and to be content with a small profit.

Another reason is this: mining and reduction works, if they are to have any prospect of success, require much more than any other technical establishment to be adopted to local circumstances. An engine—, gas—, cloth—, paper —, soda-factory, a silk-reeling establishment &c. in the South of Japan is not necessarily in any essential part different from a similar establishment in the North, while the arrangements for instance of two establishments for the reduction of silver-ores present a quite different aspect according to local circumstances, and thus we see here, how in six different mines: Ikuno, Sado, Kosaka, Innai, Mandokora, Ani the silver is extracted from the ore in quite different ways. Thorough innovations are therefore much easier adopted in any other technical establishment than in mining. And nevertheless, it is under present circumstances of the greatest importance that this be done, that is, that a rational working system be extended also to private establishments, otherwise the entire mining industry in this country must gradually decline. Formerly, when the country was closed to the outer world, the internal mining industry governed, so to speak, the metal market, that is, the price of metal depended—letting alone other circumstances, which are still unaltered—on the cost of production; now the price is influenced from abroad, and it is evident, that with the constant rise in wages here and in the price of charcoal, a point must be reached, where only the richer mines will be able to compete with the foreign mines, which are worked in a rational manner, while the poorer ones must succumb, unless a remedy be applied betimes. Already now several mines, belonging to the last named category, how had to be abandoned, and if the total produce from the mines of the country has not decreased, but has on the contrary increased, this is solely due to the larger production from those few mines, which are either entirely or partially worked on modern system.

Although, as we have just seen, the prospect is only small, that Japan will ever realize the former dreams in regard to its production of precious metals; although the experience hitherto made leads to the belief, that the produce of lead, tin, cobalt, quicksilver, petroleum never will reach any considerable figure; although the developement on a large scale of the iron-industry, according to the latest researches, must be considered problematic,—there can be no doubt, that copper-mining within certain limits, but especially coal-mining, is pregnant with a great future. While the increase in the copper-produce depends principally upon the development of the already existing mines, partly in working order partly flooded with water, and while the prospect of discovering virgin lodes is only small, a rich field offers itself for coal-mining in the opening of existing and already discovered seams, particularly those in Yesso, which are now actually taken in hand by the government. It may also be assumed with certainty, that a general geological survey of Nipon will reveal formations, from which the presence of coal-beds may be inferred, whose actual existence then has to be proved by trial-borings.

Mr. B. S. LYMAN, formerly chief-geologist under the Kaitakushi, in his geological report on Yesso * estimates the quantity of the there existing accessible coal at about 150,000 million tons, an amount, which would enable the said island during 1000 years to furnish the coal-supply at present derived from great Britain. Although the time is still far off, that such quantities of coal, when supplied, could find use here, and although the average quality of the Yesso coals may be inferior to that of the English, there can from the above said be no question, that coal mining here has a great future.

I must for a future lecture reserve the the detailed treatment of the several here occurring minerals, and of the mines in general, as well as of those mines, which are at present worked on modern system, in special, and my intention to-day is merely to consider in a general way the ancient, national methods of mining, dressing and metallurgical operations, and to suggest means of improvement. I shall here observe, that Mr. H. MUNROE, in his excellent article : "the Mineral wealth of Japan," has treated the same subject, although only briefly, and that several repetitions therefore become unavoidable. After the description of the traditional working methods, I shall add some statistical notes and conclusions drawn therefrom.

* A general Report on the Geology of Yesso by Benjamin Smith Lyman Tokei 1877.

OCCURRENCE.

The useful minerals, which are the object of mining or superficial winning, ranked very nearly according to their importance, are as follows:

Coal, copper, silver, gold, iron, kaolin, petroleum, sulphur, lead, antimony, tin, cobalt, quicksilver, marble, jasper, agate, amber, graphite.

Iron consequently at present occupies a rather secondary place. The production of ore of antimony and of crude antimony is increasing; lead, tin, copper, quicksilver, petroleum are not produced in sufficient quantities to supply the demand; nickel, zinc, arsenic have not yet been found in sufficient quantities to be of any practical value. Consequently were in 1878 imported:

Iron and steel in various shapes about..	36,000,000	catties *
Lead in pigs, sheets and tubes, about..	520,000	,,
Quicksilver	79,000	,,
Tin	212,000	,,
Smalt for about	30,000	rios.
Nickel-ware	25,000	catties.
Tinned iron-plates	9,031	boxes.
Zinc	1,000,000	catties.
Coal	47,396,160	,,
Petroleum	3,422,400	gallons.

In the same year were exported:

Coal, about	160,000,000	catties.
Copper, in various shapes	3,000,000	,,
Copper-ore	900,000	,,
Sulphur	1,500,000	,,
Sulphuric acid	1,400,000	,,

Besides at all events also a certain quantity of ore of antimony, the figure of which I, however, am unable to give. As to the form, under which the minerals won by mining occur, magnetic iron-ore, ore of antimony, sometimes also silver-ore are found in layers, the greater portion of the iron here produced is the result from the working of alluvial sands of magnetic iron. Gold and silver-ores, copper mostly only as copper-pyrites, lead as galena occur in lodes.

---

* 1 Catty=1⅓ lb. English avoirdupois.—1 £=about 5 rios.

METHOD OF ATTACK.

If we leave out of sight those mines, which are worked by the Government on modern system, and the coal-mine in Takashima, then we find, that the deposits are exclusively attacked by adits, as the machinery, requisite for the sinking and working of deep shafts was formerly entirely unknown. In order to prepare the working of a vein either an adit was driven along its strike, or where the vein was sufficiently known and the locality favorable, the connection with the surface was effected by a cross-cut. As soon as all the ore above this horizon had been extracted, then a second adit had to be driven lower down and so on. The extent of these adits is sometimes quite considerable—until about 10,000 feet—and we can imagine that such a work, carried on without the aid of blasting powder, must have demanded, not only a large expenditure, but also an enormous length of time. We are therefore in the abandoned mines still able to estimate the richness of the ore deposit worked by the length of the adits; the greater the obstacles, which were overcome in order to get at the ore, the richer the latter must have been. Of course other agencies, which can now no longer be ascertained, may have had some influence, for instance: cheap wages, compulsory labor, comparatively high value of the metals extracted etc. When finally a point had been reached, where a still lower adit, either on account of the configuration of the soil, or on account of the expense, did not appear practicable, then the working was continued below the water-adit as far down as circumstances would permit, and for hoisting the produced ores as well as the water up to the level of the adit no other motor was employed than the human hand or foot.

The depth, which was reached below the level of the adit, depended of course, on the one hand on the volume of water to be met with, on the other hand on the quantity and quality of the extracted ore. Even under the most favorable circumstances, a time must come at last, when the outturn no longer covered the expenditure on winning, haulage and drainage, that is, when in the then state of mining science it became necessary to abandon the mine. I myself know several mines, which have been abandoned evidently for no other reason, and I am convinced, that a still larger number are only waiting for the moment, when modern engineering shall have aroused them from their centenary sleep, again to yield a good profit. Under favorable circumstances, depths have certainly been reached, which, considering the absence of all aid from machinery, must be declared considerable; the Innai silver-mine is for instance yet worked fully 700 feet, the Beishi copper-mine about 800 feet below the level of the adit, and the water is lifted to this height solely by hand-pumps, which shall be described later.

Neither for connecting the several horizons with each other, nor for establishing communication between the subterranean works and the surface, are shafts used; it is preferred to make slopes, which are often very tortuous.

METHODS OF BREAKING GROUND.

The instruments here employed were until scarcely 20 years ago, when Mr. Pumpelli first used gunpowder for blasting purposes, confined to the pick, steel-gad and crow-bar. In working with such insufficient implements, it would of course be an object to reduce the dimensions of the galleries to a *minimum*, and as moreover joints and fissures in the rock were chosen preferentially on account of the ground there being less hard, the result has been that the adits and galleries are mostly very narrow and tortuous ill adapted both for a good ventilation and extensive haulage and for the passage of Europeans.

Although gunpowder has got into general use during the later decades, the limited width of the galleries imposes the necessity of drilling only small holes, or the big fragments of rock, by repeated blasting would have to be prepared for haulage. The holes drilled single-handed are about 1″ in diameter and seldom more than 14″ English in length. The tamping is generally done with needle, a bamboo-tube, filled with gunpowder, is used as "squib" and cotton or paper, dipped in oil, as "smift." Fuzes, both of European and of native make, are however also frequently used.

Fire-setting was also formerly known, although not used to any great extent, and only as preparation for working with the pick and the gad.

PRODUCTIVE WORK.

The productive work in veins has, I believe, always been done by a more or less modified stoping overhand. For the working of beds and irregular deposits a kind of pillar-work, stock-work and piling have also been used.

PAYING FOR THE ORE.

The manner, in which the labor of winning the ores is paid for is that the manager of the mine buys the extracted ores from contractors or middle men, and pays for them according to weight and contents in metal. Each of these middlemen has a number of workmen under him. The contents and solidity of the ores, as well as other conditions of winning and haulage, vary of course at the different points of the mine, and in order therefore to do everybody justice the pairs of workmen are constantly changed from one pitch to another. The manager of the mine has mostly only a very limited authority over the middlemen, who arrange among themselves about the shifts of workmen and the choice of pitches. This baneful system results of necessity in an ugly robbing, as it is in the interest of the contractors to extract only the best and richest ores, and to leave the poorer and harder ones behind. The payment for the ores includes usually the haulage underground, and often also the transportation to the reduction works and the dressing. Nay sometimes,—and especially is this the case with silver and gold-ores—it is only the metal produced that is paid for, and the winning and reduction of the ores are consequently left entirely in the hands of the contractors. The low payment for the metal produced often indirectly compels the contractors to work only the richer ores.

The keeping the mine in condition, the drainage, the dead work are to the charge of the administration of the mine, and generally contracted for by the day. The rate of daily wages varies between 8 and 25 sen a day (100 sen = 1 rio = 1 yen = about 4 shillings).

TIMBERING.

Timbering in the levels is, on account of the small dimensions of the latter, mostly unnecessary; where requisite, sets are used, consisting of a cap, supported by two vertical legs, which are channelled on top. The legs are kept asunder by a stay, placed close to the top, and where the rock is soft, rest on a cross-sill. The lowness of the galleries does not admit of a walking plank above the water-ditch. The timbering in the slopes is the same as in the levels. There are no ladders, steps cut into the rock or indented trunks of trees serve as substitutes. Ceder, pine and fir are used, or, where these are not to be had, leaf-trees.

Masonry is scarcely used at all.

HAULAGE.

The haulage is done by children with the aid of baskets or bags slung on their back; it is seldom done by men or women. In this way all the ores are carried from the pitch to the surface, without relays, up and down steps, on underground roads, often a mile and more in length. The narrow passages, which would not allow a full-grown man to pass with a load equal to his strength, necessitate the employment of children with a load of 3-6 quamme (about 25-50 lbs).

The use of any machinery whatsoever as aid, the windlass for instance or the whim is only an acquisition of modern times.

DRAINAGE.

As to the drainage, it has already been remarked, that its miserable condition very much aggravates the difficulty of working the mines, and has often been the cause of their abandonment.

Almost the only instrument for lifting the water to the water-adit, is a handpump. It consists in a prismatic, wooden box, open at top and at bottom, about 3,5^m long and about 12 centimeters square wide inside. The lower part of the box is furnished with a clack-valve, that opens upwards. In this box a valvepiston of corresponding size, with leather packing, moves up and down by aid of a piston rod, worked directly with the hand.

As for the haulage, so also for the pumps, vertical pits are avoided, and slopes are used, in which one pump is placed under the other in such a manner, that the one below discharges itself into the suction-tank of the one above. The vertical lift of each pump is between 4 and 7 feet, the piston-stroke about 3 feet, the quantity of water lifted per stroke about 5 sho.

The "pumpers" are paid either in daily wages, or at the rate of the average number of strokes; in the above mentioned Beishi copper-mine for instance, where 130 pumps are kept going to lift the water 222^m, a laborer was paid 4.9 sen for every 1000 strokes.

We will now with the aid of these figures compare the cost of this method with that of a good modern pumping-engine: 1 sho is about 65 cub." Jap.; 1 gallon about 163 cub." Jap. 1 pump-stroke = 5 sho = 325 cub." = about 2 gallons. 1,000 pump-strokes therefore deliver about 2,000 gallons. 1,000 strokes with 130 pumps, which lift the water 222 meters = about 732 English feet, cost 130 × 4.9 sen = 637 sen. To lift 1 gallon 1 foot costs consequently in wages $\frac{637}{2,000 \times 732}$ = 0.000436 sen, or as 1 gallon water = 10 lbs. Engl., 1 footpound costs 0.0000436 sen.

Now, a good Cornish pumping engine lifts, with 1 hundred weight of coals burned under the boiler, about 100,000,000 footpounds, that is: it lifts a hundred million pounds of water one foot high. Putting the price of a ton coals at yen 6, 1 cwt. would cost 30 sen. To lift the above quantity of 100,000,000 lbs. of water one foot costs then in coals 30 sen, and the cost per 1 footpound would amount to 0.000,000,03 sen.

To lift 100,000,000 lbs. of water by the Japanese method would cost in wages 0.0000 436 sen × 100,000,000 = yen 43.6, that is 145 times as much as the above engine.

In the larger mines in Europe and America, it is not an uncommon thing to lift 1,000 gallons per minute.

Suppose that this quantity was to be lifted 1,000 feet, then the cost by the Japanese method would amount to:

per minute $\dfrac{0.0000\ 436 \times 1000 \times 1000 \times 10}{100} = 4.36$ yen;

per day .. .. = 6,278.40 ,, ;

per year .. .. = 2,291,616.00 ,, ;

While the cost in using the above engine would be:

per minute $\dfrac{0.0000000\ 3 \times 1000 \times 1000 \times 10}{100} = 0.03$ yen;

per day .. .. = 43.20 ,, ;

per year .. .. = 15,268.00 ,, ;

It is needless to remark, that to this cost must be added interest and amortisation for the engine and for the shaft-sinking, as well as expenses to attendants and repairs; the example suffices to prove, that with the Japanese method it is quite impossible to work on a large scale, and this, if for no other reason, because it is scarcely feasible to procure the space required for such an enormous number of pumps.

Supposing a pump, working day and night, to make on an average 10 strokes per minute; then will during that time 10 × 2 = 20 gallons of water be lifted 5.2 feet high. To lift 1,000 gallons to the same height, would consequently require $\dfrac{1,000}{20} = 50$ Japanese pumps.

If each pump with its attendant requires a space of 9 square feet, then the pump-slope alone must have an area of 50 × 9 = 450 square feet, and to lift the water 1,000 feet would require $\dfrac{1000}{5.2} \times 50 = 8,770$ pumps, and with 8 hours' shifts 26,310 laborers.

Instead of the pumps as described above, an arrangement is used in some places, where the water has only to be lifted to an inconsiderable height, consisting in a bucket, hanging at a straw-rope, which is carried over a roll and is raised by coolies, who harness themselves to the rope.

VENTILATION.

No machinery whatsoever is employed for ventilation; by brattices, however, it is sought to regulate the direction of the air-current. The upper adit in a mine, which serves as chimney, is called the "Kemuridashi," while the lowest adit, which relieves the mine from water, is the "Midzunuki."

ILLUMINATION.

For illuminating purposes vegetable oil is burned in lamps made from shells, or well dried bamboo-sticks, about 1 c.m. in diameter, which before being used have been bruised by pounding with a hammer; these require a constant attendance to prevent them from going out. Their use has a considerable effect in fouling the air at the working places, where they are stuck to the rock with clay.

EQUIPMENT.

The further equipment of a miner consists in a breech-leather of plaited straw, "Shirishiki," which is carried at a baldric like a sabretasche.

It not only serves to protect that part of the body, from which it derives the first half of its technical name in German as well as Japanese Miner's language, but also as a mark of rank, in as much as the laborers are only permitted to wear it of quadrangular shape, while an officer may indulge in the luxury of a round one.

In those mines where protection against cold is not required, the miner's only other pieces of dress are a handkerchief around the head or sometimes a cap of plaited paper strings to guard against dust, and a pair of straw-sandals, "Ashinaka," which are cut in halves and only reach from the toes to the middle of the foot-sole. This kind of sandals are said to give a surer footing than the ordinary ones; it is also said to be unpleasant to pass through wet plates with full-length sandals, whose flapping soles send the water against the wearer's legs.

COAL-MINING.

It is only since the opening of the country, that the coal-beds are worked to any extent. Formerly coals were only extracted for the use of such salt-pans for the evaporation of sea-water as happened to be situated in the vicinity of the beds, and then only where the seam cropped out, and the winning consequently presented no difficulty.

IMPROVEMENTS.

Although those improvements, which from a technical point of view might be recommended for adoption in the mining industry, are easily inferred from the preceding description of the present condition of affairs, I shall here briefly mention them.

Where a mine, which already is being worked, is to be reformed, the first care should in most cases be to widen and regulate the passages, in order to obtain a more rational and effective transport than the present one, and to prepare the way for the use in the working places themselves of larger drill-holes and more powerful explosives.

In cases, where a thorough execution of this measure appears impracticable, because it requires either too heavy an outlay or too much time, for the beginning main-galleries might at all events be created, to which the ores could be taken from the pitches in the old fashion. These main-galleries should, if possible, be furnished with tramways, or at least with runners for Hungarian carts or wheelbarrows.

Where large quantities have to be lifted to considerable heights, mechanical aids such as windlasses or winding machines, driven by horse—, water—, or eventually steam-power, should be employed.

In all those mines, where work is carried on below the water-adit, a wide field is open for improvements in the drainage.

In many instances the conditions for affording a remedy, without any disproportionate outlay, are already in existence.

It is at the more important mines nearly always the case, that there between the upper-workings and the water-adit is a fall of several hundred feet, and also a considerable quantity of water, which at present flows into the sump, without doing any work whatsoever; if this water were collected in a proper manner, and conducted over the water-adit, it might easily be made to serve for driving a water-pressure engine or a turbine, in some instances perhaps also a waterwheel. Under favorable circumstances these motors might do service not only for the drainage, but also for the hoisting.

In such places, where there is not sufficient water-power, steam-engines might be erected in the interior of the mine, to drive suction—or force—pumps, and in many instances the old workings above the adit might by a proper arrangement be used as chimney for the subterranean boiler. By either of these, comparatively inexpensive, methods or by others based upon the application of compressed air many a mine, that is now abandoned because of the water, could assuredly again be made profitable.

In extensive mines, where large masses of water have to be lifted, it would, however, be necessary, for central hoisting and drainage, to establish regular shafts supplied with proper machinery.

Good ventilation might be procured, on the one hand in the usual way, by a proper regulation of the natural air-current, and—where requisite—by ventilators, by larger dimensions of the passages &c.; on the other hand by using for illuminating purposes a material, that fouls the air less than burning bamboo.

A further drawback, which is irreconcilable with a rational working of the mines, lies in leaving the productive work to contractors. As shown above, it is in the interest of these people to extract the more easily procured or richer ores, but to leave behind the harder or poorer ones, although these by a proper treatment might still yield a profit. After the stoppings have proceeded on their onward march, those ores become mostly irrevocably lost for the mine. A thorough change could not be effected, unless the administration hired the work out to the workmen direct, and itself kept a strict control over the latter, while it sent the contractors about their business. I certainly know from personal experience, that this is not so easily effected, nor can it be done by a stroke of the wand; but if the system were once declared doomed, it might be possible gradually to get out of the old ways and into new ones.

It is scarcely necessary to mention, that in certain instances, especially where levels of considerable extent are to be driven, or deep shafts to be sunk, or where the thickness of the ore-deposit is considerable, machine-rock-drills and generally dynamite would be used with advantage instead of gunpowder.

Besides, masonry might in many instances be advantageously substituted for timbering, as clay for brick-making is nearly everywhere to be had.

DRESSING.

The dressing is almost exclusively done by women and children, and without the aid of machinery. The output is in the first place subjected to hand-picking; those pieces, which are already sufficient rich for metallurgical treatment, are put aside, and the remainder—either with an ordinary hammer or with a tilt-hammer, similar to that used for shelling rice, and like that put in motion with the foot—pounded to a grit of a maximum size of 5^{mm}. This granulated ore is then put into shallow willow—or bamboo—baskets, ("Dsarunge"), where it is subjected to a kind of jigging operation. With this object the laborer fills the basket with about 5lbs. of stuff, seizes it with both hands, one opposite the other, and gives it in a basin, filled with water, alternately a shaking and a rotatory movement. When after the lapse of a few minutes, the coarse sands have nearly grouped themselves according to their specific weight, then the upper layer of refuse is withdrawn, the next one is put aside for a second similar treatment, while the nethermost generally yields good ore; if not, it has to be treated anew in the same manner. During this operation, the finer particles of the ore have escaped through the meshes of the basket and been caught in the basin. When these sands have accumulated in sufficient quantity, they are repeatedly passed through an oblong buddle, and the residue is further concentrated by being placed once or more on a slightly concave board ("yuri ita"), which is dexterously impelled at times rotatory, at times in such a manner, that the motion becomes a combination of that of the shaking-table with that of the jigger. From the above described process, which is principally applied to copper, lead, silver, eventually also to iron-ores and ores of antimony, the treatment of gold-ores somewhat differs.

WASHING OF GOLD-ORES.

These are in the first place pounded in the usual way, and then ground on hand-mills with the aid of water. The pulp, that flows out from the mill, is carried over inclined scarred boards into launders. In the furrows of the boards ("Neko" *i. e.* literally : cat), which correspond with the Californians' blankets and the ox-hides of the South-Americans, the heavier particles of the washings remain as sediment. They are removed by washing or knocking. The concentrations, thus procured, are then further concentrated either on the above mentioned flat boards, or in laquered dishes, similar to the soup-bowls of the Japanese table-service—, until finally gold-sand is obtained. This is then melted with borax in clay-crucibles, and by the worker handed to the administration of the mine against a certain remuneration—usually yen 2 per *momme* (1 *momme* = 3,75 grammes). The sands and slimes from the launders are occasionally again returned to the mills, and repeatedly subjected to a similar process. Nay, when ore is scarce, the tailings, which have been accumulated through centuries, are again worked over. As this renewed manipulation requires no mining expenses, it follows that it needs only a small percentage of gold to make the operation yield a profit, although it be a rather modest one ;— the limit is about $3/8$ ounce = \$7 $1/2$ per ton.

The winning and washing of gold-ores is very often carried on by each individual miner's family separately ; then the men procure the ore, the children do the transport from the pitches to the mills, the women and girls the pounding and washing of the ores. Under this arrangement, it is necessary, that each family is possessor of its own mills and launders.

IMPROVEMENT IN DRESSING.

The result of the dressing, however primitive the latter, can, generally speaking, not be pronounced bad ; nay, the product is perhaps often purer than can be obtained by the aid of machinery, and the skill of the gold-washers is so great, that the worth of only \$1 = $1/20$ ounce per ton, although of course it cannot be profitably extracted, can be detected even in pyritic ores.

But it requires no further demonstration, that the dressing—from first to last done with the human hand alone, without any machinery at all as motors—must be a very expensive one. Water power is almost everywhere obtainable—even when not always in the immediate vicinity of the mine—and the creation of dressing establishments on modern system offers therefore in most cases no great difficulties.

Complicated engines cost dear, both to buy and to work—in the hands of people who don't know how to attend to them properly—, and the transport of the larger pieces is often a matter of considerable difficulty: it would therefore suit the smaller establishments to employ some plain mechanisms, that could easily be made in the country itself, such as water-wheels, wooden stamping mills, pointed boxes or "spitzlutten," Rittinger's percussion-tables, hydraulic jiggers &c.

In working gold ores in larger guantities, amalgamation would mostly be the best method.

There exist, however, a number of poor gold-mines, which could not afford such an establishment on account of the heavy outlay for machinery and the high price of quicksilver, while they, at the present rate of wages, are able to yield a profit by the washing of the ores. These are especially those mines, which are worked by farmers at times, when they are not occupied with field-labor. There it would best serve the purpose to continue the customary method of *washing*, and to have the *disintegration*, that is, the pounding and grinding of the ores done by simple mechanisms.

METALLURGY.

As to the metallurgic treatment of the ores, the old processes are exclusively based on smelting; wet methods of extraction, amalgamation &c. are only acquisitions of modern times.

Gold—when not got by washing—is like silver extracted by liquation, lead either by roasting with subsequent reducing smelting, or by a combination of the same with precipitating smelting, copper by a repeated roasting and reducing smelting.

ROASTNG.

The roasting is almost everywhere done in a kind of rude kilns ("Yakigama"), built with quarry-stones and clay in a circular shape, about 4-6′ in diameter, and about 4′ in height, on one side furnished with air-holes. Instead of circular, rectangular kilns are also often used, 5-6′ wide and until 80′ long. Calcination in heaps is seldom used. The ore-lumps are without further preparation thrown into the kiln on a bedding of fuel, while the slicks, by the aid of brushwood mixed with the charge, are kept as loosely as possible in the furnace. The time of roasting, during which the furnace is in the main left to itself, lasts from 20 till 30 days. After the roast has cooled down, what has been badly roasted is put aside for a second calcination, while the well roasted masses, whether silver—, copper—, iron—, or lead—ores, are smelted all in the same universal furnace ("Fukidoko").

SMELTING.

The furnace consists in a hollow made in the ground, covered with brasque, of nearly hemispherical form, with a diameter of $1\frac{1}{4}'—\frac{1}{2}'$, which receives the requisite blast from ordinary smith's-bellows ("Fuigo") through 1 or 2 nozzles of clay. These bellows are hand-box-bellows, the valves packed with badger's skin; the piston-rod is moved backward and forward by a coolie, who draws it out with the hand and pushes it back with the foot. Usually two such bellows are used at each furnace. The bellows furnish about 4 cub.' air per piston stroke = about 120 cub.' air per minute, of atmospheric pressure.

The tuyeres open into the furnace in the upper border of the same, and in order to prevent the direct ascent of the blast, but on the contrary spread the latter over the entire space of the furnace, a vaulted roof of clay extends above the orifices of the tuyeres as far as half-way into the furnace. The furnace is separated from the bellows by a back-wall; the products of combustion escape through a chimney, built of frame-work and covered with loam, which is supported partly by the back-wall, partly by pillars, and commences about 7' above the bottom of the kiln.

To blow in the furnace, the latter is filled with dark charcoals; fire is lit only before the tuyeres, and the bellows are put gently in motion. Gradually the fire is increased, charcoals and charge are thrown in a heap over the furnace, and thus the charge is reduced to a state of fusion. When the furnace is filled with molten masses nearly to the tuyeres, then the blast is stopped, the heap consisting of red-hot charge and burning charcoals is pushed aside, the fire is slackened with water, the liquid slags are withdrawn from the molten bath, and the smelting is continued in the above manner, until at last the whole furnace is filled with liquid metal respectively matt, whereupon the contents are either laddled out, or lifted off in discs, or, although rarely, tapped. The red-hot furnace is then repaired with some clay, and a similar smelting repeated. When also this, and may be yet a third one, has been done, then the furnace has become so much impaired, that it is unfit for further work; it is then cooled with water, repaired with brasque, and warmed over the night, in order to be ready for use the following day.

In such a furnace not more than 400—500 *gramme* = 3,330 to 4,160 lbs. English can be smelted in a day, and the larger establishments have therefore often a number of 30 or more furnaces in operation. The fuel consumed is about 30 to 70 % of the weight of the ore.

As already observed, this kind of furnace serves with certain modifications for nearly all sorts of smelting; only for the production of pig-iron a kind of rachette-furnace on a small scale, with several tuyeres placed opposite to each other, is used here and there.

To refine copper, crucibles of clay are employed; for cupelling, tests.

THE CHARGE.

In preparing the charge, the object is to procure a tough—mostly highly silicated-slag, which can be easily removed in skins from the bath; it is thereby not to be avoided that the same, in consequence of its consistency, contains many mechanically enclosed particles of metal and regulus. The charge is either added at the same process or pounded and washed, or smelted separately, as long as a profitable result is still obtainable.

The fuel is everywhere charcoal, mostly hard one.

There is no control whatsoever with the smelting through current assays, and through smelting-books only a very insufficient one. Under these circumstances great loss of metal is of course unavoidable; scoriae for instance, which by repeated smelting yield no regulus, are thrown away, although they often contain a still considerable quantity of useful metals,—for instance lead, copper &c.—as silicate.

As the same construction of furnace serves for smelting the most heterogeneous metals, so the smelting process itself offers only insignificant variations. It would appear, that the same process and the construction of furnace, as were also customary elsewhere in Asia, for instance in India, were here originally used for copper-ore, and afterwards applied also to other metals.

DEFECTS IN THE OLD SMELTING PROCESS.

That the adoption of the same construction of furnace and of the same process in the treatment of all metals, must have its disadvantages, and these of a grave nature, is selfevident. The construction of the smelting furnaces is generally open to the following objections:

1. It causes an enormous consumption of fuel, first, because the heat from the charcoals, which are burning so to speak in an open heap, is not at all kept together; secondly, because the furnace requires every day to be warmed anew, and thirdly because, while the smelting is going on, the already red-hot charge

has to be repeatedly slackened with water, in order to enable the workmen to remove the scoriae from the metal-bath.

2. It causes a considerable loss of metal through volatilisation, as the metals, when once reduced to gaseous state have no opportunity for condensation in the upper parts of the kiln.

3. The attendance, both to the bellows and to the smelting itself, requires a vast amount of labor, at the same time as it admits of only a limited production.

4. The attendance on the furnace is extremely trying on account of the intense heat.

On the other hand it cannot be denied, that the furnace is extremely simple in its construction, is easily and quickly built and requires only a small outlay.

The fuel used for the calcinations is exclusively wood, for smelting charcoal. As the disafforestation in the neighborhood of the mines has generally been ruthlessly pursued, the fuel has now to be transported from afar, and is consequently dear (10 *quamme* cost yen 0.15—0.36 = about yen 7.05—9.72 per English ton). The dealers often deliver the coals in wet condition, to make them weigh the more.

IMPROVEMENTS.

From the above observations it is sufficiently apparent, what improvements ought to be introduced into metallurgic technics.

1. Selection of fitting process for the treatment of the various ores.
2. Use of proper furnaces for roasting and smelting.

Even if the kilns hitherto used are fit for the roasting of ores in lumps, their use for slicks must always be very disadvantageous, as they only in an insufficient degree offer opportunity for oxidation. In larger smelting works it would of course also become a matter of consideration, whether the roasting gases might not be utilized for the manufacture of sulphuric acid.

At blast-furnaces machinery, which in many cases could be driven by water, would of course have to be substituted for hand-bellows. A comparison between the cost of the present supply of blast and that of a supply, procured by good machinery, would give a result similar to that subtained in the above quoted instance of drainage.

It would carry me too far here to enumerate what furnaces are required for the several smelting processes; suffice it to say, that in almost every instance the present furnaces must be replaced by others which allow a continuous smelting. The present furnaces may at most do for trial-smeltings and for the reduction of smaller quantities.

3. Supply of the cheapest possible fuel, whether by using cokes or by the establishment of a rational forest-management.

In either case the simultaneous improvement in the means of communication —roads, rivers &c.—is an absolute condition for success.

As yet the charcoals are burned in the woods, mostly high up in the mountains, and thence carried by horses or oxen, sometimes also by coolies, to the furnace.

The wood is burned to coal, not in heaps, but in dome-shaped ovens, made from quarry-stones and clay or loam, which are abandoned as soon as the district has been denuded of its trees. The products of distillation are allowed to escape, without being utilized.

Leaving out of sight the charcoal-burner's constant change of working place, the building of carriage-roads could not pay, on account of the generally highly broken ground; the coal-transport could, however, be very much simplified by *not* burning the wood on the spot, where the trees have been felled, but by floating it on the water courses—which, where requisite, might be dammed up —to constant central coal-burning places, as near the furnaces as possible. There the ovens or heaps might also be furnished with apparatus for utilizing the products of distillation, tar, pyroliginous acid.

4. A strict control of the smelting proceedings through current assays and smelting books. For the lucidity and simplicity of the entire book-keeping, the introduction of Arabic figures would be of the greatest assistance, and the small amount of labor spent on learning the same ought not to be a matter of consideration, when compared with the advantages that would accrue therefrom. With regard to other matters, in which workmen and administration are concerned, I shall make some further remarks, at the end of this paper.

The dressing and metallurgical establishments are at present mostly situated close to the mine, and consequently generally on very steep heights, where the structures cling like swallow-nests to the rock, and in their dimensions are confined to a minimum. In order to obtain a better situation, and at the same time a greater water-power, it would often be preferable to carry the works further down toward the valley. In many instances this would also afford the additional advantage of making a joint working of the ores from several mines feasible.

ASSAYING.

The assaying of the ore is, with regard to gold, confined either to the washing of a certain quantity of ore, or to smelting the same together with lead, and successive cupellation of the rich lead. The latter proceeding is also used for silver. The smelting is done either in clay-crucibles or directly in small hearth-furnaces.

With regard to copper, iron, lead, antimony, there is no regular assaying process; but it is considered sufficient to treat certain quantities of ore in the usual manner, and then weigh the results. In this manner it of course is only ascertained, how much metal can be extracted by the method used, not how much the ore really contains.

In weighing the grains of gold and silver, the ordinary small Japanese scales, similar to the Roman balances, are used.

As curiosum I may here mention, that of late Plattner's blow-pipe-scale is used here and there in a somewhat hybrid form, that is in adopting it by prolongation of the diverging lines, for the measurement of larger grains.

The parts being placed in proportion to those on the blow-pip-scale, the results obtained must become too high. For an approximative test of the value of gold-or silver-alloys, compositions of a fixed standard, corresponding to our touch-needles, are also used. Thus for instance I have seen a collection of 100 pieces, in form of coins, strung on a wire, each of which represented a fixed standard, in gold from 0 to 100, and in silver from 100 to 0. The sample is then with the aid of Lydian stone and sulphuric acid compared with the standard alloy. The sampling is mostly done in a manner, which is far from guaranteeing a correct average.

SUBTERRANEAN SURVEYING.

Still to mention another branch of the mining industry, the subterranean surveying, it has always been the custom, to lay the main-galleries and workings down on a map.

These drawings consist usually in a rather arbitrary combination of plans, elevations and sections along the veins, showing at the same time often sketches of the surface, rivers, villages, roads etc. as well as hints as to the geological conditions.

For plotting of works in different horizons either different colours are used or smaller plans are in the proper places stuck on to the front or to the back of the main plan, accordingly as the work in question is above or below the main plan. The Japanese paper being semitransparent the perspicuity is not sensibly interfered with by this proceeding.

The instrument used for measuring horizontal angles is a sight-compass of ca. 10^{cm} diam. Upon the limb are marked from right to left the twelve signs of the zodiac: Rat, Bull, Tiger, Hare, Dragon, Snake, Horse, Goat, Ape, Cock,

Dog, Boar. Each of these signs is again divided into 3×10 parts (sometimes less) thus giving in the whole a division of the limb into 360 equal parts.

For observations, the number of degrees inside one sign is read.

For levelling is used a plumb-level and ruler; for length measurements a measuring-staff or-cord, taking as unit the ordinary shaku (foot) with its subdivisions. One mining ken is 5 shaku.

Although such surveys are far from being exact, they nevertheless have their value as guides.

OFFICERS AND WORKMEN.

Although even the private mines are able to show a numerous staff of officers the superintendence of the practical work is generally not considered of that importance which it might claim, while on the other hand great care is bestowed upon the book-keeping.

The latter comprises the keeping of stock, produce-and wages-tables,—smelting books being kept only to a limited extent—and it is, owing to the painful minuteness, with which details are recorded and the accounts kept in fractions of a hundredth part of a sen rather voluminous; principally on account of the use of Chinese figures it fails, I think, to give that clear and rapid insight which is obtained by the aid of Arabian figures.

As to the practical management of the mining operations, at least to their productive part, it has been mentioned already that the contractors or middle-men enjoy a rather far going authority, in most cases not to the advantage of the mine.

The subaltern class of overseers and foremen who fill the intermediate station between officers and workmen, is mostly recruited from people who have learnt to read, write and cipher, but who had previously no practical training in their respective functions.

Probably in order to do evenhanded justice to every one of them, to give them opportunity of becoming acquainted with all the branches of the work, etc. a frequent alternation in their functions is unfortunately the custom.

A workman can scarcely ever be promoted to any of these positions, in the first place, because there is an objection to having a coolie in the office, secondly on account of his as a rule not being sufficiently well trained in writing and ciphering.

Now, when no opportunity is offered to a workman, by industry and good behaviour to raise himself to a higher step, then he will not overexert himself and especially not, if he must apprehend, that any extraordinary exertion on his part might lead to a reduction in the contract price of task-work.

JAPANESE MINING LAW.

The Japanese Mining Law is an offspring of modern times, and carries unmistakable traces of European influence; it is therefore, strictly speaking, foreign to a description of native mining, but as it is so closely connected with the latter, I have thought it my duty to give an extract of its principal clauses, which I here subjoin:

All minerals, with the exception of those used as building stones and for agricultural purposes, are the property of the government and no one has the right to win the same, until he has obtained permission from the former.

To carry on exploration works, a license must be applied for; for the opening and working of a mine, a mining lease. Either of these is for the whole empire—with exception of Yesso, which is under the Kaitakushi—to be obtained from the Mining Department.

Any person, who opens and works a mine, has the right of expropriation with regard to the land requisite for erecting buildings on the surface and for making roads.

Explorations upon another man's land are lawful upon payment of a proper indemnification.

For every 500 tsubos contained in a mining sett (1 tsubo = $6'$ square), producing metalliferous minerals, except iron, a yearly tax of 1 yen is to be paid; for every 500 tsubos in a mining sett producing iron-ore or non-metalliferous minerals (coal, sulphur &c.), the tax is yen 0.50.

When working over old slag heaps, the same amount of tax is to be levied on every 1,000 tsubos contained in the mining sett. For each unit of measure (respectively 500 or 1,000 tsubos) contained in the mining sett leased, proof must be given every year, that a quantity of work has been executed, equal at least to the work of one hand during 300 days; otherwise the lease is forfeited.

Besides the above tax, every mine has to pay a royalty to the Mining Department, not exceeding 20 % and not less than 3 % of the value of the production.

The amount of the royalty within these limits is to be fixed yearly by the Mining Department, separately for each mine.

The lessee of a mine shall twice a year, that is, in the 1st and 7th month, forward to the Mining Department a report showing the quantity and name of the metals obtained, the number of hands employed, the working expenses, in fact the results of his mining operations.

Understatements in these reports, with the intent to avoid payment of the royalty or to pay less than due, are visited with proportionate fines.

The lease of a mining sett is *eo ipso* valid for 15 years, and may after the expiration of that term be renewed; on the other hand it may also be surrendered before the expiration of the term.

Abandoned mines must be guarded by fencing &c. in such a manner, that there shall be no danger for the public.

To engage foreign engineers, even to erect foreign machinery, requires a special permission from the Mining Department. Contracts between holders of mines and foreign engineers must be submitted to the Mining Department for its approval.

The holder of a mine is under no circumstance permitted to grant a foreigner any pecuniary interest, in the working of the mine; nor is he under any circumstances allowed to mortgage his mining lease or the future produce of the mine to a foreigner.

Transgressions of the last-named provisions give the Government the right to confiscate the mine. The structures on the surface, plant &c. may, however, be removed by the proprietor.

If the holder of a mine is unable to pay his taxes, royalty or fines, then the Government may sell the plant and buildings at public auction and after retaining from the proceeds realized what is due to itself, hand the balance, if any, to the owner.

All mining operations are to be conducted in such a manner, that the smallest possible amount of the valuable minerals, contained in the deposits, shall be left unworked, and care must be taken, that the underground works do not endanger houses, railways, castle-walls &c. If through infraction of this rule injury be done, then the lessee of the mine shall pay double the amount of the damage caused.

It is permitted to drive general galleries of a certain area, and the mine-owner, who does so, is entitled to recover from those mines, which thereby have been relieved from their water, a compensation, the amount of which is to be settled by amicable arrangement, or eventually by the Mining Department.

As already said, this law has many points of contact with the mining laws of European countries, from which it in the main differs in the strict measures, taken to prevent foreigners from becoming interested in mining, and also by the total absence of mining-police regulations for the protection of the workmen in the mine. The facts, that robbing, the prohibition notwithstanding, is carried on in many mines, and that the stipulated royalty of from $3-20\%$ has never been levied, show that the law is not strictly observed in all its points.

In the above remarks we have considered the state of the mines and mining in Japan, and indicated the outlines of such technical reforms as are desirable; it now remains for us to examine, what general measures might still be taken with the object of raising the mining industry in this country.

There can be no doubt, that the speediest, the most effective and cheapest means to raise the mining industry to the height of modern times lies in admission of foreigners to work the mines, and the question is only, how far this means would be to the interest of the country. The objection, that the foreigners in a comparatively short time would possess themselves of and export the mineral treasures of the country, so that the pecuniary condition of the latter although momentarily somewhat improved, would later, when the mines had been exhausted, become very much deteriorated—is scarcely tenable. In the first place, the existing deposits, which have hitherto only been worked in their superior levels, run for many years to come no risk of being exhausted, even by an energetic production; in the second place, the mines, when worked by modern methods and under foreign management, will utilize ores, which are now entirely lost; and finally a flourishing mining industry, although the outturn were largely exported, would yield a considerable revenue for the finances through their royalties to the treasury as well as by affording encouragement to industry in general. But there is another reason, which may well have caused the government to shrink from giving the right of mining free, and this lies in the circumstance, that when once the interior of the country has been opened, it becomes impossible to prevent it being swamped by a Chinese immigration.

When we consider, to what troubles even a country with such enormous demand for labor as the United States has been exposed through an unlimited, pigtailed immigration; when we farther remember the short distance between Japan and China, the kindred manners, the similarity in culture and mode of life in the two countries, then it is impossible to shirk the conviction, that Japan, through an illimited Chinese immigration, would not only get into temporary troubles, but would find its national existence seriously jeopardized, and this the more, because a comparison between the Japanese and the Chinese workman does scarcely result to the advantage of the former. The Japanese workman is undoubtedly clever and skilful, but he is generally lighthearted and open-handed, and if he receives high pay, this rather prevents him from than stimulates him to continued working, while the Chinaman is industrious, frugal and saving, and by high wages is animated to still greater industry,—all of them qualities which cannot but recommend him to the employer of workmen. The manager of every mine, or any other establishment, worked by a foreigner, would therefore in all probability sooner or later surround himself with a staff of Chinese workmen. Even if the amount of the average *daily* wages, especially when compared with the same in the United States is not alluring, the money to be made by *task*—work, would in itself be sufficient to encourage immigration. It may now easily be conceived, in what condition the Japanese workman would find himself, when also the necessaries of life rose in price, in consequence of the increased population, while at the same time the means of procuring the same were taken away from him, or at all events reduced through the presence of his preferred rivals. In the face of these circumstances, it is not to be wondered at, that the government recoils from admitting foreigners and opening the interior of the country as a means for promoting the mining industry.

The case would be otherwise, if foreign capital were allowed to be invested in mining enterprises, perhaps under some such conditions as proposed by Mr. Lyman for Yesso ("a general Report on the geology of Yesso," by B. S. Lyman, 1877.) That the government with the most painstaking scrupulosity tries to prevent this also, is probably due to the circumstance, that it in this manner wants to put a stop to every attempt made by foreigners to get a foothold in the interior, and to avoid the risk of disputes and lawsuits. We will therefore in the following considerations renounce on all assistance from foreign capital, and examine in what directions reforms might still be introduced.

In the first place it is requisite, that care be taken to create a staff of able officers and workmen.

With regard to the technical education of future officers, the Government is alive to its duty, and has with this object established well provided classes for mining and metallurgy in the *Tokio Daigaku* as well as in the *Kobu Daigaku*. But those officers also, who are already employed in practical service, might obtain a certain instruction by attending a brief course of studies arranged in Tokio for their special benefit. Even if it would scarcely come within the plan of such a course of studies to enable these students *on their own hand* to establish thoroughly modern works, a great deal would already be gained, if they were taught to appreciate the usefulness, nay the necessity of such reorganisations, both in great and in small things, and if they would therefore kindly assist the young men of the new era with their own long experience, instead of treating them with mistrust.

But the creation of a reliable staff of officers requires something more than the mere technical education, be the same ever so good. In whatever country it be, as long as an officer has no guarantee, that a faithful performance of his duties will secure him his place in Government service, and that, when old age or sickness compels him to retire from active service, the future support of himself and family will nevertheless be provided for,—so long the temptation must always be there, to use his position, while he has it, as a milk-cow, and to take his work as easily as possible. To procure him that security, pension— and widows'—funds, as we have them in our Government service and in large private establishments, would be the most fitting means. Only then, however, would such funds be able to subsist, if on the one hand arbitrary dismissals from service were put a stop to, on the other hand the capacities of the candidate became the principal consideration in making new appointments.

Reforms in the workmen's class are of no less importance than the reorganization of the officers' department. In the present condition of things, a man may come to work or not, just as he pleases. The consequence is, that at the time of field-work, or after pay-days, on festivals &c. he is simply *bioki*, that is, does not make his appearance. In this case he of course receives no wages, but neither does he, when he is actually laid up with sickness. The result of this liberty for the workman to remain away whenever he likes, is that the works at times are denuded of workmen, or—and this is more frequently the case—that they engage more workmen than necessary in order to be secured against all eventualities. Here also an improvement could be made by the establishment of workmen's funds. Into these the workmen should pay a certain percentage of their wages as well as eventual fines for transgression of the working regulations, for unauthorised absence from work, while any deficiency is supplied by contribution from the works themselves. From this fund the workmen would receive assistance in case of sickness, and when he had been a contributing member for a certain time, and had become unfit for work, a pension. To prevent the men from shamming sickness, and also to attend the sick, the presence of a physician would of course be absolutely necessary.

MODEL-WORKS.

Another means, which the Government possesses for improving the mining, consists in setting private mine-owners a good example by the establishment of modern model works. It must be admitted, that in this respect as well as in the establishment of colleges the Government has done what lay in its power, even if—as already observed—the success not always has been in proportion to the efforts made. The Gorvenment is now again occupied in organizing on modern system two works, which may be made very productive, and of which it has lately become possessed. Their success, which may safely be predicted, must have the more influence on private mining, as one of them is a coppermine, and copper is the very metal, which is profitably produced also by private mine-owners, while hitherto no establishment on a large scale for working the same on modern system has been in existence here.

Even if, as already remarked, not all the mines and reduction works of modern style have had the desired success, it is the duty of a Government by its own initiative to open the way for new methods. As it, however, is a notorious fact that a Government always works at a higher cost than private individuals, a Government acts wisely when it surrenders well organized establishments to be worked by private citizens, and this the Government has recently done with regard to several mines. As observed at the commencement of this paper, the want of capital is an obstacle to private individuals taking the initiative in the establishment of large mining works, even in places, where there can be no doubt about their profitable nature.

FORMATION OF PRIVATE COMPANIES.

Instead of constantly applying the floating capital of the country to the creation of new banks, part of it might be more advantageously used for the formation of companies, which besides other industries would devote their attention to mining. Such a company would have to become owner of all the mines in an entire mining district, in order by consolidation of neighboring mines to become possessed of the great advantages to be derived from a common management, common working of the mines, drainage, reduction.

CENTRAL REDUCTION—WORKS.

Another not less important measure would be the erection of central reduction-works and also of central dressing-establishments, at favorably situated places.

Suppose for instance, that such a central establishment for the working of all the ores, as well from the immediate as from the more distant neighborhood, were created either by government or by a company, at some favorably situated point on the coast of the inland sea, say in the vicinity of Kobe. The copper—, silver—, gold—, lead—, sulphur-ores would be delivered from the mines— whosoever their owners—at the smelting-works, where they would be accurately assayed and, according to their ascertained contents, paid for at fixed rates. The advantages, which centralization offers, not only in respect to the management, but also to the technical superintendence of the works, composition of the charge, utilization of the roasting gases for the manufacture of sulphuric acid &c., would enable the reduction-works, organized on the latest system, to pay the mines a higher price for their ores than the mines themselves, with their defective smelting methods, costly administration, high charcoal-prices, are at present able to make, and both parties would thus be gainers by the arrangement. The cokes or coals would have to be got from the South, Karatsu, Nagasaki, Miike.

These reduction-works would work the ores from the following mines, which are all situated more or less in the neighborhood: Copper-mines: Tenwa, Tsubouo-uchi, Ishibe, Wake, Akasaka-Ida, Beishi, Kumayama, Kawato, Tada, Kanahira, Ono-Omodaui, Hosono, Maibira, Shikama, Wurushiyama; the lead-mines of Mandokoro and Odome, and eventually the silver—and copper-ores from Ikuno and the ores of antimony from Ichinokawa, near Saijo. According to the report on the Uyeno Exhibition in 1877, the present produce from these mines—with exception of Ikuno, which works annually about 20,000 tons of ore—amounts to the aggregate sum of 18,000—19,000 tons of ores per annum. Of all the mines quoted above, Ikuno is the only one, where ores are worked by modern methods.

The transport of the ores might here and there be rather expensive; it would, however, in nearly all instances be down-hill work, that is, from the mines to the coast, and in many cases rivers, canals, the lake Biwa, the railroads between Kioto or Tsuruga and Kobe, and the sea may be availed of. Where requisite the transport by land must certainly be facilitated by good carriage-roads, as on the whole the establishment of proper means of communication through the interior of the country is a *conditio sine quâ non* for the progress of industry in general and of mining in special. The objection might be raised, that the transport of the ores to the central reduction-works would enhance their price too much; if it, however, be borne in mind, that ores from South-America—even from the west-coast—are profitably smelted in Swansea, and ores from the west coast of Mexico smelted in large quantities in Freiberg, that is, deep in the interior of continental Europe, then it may be presumed, that the comparatively infinitesimal short distances in the instance quoted by us are not of so very great consequence, even if the ores should prove less rich than those from America.

In a similar manner as in the South central reduction-works might be established at a convenient place on the northwest coast, perhaps in Funakawa.

ENGINEERING BUREAU.

A still further means for assisting private citizens in their mining enterprises would be the establishment of an engineering bureau, under the Mining Department, where on payment of a reasonable fee ores could be assayed and analyzed, plans and estimates be obtained for such establishments as were required by the works, a bureau in fact, where holders of mines could always obtain information on technical questions. The Chief of this bureau should at the same time take charge of the hitherto entirely wanting mining-police, that is, see that laws issued with the object of procuring the workmen the greatest possible safety in the mines, of securing a proper technical working method, of preventing robbing &c. are observed.

GEOLOGICAL SURVEY.

Finally, it would be of great importance, not less in respect of mining than of many other branches of industry, if a *systematical* thorough geological survey were made, having for its object, not merely the rendering of the topography of the country and the study of its geological condition in general, but also registering all hitherto known places, where useful minerals occur, searching for new ones, explaining the local laws of the occurrence and formation of ore-deposits, indicating those places, where further explorations are to be made and those where not; in short, collecting and making accessible to the general public all the information, that can be of interest for mining. Besides it would have to embrace all the examinations concerning the development of the country from an agricultural and general technological point of view.

There has been made a beginning already in regard to a geological survey of some places of the main island and of Yesso, the examination having chiefly been conducted from a topographical, geological and mining standpoint. It seems that the government has now in view to extend the researches to such a degree that all the branches of a modern geological survey are fully investigated.

In the subjoined plates, which have been prepared by Mr. Ota after sketches made by my assistant Mr. W. Watanabe, the principal mining and smelting apparatus and tools are represented.

ENUMERATION OF THOSE MINES, WHICH ALREADY ARE WORKED ON MODERN SYSTEM.

After having in the foregoing remarks examined the traditional native mining, I desire here to repeat, that, as far as technics are concerned, the state of things has already, especially in the Government-mines, in many cases been considerably improved.

The following mines, the production of which appears from the tables inserted below, are worked on modern system :

1. BELONGING TO THE GOVERNMENT.

SADO.—Gold—and silver-mine. Mechanical dressing, smelting and pan-amalgamation. Organized by foreigners, now worked by Japanese only.

IKUNO.—Gold—and silver-mine, province Tajima. 100 iron revolving stamps, dressing by Rittinger's percussion tables, Freiberg barrel amalgamation. Had formerly 12, at present still 8, Frenchmen.

KAMAISHI.—Iron-mine and—works, province, Rikuchiu. 2 charcoal—blast-furnaces, puddling furnaces. Formerly 4, now 1 foreigner there; but metallurgists have again been engaged in England. The ore is magnetic iron.

NAKAKOSAKA.—Iron-mine and—works, province Kozuke. 1 charcoal- blast-furnace, built by English engineers for private individuals, recently taken over by the Government. Worked formerly with loss, is not yet worked anew. *

MIIKE —Coal-mines, province Chikugo. English engineer.

Besides these mines, the copper-works at Ani and the silver-works at Innai, both in the province of Ugo, have lately come into possession of the Government; they were hitherto worked on the Japanese system, but are now by German engineers being organized on foreign system.

2. PRIVATE.

OQUUSU.—Gold-mine, province Ugo. Amalgamation in Californian pans and in Hungarian bowls. 10 iron stamps. As yet the mine has not been able to produce the quantity of ore required by the works. Organized by an American engineer, now worked by Japanese alone.

KOSAKA.—Silver—and copper-mine, province Rikuchiu. Raw Smelting. Ziervogel and Hunt—Douglass process. Erected by German engineers, now worked only by Japanese.

The modern establishments in Oqunsu and Kosaka were erected by the Government, and, when completely fitted up, handed over to private people for working.

NAGANO.—Gold-mine, province of Satsuma. Passed once for one of the best gold-mines, but is now said to be poor in ores. Californian amalgamation. 10 iron stamps. Has a French engineer.

---

* Has been started again lately.

HANDA.—Silver mine, province Iwashiro. Wooden stamp-mill, Freiberg barrel-amalgamation. This is the only establishment, which by Japanese alone has been furnished with European machinery. The production is insignificant.

TAKASHIMA.—Coal mine, province Hizen. Now together with Miike the most productive mine in Japan. Has 12 English engineers and overseers.

Besides, the coal-fields in Yesso are now being opened by American engineers, in the employ of the Kaitakushi.

The following tables will help to fill up the outlines of the picture now drawn of Japanese mining. The material for the production-tables has been taken from recently published reports from the Kobusho.

NOTES TO THE FOLLOWING TABLES.

The weight of gold and silver is given in ounces Troy, of copper, lead and iron in lbs. English and that of coal in English tons.

The value of an ounce of gold was taken at						....	yen 20.7
,,	,,	,,	,,	silver	,,	,, ...	1.27
,,	,,	a	lb. of copper		,,	,, ...	0.17
,,	,,	,,	,,	,, lead	,,	,, ...	0.048
,,	,,	,,	,,	,, iron	,,	,, ...	0.01
,,	,,	a ton coal (lumps, dust and coke) from private mines.					4.50
,,	,,	,,	,,	from government mines			3.50

The prices have of course varied according to time and place; those quoted above, which correspond pretty closely with the actual state of the metal-and coal-market, are rather too low than too high, considering that since the time, to which the tables refer, most of the above-mentioned articles have fallen in price. The expenditure, as stated in the tables, comprises both first outlay and the working expenses. The decimals have been left out.

NOTES TO TABLE I. Table I shows the produce from the mines at Sado, Ikuno and Miike since the time, when modern methods were there being introduced; the expenses therefore cover all the new constructions, machinery &c., and as a matter of course the production could only be on a small scale as long as the works were under construction.

The mines at Ani and Innai were only recently taken over by the government, and the purchase price of the mines is included in the expenditure of yen 609,725 and yen 253,405 respectively.

The production of copper from government-mines has hitherto been very small, as the government, until it bought Ani, had no real copper-mines at all.

Iron has not yet been worked by the government; large iron-works, on which

TABLE I.

a.—Production of the Government mines since 1868 and 1875-77.—*b.*—Production of private mines 1874-1877 incl.

PRODUCE.

	Name of the Mine.	Period of Working.	Gold. oz.	Value. yen.	Silver. oz.	Value. yen.	Copper. lb.	Value. yen.	Value. yen.	Lead. lb.	Value. yen.	Iron. lb.	Value. yen.	Coal & Coke. tons.	Value. yen.	Total Value of Produce. yen.	Total Expense. yen.	Profit and Loss. yen.
a.	Sado.	Dec. 1868–June 1878 9 years 7 Months.	9,441	105,423	375,079	476,350	79,875	13,579								685,368	1,375,842	– 690,484
	Ikuno (Tajima).	Jan. 1869–June 1878 9 years 6 Months.	21,678	496,315	179,146	227,506										668,920	1,759,312	– 1,095,452
	Mike (Chikugo).	June 1873–June 1877 5 years 1 Month.													750,303	1,225,060	1,225,060	561,053	+665,001
	Ani (I go).	Nov. 1875–June 1878 2 years 8 Months.	68	1,409	47,529	59,374	2,111,697	364,089	531,552	27,914							462,785	609,725	– 156,940
	Innai (I go).	Nov. 1875–June 1878 2 years 8 Months.	1,489	30,343	143,408	182,123											212,971	253,465	– 40,494
	Sum.		32,676	633,996	745,178	945,357	2,221,572	377,675	581,552	2,914					350,303	326,460	3,240,994	4,559,403	– 1,318,409
	Kamaishi (Rikuchu).	May 1874–June 1878 4 years 1 Month.									Under construction.							1,110,843	– 1,110,882
	Nakakosaka (Kozuke).	June 1878 1 Month.									Under construction.							42,457	– 42,457
																	Summa.	3,742,743	– 2,501,749
b.	All the private mines.	Jan. 1874–Dec. 1877 incl. 4 years.	3,515	72,760	339,358	431,035	27,464,673	4,669,977	931,141	39,356	97,347,679	373,477	1,151,516	5,181,822	10,767,493	15,811,408	+4,936,01

(*) In the Mining Department's table this number is by an error given as 270,461,572.

TABLE III.

					PRODUCE.										
Name of the Mine.	Period of Working.	Gold. oz.	Value. yen.	Silver. oz.	Value. yen.	Copper. lb.	Value. yen.	Lead. lb.	Value. yen.	Iron. lb.	Value. yen.	Coal and Coke. tons.	Value. yen.	Total value of produce. yen.	Total expense. yen.	Profit and Loss. yen.
a. (Government mines.) SADO.	Yearly average from 9 years 7 months, 18⅞⁷/₁₂.	934	78,746	59,132										71,520	143,460	−71,940
IKUNO.	Total in 18⁷⁷/₁₂.	2,408	213,637	105,944										181,476	161,619	+22,857
	Average from 9 years 6 months, 18⁷⁷/₁₂.	2,220		18,823										69,876	185,181	−115,308
	18⁷⁷/₁₂.	7,020		65,021										210,951	158,479	+55,472
MIIKE.	Average from 5 years 1 month, 18⁷⁷/₁₂.	—		—								63,904	211,164	211,164	160,161	+132,039
		—		—								67,903		267,670	130,163	+107,194
AXI.	Average from 8 years 8 months, 18⁷⁷/₁₂.	24		17,840		805,186		218,076						160,788	223,618	−59,860
		—		23,859		808,431		360,429						104,720	132,933	+51,784
INNAI.	Average from 2 years 8 months, 18⁷⁷/₁₂.	552		53,172		—		—						79,860	117,937	−15,192
		620		51,744		—		—						76,622	95,052	+13,494
	Total in yearly average. Total in 18⁷⁷/₁₂.	3,780		129,596	103,511	813,476	138,230	218,076	10,467	—		63,904	211,164	632,218	761,503	(†) −129,300
		10,553		214,049	233,327	531,431	153,631	535,122	11,564	—		67,903	211,164	902,423	645,716	+257,243
	Difference i.e. excess in 18⁷⁷/₁₂.	6,778		114,453		120,005		85,344		9,336,919		−1,004		307,221	−74,792	+382,032
b. ALL THE PRIVATE MINES.	Yearly average from 4 years, 18⁷⁴/₁₂–1877.	870		84,849		6,865,143		225,785				297,870		2,632,850	1,452,852	+1,210,007
		723		110,344		7,378,946		246,903		9,675,013		335,713		3,929,955	1,725,816	+1,204,110
	Excess in produce in 1877.	−156		25,495		647,303		63,197		1,438,992		39,834		337,097	272,991	64,103

(*) Besides, yen 175,948 were spent on Kamaishi. (**) Besides, about 7,500,000 catties copper ore were exported in 1873–76 incl. 830,000 " " " " 1877.

(†) Exclusive of the expenditure on Kamaishi and Innka-kosaka.

TABLE XII.

PRODUCE.

	Gold. oz.	Value. yen.	Silver. oz.	Value. yen.	Copper. lb.	Value. yen.	Lead. lb.	Value. yen.	Iron. lb.	Value. yen.	Coal and Coke. tons.	Value. yen.	Total Value of produce. yen.	Total expenses. yen.	Profit and Loss. yen.
Average yearly produce from all the Government mines.	3,780	79,746	129,596	103,541	813,476	138,290	218,076	10,467	—	—	68,904	241,164	632,208	761,508	−129,300
Average yearly produce from all the private mines.	879	16,195	84,840	107,728	6,866,143	1,167,244	225,785	10,838	9,336,919	93,369	287,879	1,295,455	2,692,859	1,452,852	+1,240,007
Average yearly produce from all the mines in Nipon.	4,659	96,941	211,415	271,239	7,679,619	1,305,534	443,861	21,305	9,336,919	93,369	356,783	1,536,619	3,325,067	2,214,360	+1,110,707
Produce from the Government mines in 18⁷⁷/₇₈.	10,358	218,697	211,049	309,927	933,431	169,691	303,420	14,561	—	—	67,906	237,630	939,499	686,716	+252,783
Produce from the private mines 1877.	723	14,976	110,314	141,137	7,513,946	1,277,370	238,952	13,871	10,775,918	107,750	327,741	1,474,843	3,629,936	1,725,846	+1,904,110
Total produce (*) from all the mines in Nipon in 1877.	11,251	233,643	354,302	451,014	8,447,427	1,436,061	592,402	28,435	10,775,918	107,759	395,643	1,712,493	3,969,435	2,112,362	+1,856,833
Annual average produce from all the mines in Nipon (Tab. III a.)	4,659	96,941	211,415	271,239	7,679,619	1,305,534	443,861	21,305	9,336,919	93,369	356,783	1,536,619	3,325,067	2,214,360	1,110,707
Difference i. e. excess in 18⁷⁷/₇₈.	6,622	136,702	139,917	179,765	767,808	130,422	148,511	7,130	1,438,999	14,391	38,860	175,874	644,358	198,202	446,186
That is an increase of:	142°/₀		65.2°/₀		10°/₀		33°/₀		15.4°/₀		10.9°/₀		19.4°/₀	9°/₀	40°/₀
The produce from the mines in 1874, as estimated by Mr. J. G. H. Godfrey.	12,000		312,000		6,722,000		414,000		11,200,000		390,000				

(*) With regard to the produce of petroleum, antimony as also of sulphur and sulphuric acid vide further below.—

according to the table yen 1,140,883 have been expended, are, however, under construction in Kamaishi, while another, previously existing, but at present not working establishment, has been purchased for yen 42,457.

The second part of the table gives a synopsis of the winning from the Japanese private mines during 4 years (1874-1877).

The favorable financial result of the latter, when compared with that of the government mines, may be explained, partly by the circumstance, that the best mines are private property, and that private mines work cheaper than those under government administration, partly by the fact, that in the former scarcely any innovations have been made, while in the latter by the erection of machinery, the construction of furnaces, the sinking of shafts &c. a future extensive and remunerative working has been prepared.

NOTES TO TABLE II. In table II the annual average for the several government and for the private mines are calculated from the preceding table, and compared with the results of the workings for the year $18\ ^{77}/_{78}$.

It appears therefrom, that in the government mines the production of all metals has increased, and in some instances very considerably, while the production of coal (in Miike), has remained nearly stationary. Whether the latter fact be due to commercial or local conditions, or to the circumstance, that in later years machinery has been erected, and the working perhaps thus interfered with, I am unable to tell. As in $18\ ^{77}/_{78}$ the new establishments (with exception of Miike) were completed, a surplus of more than a million yen was obtained.

If we in the Sado mine consider the excess of the total expenditure over the total income, yen 690,484 (Table I), as the capital invested in establishing the works, then the said mine would in $18^{77}/_{78}$,—as Sado in that financial year, according to table II, yielded a net profit of about yen 23,000—have paid $\frac{23,000 \times 100}{690,484} = 3^1/_2 \%$ interest (exclusive of the increase in the principal, arising from interest accrued in the meantime).

In Ikuno, where the deficit amounted to yen 1,095,492, the net surplus in $18^{77}/_{78}$ to about yen 57,000, a similar calculation would give the interest at $5^1/_2\%$. Unfortunately the vein, which is principally worked by that mine, does not promise much for the future, so that another yield like that of $18^{77}/_{78}$ can scarcely be expected any more.

If we make similar calculations from the total deficit and the total surplus in $18^{77}/_{78}$ for Ani and Innai, the latter being for Ani yen 156,040 against yen 51,786 and for Innai yen 40,494 against yen 13,484, then we find Ani paying an interest of 33% and Innai of 33%, a result, which fully supports the view I expressed above with regard to the productivity of these mines.

The deficit in working the government mines, that is, the total outlay on government mines (with exception of the two not yet active iron—works), which has not been covered by the outturn, amounts according to table I to yen 1,318,409, on which the surpluses in $18^{77}/_{78}$ ($=$ yen 252,783) would pay an interest of $\dfrac{252,783 \times 100}{1,318,409}$ = about 19%.—Or, if the two mines at Oguusu and Kosaka, which have been taken over from private owners, but not yet paid for, are taken into account with a first outlay of yen 350,000, then this would give an interest of $\dfrac{252,783 \times 100}{1,318,409 + 350,000}$ = about 15%, a rate of interest, from which, however, would still have to be deducted the expenditure connected with the administration of the Mining section (Kozan Kioku) in Tokio, under the Ministry of Public works.

It should not be forgotten, that this at all events tolerable result is due, not to the production of precious metals, but to that of coal and copper, a circumstance, which corroborates what I have said above with regard to the prospects of mining in Japan. Among the silver mines, Innai would seem to be the best, as it, although worked solely on Japanese system, yielded on an average much more than Sado and Ikuno, that is, at the time of their partial Japanese working. In the private mines the production of gold has, according to the synopsis in tab. II, somewhat decreased, the production of all the other minerals increased. The production of coal would at all events have been larger, if it had not in that year become necessary to put Takashima under water on account of subterranean fire, in consequence of which the mine was for a long time unable to yield any output.

NOTES TO TABLE III. In table III the annual average productions from the government mines and the private mines are compared with each other, and the comparison shows, that the government is at the head with regard to bullion, while private industry takes the lead in all other produce.

In the 2nd part of this table a synopsis is made of the winnings of both categories in $18^{77}/_{78}$ (government mines) and in 1877 (private mines).

Finally, in order to compare a previously published estimate by Mr J. G. H. Goldfrey of the mineral produce in 1874 (Mr. Plunkett: "On the Mines of Japan." Report to H. B. M.'s Minister in Yedo, 1875)—made to my knowledge before the materials had been officially collected—with the average numbers given by me (the official statistics for that year are not in my possession), I have placed that estimate at the foot of tab. III. With the exception of gold, the difference is unimportant.

It appears from the 2nd. part of the table, that the ratio between the government and the private mines has remained about the same as before, while the total production, as against the previous average, has increased, of gold with

14⋅2%, of silver with 65.2%, of copper with 10%, of lead with 33%, of iron with 15.4%, of coal with 10%. The production of copper has not much increased, because as yet no large copper mine has been organized on modern system.

PRODUCTION OF IRON.

The production of iron is as yet very insignificant, and does not much exceed that of copper; the total annual production of iron, stated for convenience' sake in tons, does not amount to more than 4,800 tons, a quantum, which one large blast-furnace can turn out in about 60 days. The reason of this is, that with the hitherto used ancient proceedings a large production is both technically and economically impossible; that the apparatus requisite for the further working of iron were hitherto wanting (it was therefore thought preferable to import manufactured iron), and finally that for many purposes the native, very soft, wrought iron is as useless as the brittle, hard cast iron. Even when the new iron-works are set going, and the apprehensions, that have been entertained with regard to the extent of the deposits of magnetic iron-ore at Kamaishi, should, prove groundless, it still remains a question, whether the national iron-industry, in the face of the fact that coal and iron do not occur in each other's vicinity, that charcoal costs dear, that the means of communication are difficult and undeveloped, and being moreover hampered by a circumstantial administration, is able successfully to oppose foreign competition.

On the other hand, the question is worthy of consideration, in what proportion the *supply* of pig-iron from the three nearly finished charcoal-blast-furnaces, besides the two more, that are under contemplation, stands to the country's *demand* for pig-iron.

Table IV represents as nearly as possible the amounts of iron and steel imported 1868—1878 inclusive.

In that table the total amount of imported machinery must appear rather low, if we consider the quantity of plant and stock, required for railways, mints, arsenals, printing-, reeling-establishments, mines &c.; but I have not thought myself justified in making arbitrary alterations in the above figures, which are taken from the custom-house-reports. Iron, imported in the shape of ships, is not included in the table.

TABLE IV.

IMPORT OF MANUFACTURED AND ROUGH-STEEL,

CAST-AND WROUGHT-IRON,

1868—1878 INCL.

Imports.	Catties.	Value in yen.	Average price. per catty.
			yen.
1. Manufactured iron	127,917,345.	5,021,578.	0.039.
2. Cast iron	19,504,676.	314,941.	0.016.
3. Kentledge	1,336,624.	18,558.	0.014.
4. Steel	3,125,880.	257,803.	0.082.
5. Ammunition, cannon, rifles etc.	20,096,465.	4,019,293.	0.20. (*)
6. Iron-ware	13,833,880.	1,383,388.	0.10. (*)
7. Machinery	16,412,040.	3,282,408.	0.20. (*)
8. Iron-wire	3,629,827.	272,886.	0.075.
9. Anchors and cable	1,097,000.	76,790.	0.070. (*)
Total	206,954,743.	20,147,577.	—
Annual average	18,814,068.	1,831,577.	0.0923.
„ „ …… tons	11,200.	—	—

(*) In the items marked (*) only the value of the imports is known, and the quantity has been calculated therefrom.

The blast-furnace in Inaka-Kosaka has been constructed with a view to a daily outturn of about 15 tons, while either of the two nearly completed blast-furnaces at Kamaishi is intended to supply a quantum of about 20 tons a day. The three blast-furnaces would consequently in 300 working days deliver 16,500 tons pig-iron. Supposing, that for the moment only the import-articles, mentioned in the table sub 1—4, were to be replaced by national produce, then a quantum of ca. 10,000 ton pig annually would be sufficient, because the sum total of these articles during 11 years aggregated 151,884,531 catties, or on an annual average about 8,220 tons. If, moreover, the hitherto existing *private* *national* production should be supplanted by the new government works, then a still further quantity of about 10,000,000 lbs. English (Tab. III), that is, in round numbers 5,000 tons, would be required annually. Consequently about 15,000 tons pig-iron would be needed annually.

The total weight of *all* the iron imported (both in pigs and manufactured) amounts, according to table IV, to a round sum of 12,000 tons annually. If then *all* the iron, that is consumed in the country, in whatever shape, should be produced by the new works, and the iron, that was hitherto produced by the traditional methods, be driven out of the market, then there would—taking into account the diminution resulting from working the pig—annually to have been produced a quantity of:

   15,000 tons as substitute for imported iron,
    5,000 ,, ,, ,, ,, native iron-production
Total: 20,000 ,, pig-iron.

Let us now examine, whether there is any prospect, that this hitherto maximum demand for about 20,000 tons will increase in the future.

If the building of roads and the bridging over of the numerous rivers by aid of iron-structures were taken energetically in hand, then certainly a considerable quantity of iron would be required. It is moreover not impossible, that the government, eventually by creations in the Navy Department and by constructions for the coast-defence, as well as by building new railways, may open an outlet for the iron produced, although, as far as railways are concerned, it has I think already been proved, that under present circumstances in Japan the development of the coasting trade, the creation of an extensive net of roads and canals is of far more importance than the building of railroads, which only then are able to prosper and to diffuse prosperity, when proper means of communication allow of their being supplied with freight of sufficient quantities. The example, drawn from America, where the quick progress of some states for a great part is due to the railways, does for several reasons not hold good here.

It only requires to call attention to the geographical formation of the two countries, and it needs no demonstration, why rail roads are of much more importance on a large continent than in a prolongated group of islands. Besides, in America, as well as in England—which latter country has been hold up to Japan as a model on account of its possessing so many railways, notwithstanding its insular position,—the districts, which are opened by railroads, are generally already able to supply large masses of produce from agriculture, mining or manufactories. Here it is otherwise: the principal article of produce, the rice, with which all the plains are planted, is consumed within the country, and requires consequently only a limited transport. Tea and silk, the two chief-articles of the export-trade, are not weighty enough to require to be transported by rail. Although the mountains and table-lands still offer a wide field for the cultivation of other kinds of agricultural produce, the same must first be opened to traffic by the means of regular roads. As long as every trunk of tree, every bag of grain has to be carried for miles after miles, by tracks hardly passable, on the back of horses or coolies, until it reaches the railway, as long as nearly every river offers an obstacle to circulation instead of a facility for transport,—so long it scarcely will pay to raise produce for distant markets. In the few instances, where it is required to connect iron- and coal-mines with the sea, care has already been taken to build railroads. Even if therefore a short railway-line may still be built here or there, it is not to be presumed, that the consumption of iron will be greatly increased in consequence of large railway-enterprises.

How far the iron here produced would find an outlet in China, would depend, on the one hand, on the price and quality of the product, on the other hand, on the development of Chinese iron-works, of which it is now for instance under consideration to make an establishment as Kaiping. As a set-off to those circumstances, which eventually might cause an increase in the average-demand, it is to be borne in mind, that the latter, during the last decade, has been comparatively high on account of purchases for the foundation of railways, navy, army, arsenals and all sorts of industries. It may moreover with certainty be predicted, that, all the efforts of the government to the contrary notwithstanding, the use of machinery &c. in this country will yet for some time to come remain a limited one, and that consequently the import, at least of manufactured iron, will still continue. The state of transport and other local circumstances, habit &c. will likewise for a long future protect the old, national iron-industry against being replaced by new, modern establishments, and finally the iron here produced will, for reasons already mentioned, scarcely be offered at so low rates as to cause a rapid increase in the consumption. Under these circumstances the conclusion appears justified, that the three charcoal-blast-furnaces, now under construction, always provided that they as well as the ore-deposits realize the expectations entertained, for the moment suffice to meet the demand, and that the building of more blast-furnaces does not appear urgent.

While thus the prospects for a large, *natural* development of iron-production in Japan for the moment can scarcely be called brilliant, an examination of another branch of mining-industry, coal-mining shows favorable results.

PRODUCTION AND EXPORT OF COAL.

It appears from table V, that the export is continually increasing, and exceeds the import nearly tenfold; although the production, when compared with that of other countries, is still very small, it should be borne in mind, that only two mines have recently commenced to be worked on modern system, and that a wide field is open for further progress.

The fact, that there is still an import of coal and cokes, nay that the same is even on the increase, is explained in this manner, that the Japanese coals are not fit for all purposes, especially do not afford so good heating material for steamers as the best English coals and that English coke is generally preferred for foundry purposes. A comparison between tables V and III show, that on an average

TABLE V.
COAL-EXPORT AND-IMPORT 1868-1878 incl.

Year.	Export.				Import.		Average yearly production tons (*)
	Actual Export.		For ships' use.		English tons.	Value in yen.	
	Engl. tons.	Value in yen.	Engl. tons.	Value in yen.			
1868	15,584	79,519	945	4,760			
1869	14,581	82,978	18,665	99,603			
1870	26,164	130,085	30,845	150,258	55,232	812,884	
1871	18,744	100,429	45,008	224,552			
1872	27,389	180,279	30,883	155,637			
1873	47,172	225,158	99,194	462,981			
1874	31,408	146,470	81,768	408,870			
1875	22,268	94,706	83,560	452,811	5,353	92,716	
1876	49,040	200,823	136,388	717,270	10,977	149,120	
1877	49,697	185,723	82,661	404,369	17,084	182,608	
1878	95,064	335,015	111,785	576,635	28,212	177,780	
Total	399,880	1,773,184	721,630	3,656,696	122,858	1,115,104	
Yearly average.	36,353	161,744	65,698	327,881	11,167	129,555	856,783
Average price per ton.	yen 4.45		yen 4.97		yen 11.52		

(*) According to Table III.

about 28% of the coal produce leave the country, to wit: about 10% are actually exported, about 18% supplied as fuel to foreign steamers, which touch here, while 72% of the produce remain for consumption in the country, the principal consumers being the Mitsu Bishi Company and the railroads. The construction of coke-blast-furnaces would of course have a favorable influence on the development of the coal-industry. How far the impending working of the Chinese coal-mines on modern system may influence the coal-mining in Japan, the future will show; the interference can, however, never be great, considering that the actual export even now only figures with 10% of the produce, and that China's coal-production, according to von Richthofen's estimate, in late years already amounts to about 3,000,000 tons annually, that is, about eight times Japan's production of coal.

JUXTAPOSITION OF JAPAN'S MINERAL PRODUCTION WITH THAT OF OTHER COUNTRIES.

The following juxtaposition of the mineral production of Japan with that of other countries, as far as known, enables us to make a comparison, even when only approximatively.

The statistics have been collected from:

Berg- und Huettenmaennischer Kalender, 1879.
Handbuch für vergleichende Statistik, von Kolb.
Zukunft des Goldes, von E. Suess.
Edelmetall-Production, von Ds. Neumann-Spallart.
Reports from the Imperial Japanese Ministry for Public works.
Report on the Exhibition in Tokio. 1877.
Engineering and Mining Journal, Mining Journal, Berg- und Huettenmaennische Zeitung &c.

GREAT BRITAIN 1876.

Coal............	2,709,565,645 cwt.	=	933,413,360 Mark.*
Ores............	486,499,028 „	=	217,696,720 „
Rocksalt........	46,192,562 „	=	22,732,560 „
			1,173,836,640 „
Pig-iron........	133,217,859 „	=	321,243,840 „

BRITISH COLONIES.

CAPE COLONY.

In 1875, *exported*:

Copper ores......	248,330 „	=	4,970,740
Diamonds........	für		21,000 „
Gold............	„		3,619,160 „

AUSTRALIA.

Bullion produce in 1875:

Victoria..........	1,068,418	oz.
New Zealand.....	355,322	„
New South Wales..	230,883	„
Queensland......	359,076	„
Tasmania........	3,010	„
South Australia...	1,000	„ (?)
Total...........	2,017,709	i. e. ca. 140,000,000 „

From New South Wales exported, 1875, coals

19,567,160 cwt = 13,488,200 „

* 1 Mark = 1 Shilling.

In Queensland and Tasmania, 1873, produced 890,000 cwt.
From New South Wales exported,
                1875, copper 238,672 cwt. = 10,027,740 Mark.
From Australia to England exported in the
year 1875, tin .... 144,360 „ = 12,992,400 „
    STRAITS SETTLEMENT.
In 1875 exported to England, tin ...220,000 „
    BRITISH EAST INDIA.
In 1875 coals produced about .....2,000,000 „
    BRITISH COLUMBIA (with a part of Mexico).
Bullion produced in 1877 .... 10,440,000 „
    BRITISH NORTH AMERICA,
           1875 produced coal 1,618,440 „
           1876 „ pig-iron ca. 150,000 „
    NOVA SCOTIA in 1875, gold; ......10,957 oz. = ca. 800,000 „
UNITED STATES.
    1876, Coals.................965,468,940 cwt.
    1877, Gold to the value of........................181,200,000 „
    „   Silver   „   „ ....184,000,000 „
    „   Lead   „   „ .... 11,900,000 „
    „   Copper „   „ .... 3,900,000 „
    1876 Quicksilver................................ 6,561,690 „
    „   Pig-iron ....37,977,660 cwt.
    „   Petroleum exported.... 261,132,348 gallons.
GERMANY 1876.
    Coal, graphite &c. .... 991,760,966 cwt = 302,620,298 „
    Ores .... 93,223,778 „ = 69,479,321 „
    Rock-salt .... 15,021,128 „ = 5,903,766 „
    Common auk Abraum-salts .... 9,720,703 „ = 17,494,736 „
                                          395,498,121 „
    Pig-iron production .... 36,165,631 „ = 109,079,554 „
LUXEMBURG.
    Iron ores (1876)............. 23,934,580 „ = 2,666,538 „
    Coal (1871)..:.............. 1,063,540 „
AUSTRIA, 1877.
    Coal...................... 240,488,586 „ = 65,251,240 „
    Ores....................... 16,721,781 „ = 26,769,256 „
    Rock-and common-salt .... 35,140,578 „ = 44,647,028 „
                                                136,668,124
    Pig-iron-production ....: 10,361,400 „ = 27,474,096 „
HUNGARIA, 1875.
    Coal .... 29,023,160 „ = 11,053,533 „

Rock-salt	1,994,950 cwt.	=	18,950,000 Mark.
Metals (iron excepted)	for		11,014,343 ,,
Pig-iron	3,194,074 ,,	=	15,043.244 ,,
			66,061,120 ,,

FRANCE.

Bullion (average 1869-74)			8,336,776 ,,
Coal, 1877	337,784,020 ,,		
Pig-iron, 1876	28,990,754 ,,		
Ores	?		

BELGIUM, 1876.

Coal	286,591,560 ,,	=	152,243,276 ,,
Ores	6,858,580 ,,	=	5,824.617 ,,
			158,067,893 ,,
Pig-iron produced	9,810,160 ,,	⇒	1,966,395 .,

RUSSIA IN EUROPE, 1875.

Coal	21,983,448 ,,
Rock-and common-salt	4,582,186 ,,
Metals	about 128,000,000 ,,
Petroleum	2,725,000 ,,
Pig-iron produced	8,475,136 ,,

ASIATIC RUSSIA 1874.

Gold	33,955 kilogr.	= ca.	94,750,000 ,,

FINLAND, 1876.

Silver	12, 350 ,,	= ,,	2,220,000 ,,
Pig-iron	613,857 cwt.		
Copper	?		

SWEDEN.

1876, coals	1,847,952 ,,
1874, Silver	1,740 lbs.
,, Gold	9.83 lbs.
,, Copper	22,574 cwt.
1876, Pig-iron	6,487,527 .,

NORWAY (annual average from 1871-75),

Copper-iron-and silver-ores and iron pyrites	2,840,400 ,,	=	5,092,136 ,,
Cast-iron, rod-iron, steel	546,296 ,,		

TURKEY, 1872.

Coal, about	2,000,000 ,,
Pig-iron	240,000 ,,

GREECE (annual average from 1867-74).
 Coal .... 120,000 cwt.
 Ores and earths .... 796,000 ,, = 1,012,360 Mark.
ITALY, 1873.
 Coal .... 2,042,800 ,,
 Sulphur .... 5,604,220 ,, = 27,627,984 ,,
 Lead-ore .... 665,660 ,, = 5,866,004 ,,
 Zinc-ore .... 158,940 ,, = 4,322,887 ,,
 Iron-ore .... 5,203,980 ,, = 2,654,587 ,,
 Pig-iron produced in 1873 .... 520,000 ,,
SWITZERLAND.
 Coal (1876) .... 380,900 ,,
 Pig-iron ,, ... 175,000 ,,
SPAIN.
 1872, Silver .... 65,966 lbs = 5,936,910 ,,
 1876, coal .... 14,136,280 cwt.
 ,, Quicksilver ca .... 15,000 ,,
 Pig-iron, 1872, ... 1,460,000 ,,
 Besides copper, zinc, phosphorite, much lead.
PORTUGAL. ($18^{71}/_{72}$).
 Ores .... 180,054 ,, = 5,559,520 ,,
 Coal (1872) .... 420,000 ,,
DUTCH COLONIES, 1875.
 Tin exported to England : from Banca   88,000 ,,
        ,, Billiton   70,470 ,,
             158,470 ,,
MEXICO, 1875.
 Silver .... 601,800 kilogr. = 108,324,000 ,,
 Gold .... 2,020 ,, = 5,636,000 ,,
COLUMBIA, 1874.
 Bullion .... 9,200,000 ,,
HONDURAS, 1877.
 Bullion .... 2,400,000 ,,
PERU.
 1860 { Guano .... 10,251,140 cwt. = 80,780,584 ,,
    { Saltpetre .... 2,944,000 ,, = 26,496,000 ,,
 1875, Silver .... 70,000 kilogr. = 12,600,000 ,,
 ,, , Gold .... 360 ,, = 1,004,000 ,,
 1876, Quicksilver, about ...... 3,000 cwt.
CHILI, 1875.
 Coals (1876), about .... 8,000,000 ,,

Copper ....56,000,000 Mark.
Silver ....11,600,000 ,,
Gold ....1,116,000 ,,

BOLIVIA, 1875.
Silver .... 222,500 kilogr. = 40,050,000 ,,
Gold .... 2,000 ,, = 5,580,000 ,,

ARGENTINIAN REPUBLIC, 1863.
1875 Gold .... 4,000 oz. = ca. 300,000 ,,
,, Silver .... 450,000 ,, = 2,300,000 ,,
1863 { Copper.................. 13,829 cwt.
     { Lead.................... 20,000 ,,

BRAZIL, 18 $^{73}/_{76}$.
Diamonds about..................................33,660,000 ,,
Gold   ,, ... 2,320 kilogr = 6,400,000 ,,
Pig-iron produced in
Brazil and the rest of
South-America together   ca. 340,000 cwt. =

THE ORANGE STATE, 1872.
Diamonds... ....3,000,000 ,,

CHINA.
(According to von Richthofen's estimate in yearly average from
1869-1878 :
Coals......................60,000,000 cwt.

JAPAN, 1877.
Gold .... 11,281 oz. =   934,572 ,,
Silver .... 354,392 ,, = 1,804,256 ,,
Copper .... 75,423 cwt. = 5,744,244 ,,
Lead .... 5,289 ,, =   113,740 ,,
Pig-iron .... 96,213 ,, =   431,036 ,,
Coal .... 7,912,860 ,, = 6,849,972.
                                            ─────────
                                            15,877,820 ,,
Besides :
1877, Sulphur .... 22,224 cwt. = 133,232 Mark. { export-
1878, Sulphuric acid .... 15,767 ,, = 379,116 ,, { ed.
1876, Petroleum, refined 287,662 ,, = 238,316 ,,   (†)
 ,, , Ores of antimony   5,514 ,, = 44,112 ,,   (†)
 ,, , Tin...............   392 ,, =   27,440 ,,   (†)

The value of the total produce from the mines in Japan would consequently
amount to about 17,000,000 Mark (‡).

(†) According to the Report on the Uyeno Exhibition, Tokio, 1877. (‡) 4 Mark = 1 yen.

TABLE VII.

EXPORT AND IMPORT OF BULLION (IN BARS AND IN SPECIE), COPPER-COIN AND PAPER-MONEY.

YEAR.	EXPORTS, VALUED IN RIOS.					IMPORTS, VALUED IN RIOS.						
	GOLD.	SILVER.	COPPER COIN.	PAPER CURRENCY.	TOTAL.	GOLD.	SILVER.	COPPER.	PAPER CURRENCY.	TOTAL.	MORE EXPORT THAN IMPORT.	MORE IMPORT THAN EXPORT.
1650–1671.	Said ca. 500,000,000											
1671–1871.	Unknown.											
1872.	2,684,786	1,796,109	—	—	4,480,895	—	3,691,409	—	—	3,691,409	789,386	—
1873.	2,614,655	2,508,871	3,200	—	5,126,726	2,013,007	1,066,635	—	—	3,080,542	2,045,684	—
1874.	8,126,290	5,060,912	—	—	13,187,202	2,700	1,069,030	—	—	1,071,730	12,115,472	—
1875.	7,134,340	2,320,935	—	—	9,455,275	21,890	64,645	—	—	86,541	9,368,731	—
1876.	7,091,486	5,373,054	—	60,482	12,525,022	1,616	1,596,298	—	37,990	1,635,904	10,889,118	—
1877.	2,853,850	4,527,962	—	13,488	7,395,300	882,811	7,087,736	—	6,116	7,976,663	—	581,363
1878.	6,211,774	4,584,464	131,000	13,500	10,940,738	—	1,906,676	—	5,996	1,912,672	9,028,086	—
Total	36,716,581	26,172,227	131,200	87,470	63,110,678	2,925,533	16,479,529	—	50,102	19,455,464	43,655,114	—

1872-78.—Total Export of Gold .... yen 36,712,327.
 ,,   ,,   Import   ,,   ,, ... yen 16,179,529.
More Export than Import: Gold .... yen 9,692,798.
1872-78.—More Export than Import of bullion ..... yen 33,790,648, and Silver
                                                  yen 15,183,416.

Although the export of bullion during the period 1868—1878 is not precisely known, it may easily be estimated, as its amount is pretty accurately indicated by the excess in goods imported over and above exports.

TABLE VIII.

In the year.	More Export of goods than Import. Yen.	More Import of goods than Export. Yen.
1868.	4,860,401	—
1869.	—	7,874,655
1870.	—	19,198,625
1871.	—	3,984,119
	Total. 4,860,401	31,057,399
		4,860,401
		26,196,998
1872.	—	9,148,168
1873.	—	6,475,249
1874.	—	4,144,508
1875.	—	8,076,695
1876.	—	7,665,275
1877.	2,381,560	—
1878.	—	5,020,663
	2,381,560	40,530,558
		2,381,560
		38,148,998

The excess in imported goods over and above exports during the period 1868—1871 was consequently............yen 26,160,998
and during the period 1872—1878 incl....., ,, 38,148,998.

(The difference of more than yen 5,000,000, which exists between the last mentioned amount and the amount of bullion exported to cover the excess in imports [yen 43,483,446], is probably due to the fact, that the values of goods were not correctly declared at the custom-house by the interested parties).

Our estimate will therefore at all events be rather too low than too high, if we take the export of bullion during the period 1868-71 incl. to have been equal to the excess in imported goods over and above exported goods, or with a round sum yen 26,000,000.

The total export of bullion during the period 1868-78 would consequently provided that gold and silver were represented in the same proportion as in 1872-78, amount to:

TABLE VI.

EXPORT OF MINING-PRODUCTS (With exception of bullion) 1868-1878 incl.

Year.	Copper.	Copper in bars.	Copper in slabs and wire.	Copper ware.	Copper shafts.	Copper ores.	Bronze.	Bronze ware.	Sulphur.	Coals.	Coals for ship's use.	Total in yen.
	catties.	catties.			catties.	catties.	catties.		catties.	catties.	tons.	
1868	109,556	—			—	5,276	—		196,675	26,181,479	945	
1869	603,616	—			—	—	4,590		169,000	21,447,840	18,663	
1870	550,199	—			—	157,266	70,562 10,000		195,040	42,273,073	30,845	
1871	4,384,674	—			244,778	252,373	211,634		518,020	31,569,815	46,003	
1872	4,950,310	—			666,282	1,267,000	631,269 1,291,172		843,825	46,013,563	30,883	
1873	162,571	—			290,165	1,246,026	322,216 1,034,813		1,112,749	79,218,531	99,194	
1874	3,046,671	—			131,913	99,463	190,118 415,979		3,169,254	60,205,140	81,763	
1875	825,672	119,719			—	140,330	35,500		157,910	37,410,662	83,560	
1876	961,118	195,237			—	523,096	38,766		2,120,530	83,914,973 7,120,993	136,396	
1877	356,375	773,249			—	929,912	1,234		1,666,835	83,223,778	82,661	
1878	409,350	2,589,351			—	855,803	325,545		1,556,064	159,707,663	111,785	
Total....	16,385,121	3,677,356			1,336,138	5,405,565	4,743,737		10,967,892	676,419,395	721,690	
	lbs.	lbs.			lbs.	lbs.	lbs.		lbs.	tons.	tons.	
Engl. Weight.	21,844,101	4,903,115			1,781,544	7,207,553	6,324,983		14,623,909	393,189	721,690	
	yen.	yen.	yen.	yen.	yen.	yen. (†)	yen.	yen.	yen.	yen.	yen.	11,747,139
Value in rios.	2,677,999	730,639	803,163	50,968	136,847	961.31	622,600	114,439	200,630	1,779,184 Yearly	3,606,093 Average...	1,067,922

(†) The value of the copper-ore is very high, probably on account of the ores containing some gold and silver.

EXPORT OF MINERAL PRODUCE.

Table VI shows the export of produce from all the mines in the country, with exception of bullion, sulphuric acid and ores of antimony.

Both value and quantity of the copper exports is taken from the customhouse-reports; as it is to the interest of the exporter to declare the value of the copper—on which formerly an *ad valorem* duty was levied—as low as possible, the values given in the table are not quite the actual values.

According to table VI, the total export of copper, whether in the shape of metal, copper-ware, bronze or ore, amounted during the period 1868-1878 incl. to:

	VALUE IN YEN.		CATTIES.
Coarse copper	2,677,999		16,383,121
Old copper	196,847		1,336,158
Copper in sheet and wire	805,163		3,660,000 (*)
Copper-ware	50,988		200,000 (*)
Copper in bars	730,639		4,903,115
Bronze	622,600	with	119,520 (*)
Bronze-ware	114,455	„	38,000 (*)
Copper-ores	961,934	„	720,953 (*)
	6,160,524 yen	„	27.360,867 catties copper.
Yearly average	560,067. yen		2,487,351 „

The 2,487,000 catties, which were on an average annually exported, would represent about 15,000 English tons, or in round numbers 3,300,000 lbs. English, that is, an export of about 43% of the production. According to an estimate made by Dr. Geerts (*Transactions of the Asiatic Society*, vol. III. p. 41), the Dutchmen exported during the period from 1619—1858 a quantity of

280,000 American tons, and

the Chinese 250,000. „ „

Total 530,000 American tons, or on a yearly average 2,001 English tons, a quantum, which certainly, when compared with the average as stated above, must appear somewhat large, especially when it be remembered, that this export is said to have continued uninterrupted during two centuries and a half.

EXPORT OF BULLION.

If we now finally ask, what proportion the mineral production of Japan bears to its export of bullion, then table VII will show us the details of the latter for the years 1872-1878 incl.

(*) In the entries marked (*), the quantity of the copper has been estimated from the declared value.

Gold yen, to the value of............yen 54,141,307 and
Silver „ „ „ „ „ .... „ 15,539,109.
                                Summa „ 69,683,446, in bullion

or on a yearly average :

Yen 4,922,191 in gold = 77.7% of the bullion export : Gold.
„ 1,412,668 in silver = 22.3 „ „ „ „ : Silver.
Yen 6,334,859 bullion   100.0 „.

COMPARISON OF THE PRODUCTION AND THE EXPORT OF BULLION.

The average annual production amounted, according to table III,

of Gold to yen 96,941
„ Silver „ „ 271,299
„ Bullion, „ 368,240.

The production in the year 1877 was :

Gold,..................... Yen 233,643
Silver.................... „ 451,064
Bullion,................... „ 684,707

Consequently :

1. The average production of gold amounted .... to 1.9" „ of the average gold export.
2.- The gold production in 1877 .... „ 4.7 „ „ „ „ „
3. - The average production of silver .... „ 10.2 „ „ „ silver export.
4.—The silver-production in 1877.............................. „ 12.0 „ „ „ „ „
5.- The average production of bullion .... „ 5.8 „ „ „ bullion export.
6.- The bullion production in 1877.......................... „ 11.5 „ „ „ „ „
7.- The average net proceeds from all the mines .... „ 17.5 „ „ „ average bullion „
8. The net proceeds from all the mines in 1877 .... „ 24.0 „ „ „ „ „
9.- The average total production of all the mines .... „ 52.9 „ „ „ „ „
10. The total production of all the mines in 1877 .... „ 62.6 „ „ „ „ „

These figures need no further comment ; it is no wonder, that there is a high premium on gold, when in the most productive year (1877 and 187⁷⁄₇₈) only 4.7% of the export is covered by gold produced in the country, when in fact an export of bullion, which is from 9 to 17 times larger than the production of the country, is ruining the credit of the empire. Although there, according to table III, in 1877 was an increase of 19.4% in the total mineral production, and of 40% in the net proceeds, when compared with the average of the working period in question, it is not to be expected, that Japanese mining, however susceptible of development in certain directions, will soon be able, even but approximatively, to meet a bullion-export of such a magnitude, so much the less, as there is no prospect of such a rapid increase in the production as the above mentioned, at least not in the nearest future.

PROBABLE FUTURE MINERAL PRODUCTION.

As to the probable mineral production in the nearest future, it seems under present circumstances most likely, that the production of gold and silver from the government mines will decrease on account of an inferior output from Ikuno, (*) until the new establishments in Innai can commence operations. The copper-production will remain nearly stationary, until the reorganisation of the Ani mines enables to obtain an increased output.

The iron-production may be predicted to increase considerably, as soon as the new works are set going.

As Miike has lately been furnished with new machinery, it may be assumed that the production of coal will increase, provided Takashima is successfully protected against fire from spontaneous ignition of the coals. Coal-production from the new coal-fields of Yesso cannot be expected in the next future.

Finally, not to omit two products, which more or less come under the mining industry, petroleum and sulphuric acid, the production of the former has no prospect of any considerable increase. The wells may, as long as they are worked by private owners at small expense, yield a profit, but it would scarcely pay for the government to take them in hand and work them energetically.

The production of sulphuric acid, the export of which—exclusively to China, in 1878 amounted to 1,324,456 catties, will probably flourish as long as China does not establish works of her own; there is no prospect of a large consumption within the country, until either the discovery of rock-salt-deposits makes it possible to establish a soda-industry, that can compete with foreign manufactories, or the discovery of phosphorite-deposits offers the materials requisite for the manufactory of mineral manure.

(*) In Mikobata, four *ris* from the present mine, silver-ores have recently been discovered and further explorations are proceeded with.

EXPLANATION OF THE PLATES.

TOOLS AND IMPLEMENTS.

I. For Mining

Plate I.
- Fig. 1.—Handpump.
- „ 2.—Basket for carriage.
- „ 3.—Tray.
- „ 4.—Sandals.
- „ 5.—Breech-leather.
- „ 6.—Timber-Set.
- „ 7.—Ladder.
- „ 8.—Gad.
- „ 9.—Wedge.
- „ 10.—Tongs for holding gad.
- „ 11.-12.—Lamps.

Plate II.
- Fig. 13.—Gad.
- „ 14.—Sledge.
- „ 15.—Hammer.
- „ 16.—Drill.
- „ 17.—Scraper.
- „ 18.—Pick.
- „ 19.—Match (Bamboo cane filled with gunpowder and enveloped in paper.)
- „ 20.—Tamping bar.
- „ 21.—Loop-drag (Bamboo with cotton rag).

II. For Dressing.

Plate III.
- Fig. 22.—Dressing hammer.
- „ 23.—Hand-mill.
- „ 24.—Tilt-hammer.
- „ 25.—Buddle.
- „ 26.—Jigging-basket.
- „ 27.—Scarred board.
- „ 28.—Wash-dish with basin.
  (Besides *Nadeki* and *Mizusagashi*, tools for working at the scarred boards).

III. For Metallurgic Operations.

Plate IV.
- Fig. 29.—Rectangular roasting kiln.
- „ 30.—Blast-furnace (Coarse charcoals at the bottom, in the middle finer ones, brasque on top).

Plate V.
- „ 31.-32. & 33.—Scrapers.
- „ 34.—Shovel.
- „ 35.—Wooden hand-box-bellows.
- „ 36.-45.—Furnace tools.

IV. For Copper Refining.

Plate VI. { Fig. 46.—Furnace and crucible.
" 47.—Mould for casting slabs.
" 48.-59.—Refining tools.

ERRATA.

1.	page.	6.	line	fr.	b.	r.	market	instead	marcket.'
2.	,,	8.	,,	,,	,,	,,	thoroughly	,,	throughly.
3.	,,	18.	,,	,,	t.	,,	preferred	,,	prefered.
3.	,,	13.	,,	,,	b.	,,	Mandokoro	,,	Mandokora.
4.	,,	2.	,,	,,	t.	,,	have	,,	how.
4.	,,	10.	,,	,,	,,	,,	scale	,,	scale.
4.	,,	16.	,,	,,	,,	,,	coal	,,	coat.
4.	,,	10.	,,	,,	b.	,,	the detailed	,,	the the detailed.
7.	,,	13.	,,	,,	t.	,,	tortuous, ill	,,	tortuous ill.
9.	,,	18.	,,	,,	b.	,,	average	,,	avarage.
11.	,,	8.	,,	,,	,,	,,	vicinity	,,	visinity.
16.	,,	9.	,,	,,	t.	,,	1½—2½′	,,	1½—½′
17.	,,	6.	,,	,,	,,	,,	Rachette	,,	rachette.
30.	,,	15.	,,	,,	,,	,,	mine	,,	mince.
33.	,,	11.	column	,,	,,	,,	10,775,918.	,,	70,775,918.
33.	,,	16.	,,	,,	,,	,,	109,164	,,	169,164.
41.	,,	3.	,,	,,	,,	,,	180,278	,,	180,279.
42.	,,	10.	line	,,	,,	,,	Dr	,,	Ds.
43.	,,	13.	,,	,,	b.	,,	and	,,	ank.
44.	,,	17.	,,	,,	,,	,,	Finland	,,	Finlad.
47.	,,	6.	column	,,	,,	,,	Scraps	,,	Sraps.
47.	,,	10.	,,	,,	,,	,,	Sulphur	,,	Salphur.
47.	,,	7.	,,	,,	,,	,,	961,934	,,	961,34.
48.	,,	14.	line	,,	b.	,,	1,500	,,	15,000.

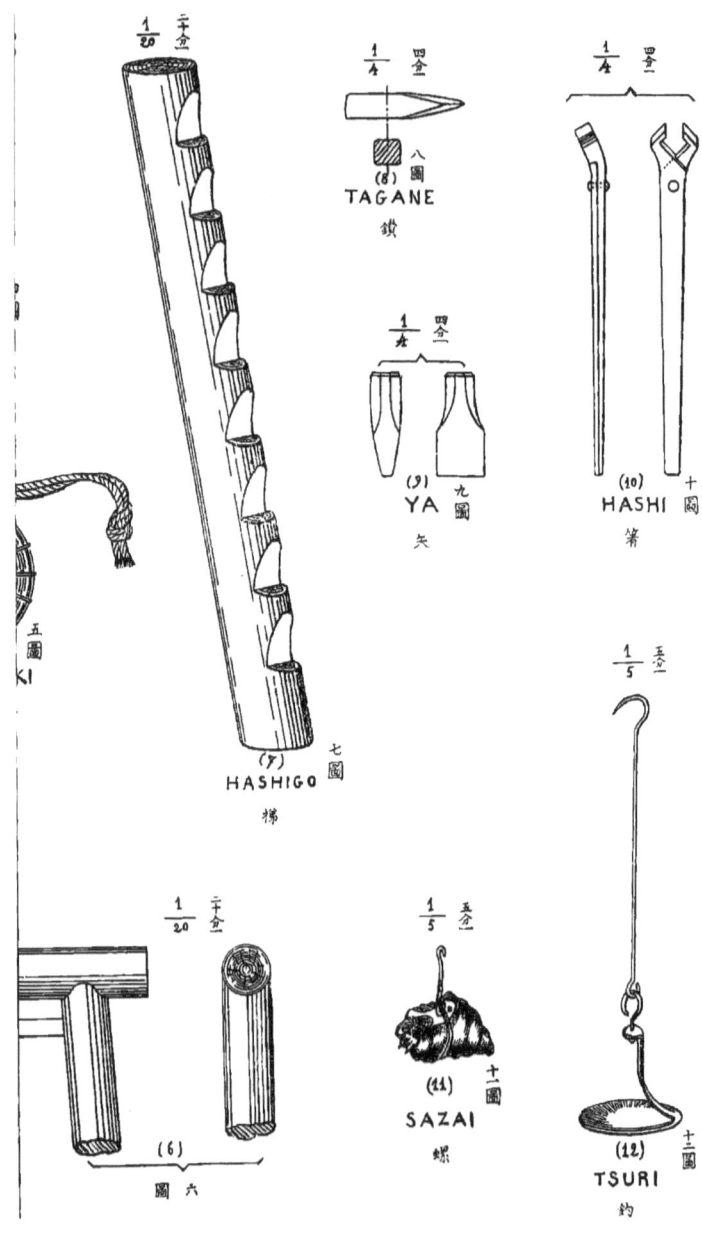

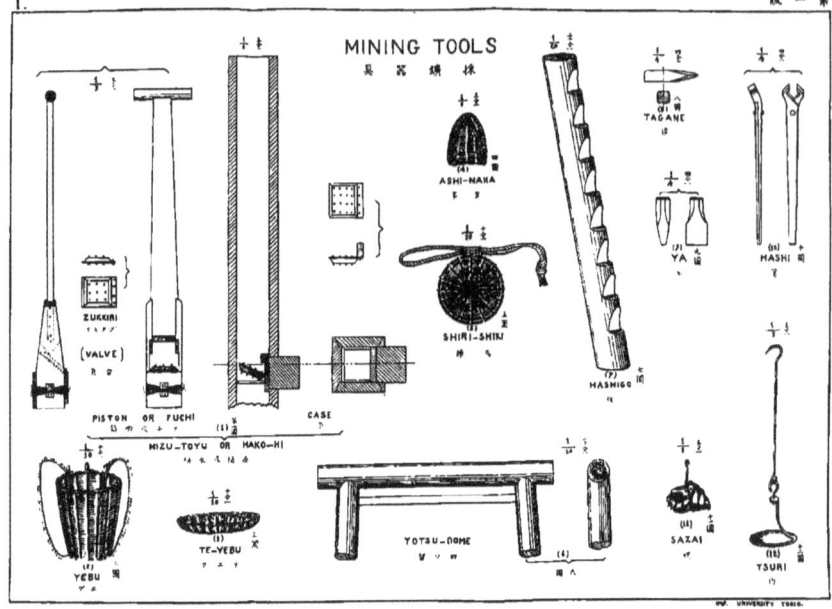

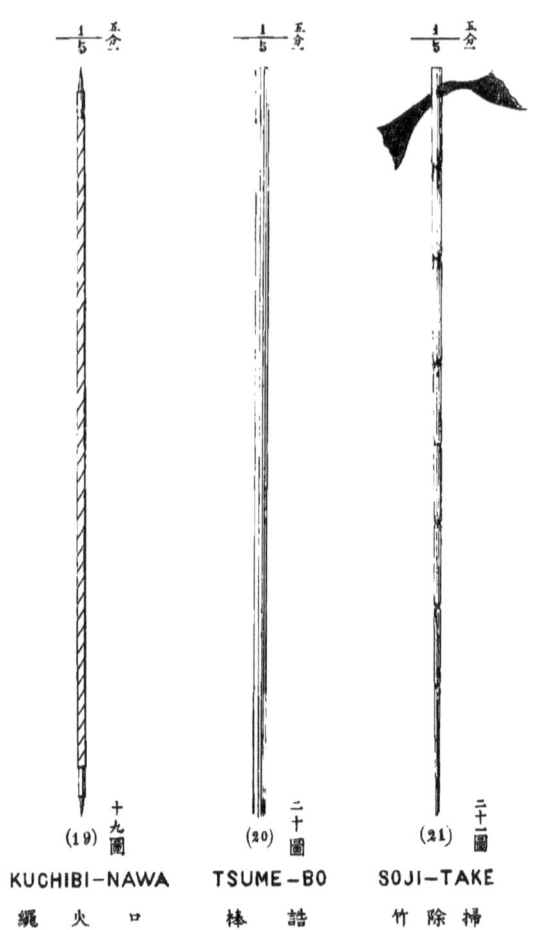

(19) KUCHIBI-NAWA 口火繩

(20) TSUME-BO 詰棒

(21) SOJI-TAKE 掃除竹

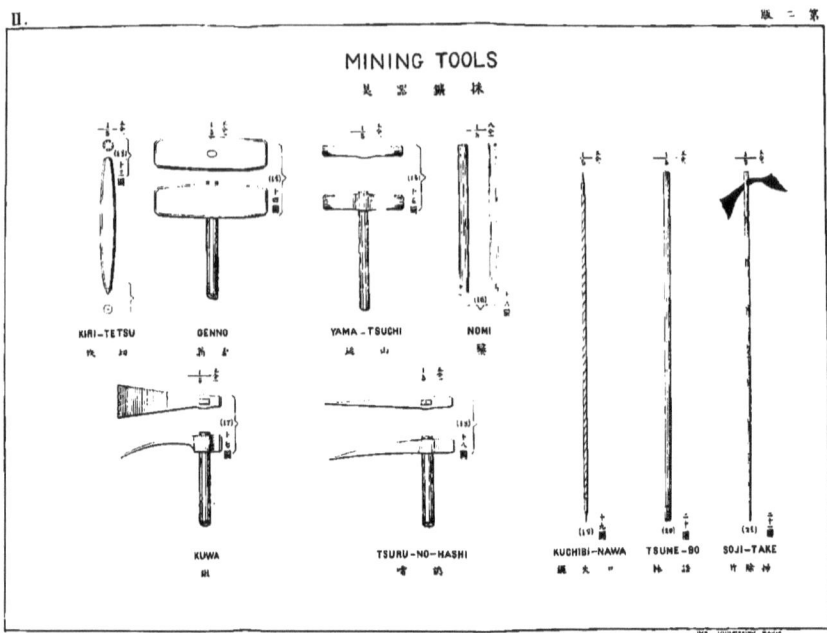

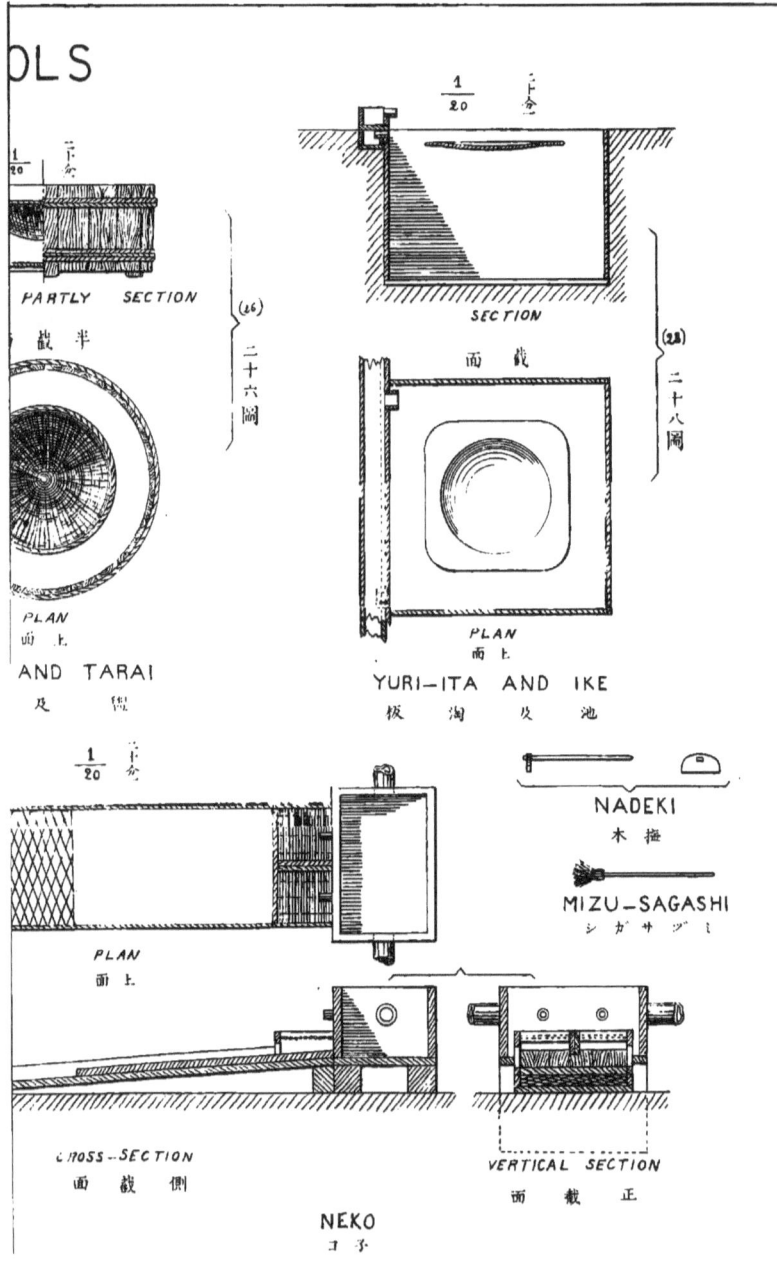

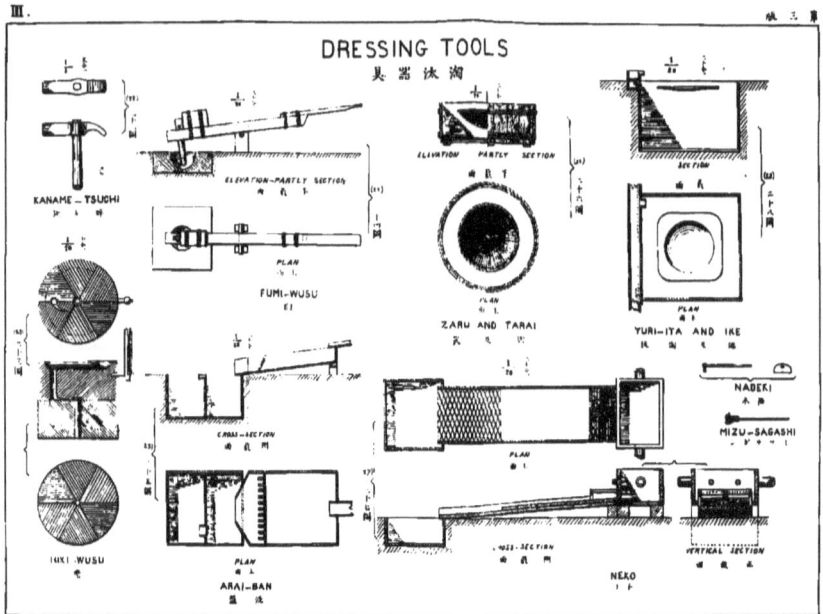

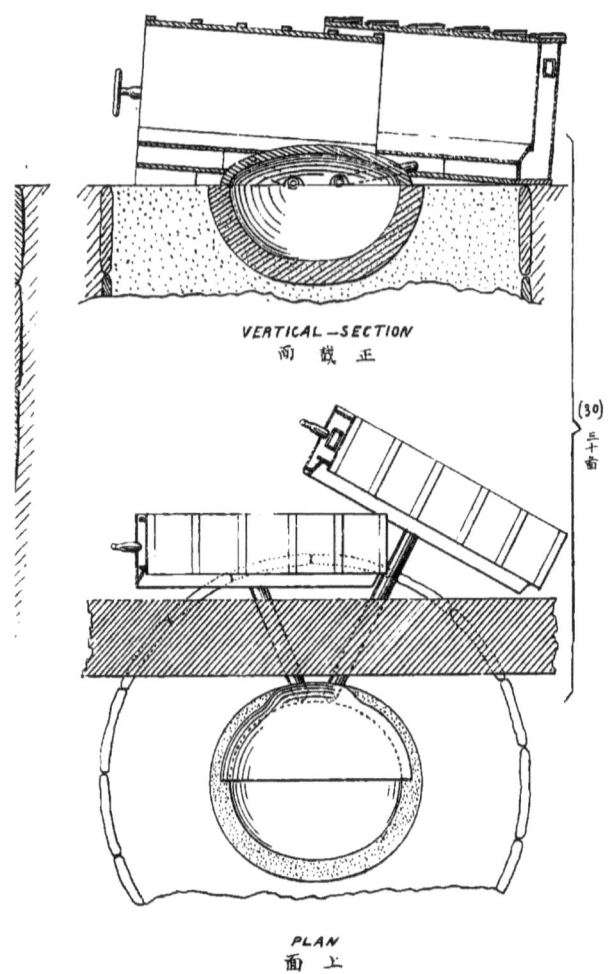

FUKIDOKO

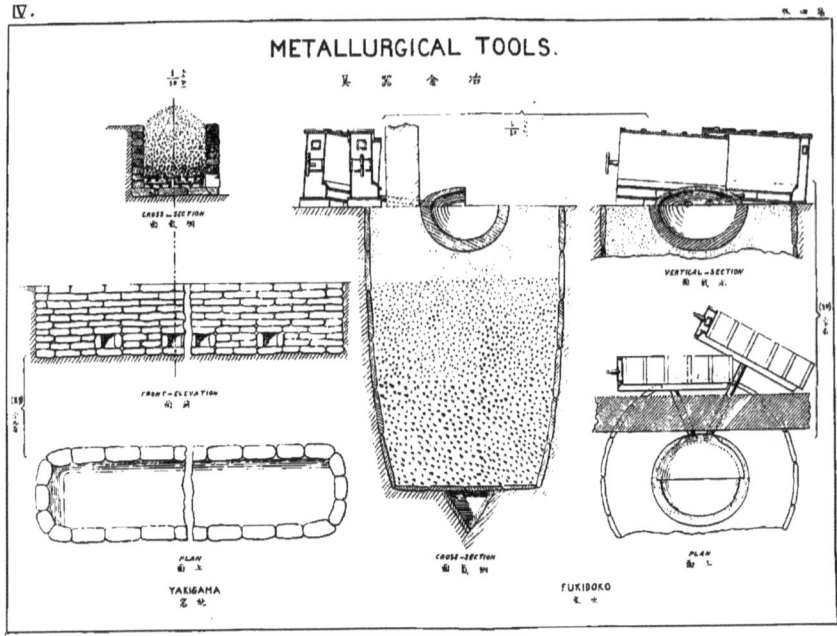

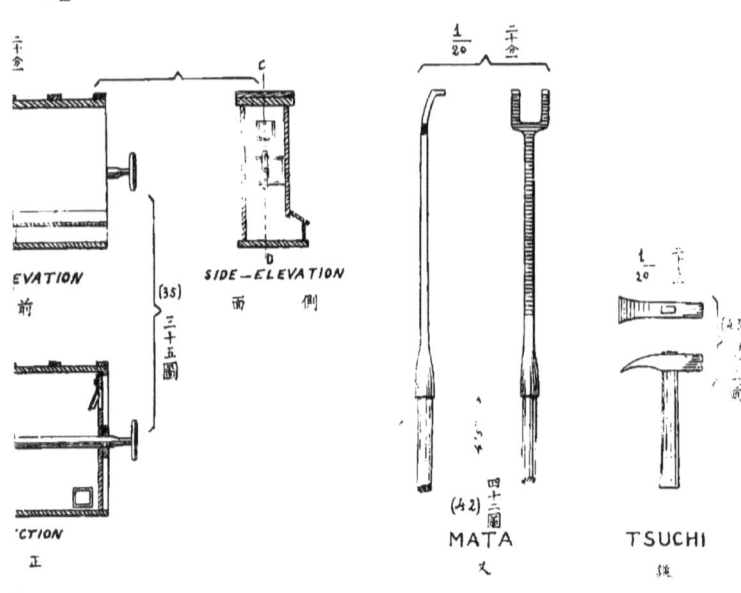

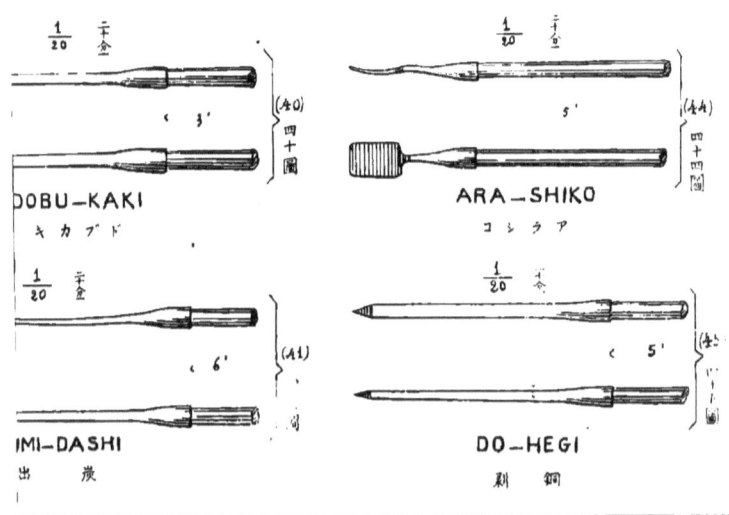

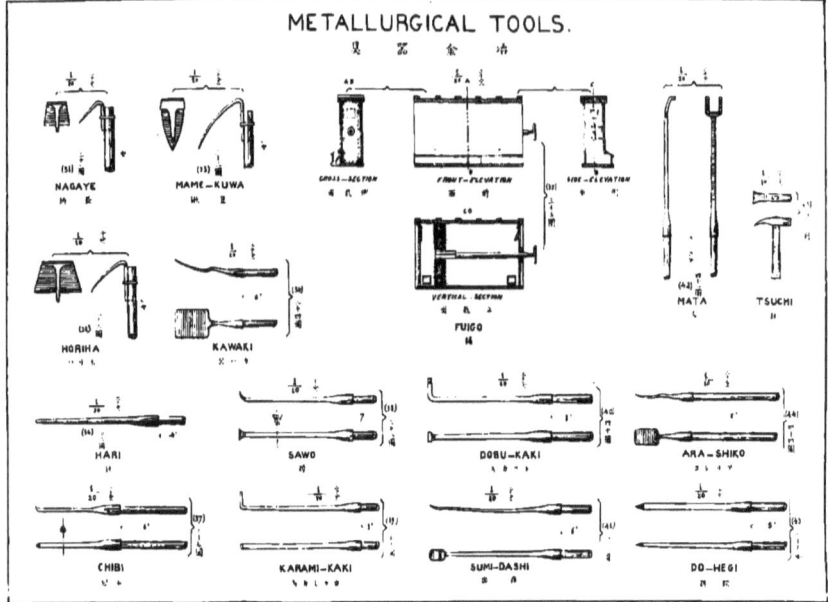

REFINING

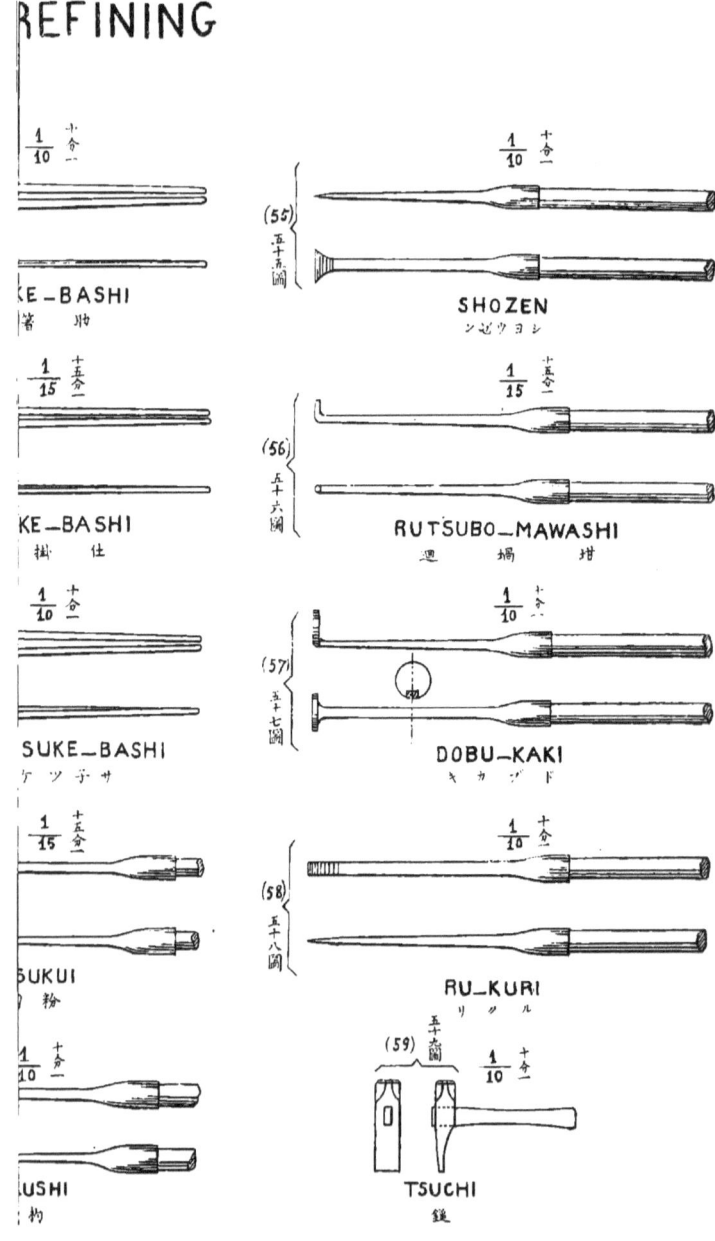

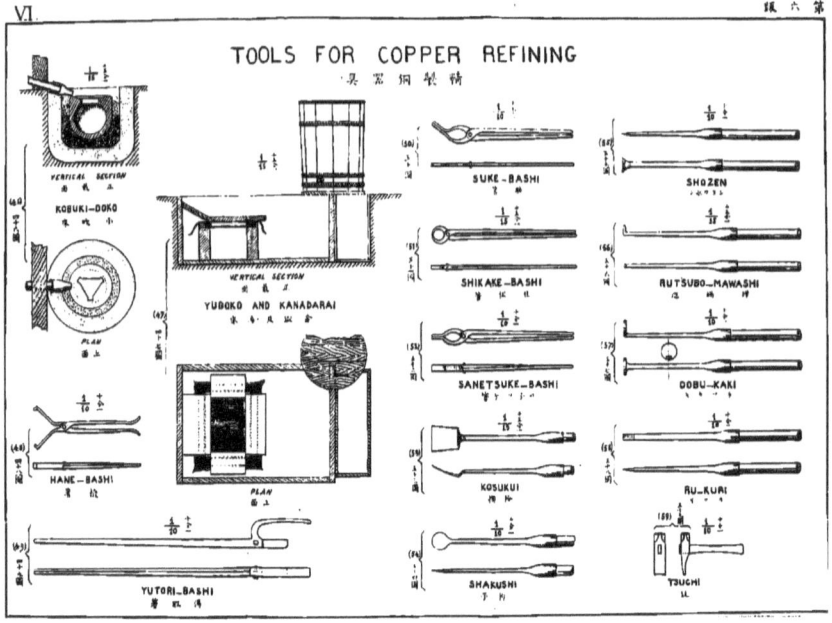

版權所有

MEMOIRS

OF THE

SCIENCE DEPARTMENT

UNIVERSITY OF TOKIO, JAPAN.

VOLUME III. PART I.

REPORT

ON THE METEOROLOGY OF TOKIO.

FOR THE YEAR 2539 (1879).

T. C. MENDENHALL.

Professor of Experimental Physics University of Tokio.

PUBLISHED BY THE UNIVERSITY.

PRINTED AT THE GOVERNMENT PRINTING OFFICE.

2540 (1880).

MEMOIRS

OF THE

SCIENCE DEPARTMENT

UNIVERSITY OF TOKIO, JAPAN.

VOLUME III. PART I.

REPORT

ON THE METEOROLOGY OF TOKIO.

FOR THE YEAR 2539 (1879).

T. C. MENDENHALL,

PROFESSOR OF EXPERIMENTAL PHYSICS UNIVERSITY OF TOKIO.

PUBLISHED BY THE UNIVERSITY.

PRINTED AT THE GOVERNMENT PRINTING OFFICE.

2540 (1880).

PREFACE.

This Report makes no pretensions to be other than an arrangement and classification of the principal results of the meteorological observations made during the year 2539 (1879) at the meteorological station established by the University of Tokio. A good deal of care has been bestowed upon the classification of these results, especially in the construction of the charts which not only exhibit the more pronounced results in a much more intelligible manner but also invite attention to many relations and probable dependencies which might otherwise remain hidden in the numerical tables. In no other way can a comparison of meteorological conditions be so easily made as by these graphical methods. At the end of the present year it will be possible to construct a series of diagrams representing the combined results of two years' work. These will doubtless take the general form of those here presented, modified by such variations as will undoubtedly occur in the present year.

A study of the changes which are wrought in these weather charts from year to year cannot fail to be of use in determining to what extent the climate may be regarded as constant and in revealing, as far as possible, what the normal climatic conditions may be.

For the liberality with which this volume is illustrated, I wish to express my indebtedness to the Directors of the University, Mr. Kato and Mr. Hamao, whose constant desire has been that it should be rendered as complete as was possible. I must also bear testimony to the faithfulness with which the original diagrams have been reproduced by the Gengendo Engraving House. In common with its predecessors in this series, this volume is throughout, in its material and its mechanical execution, the product of the country and I may be permitted to say that, in that particular, it is equally with them deserving of credit.

I must express my thanks to W. S. Chaplin Esq. Prof. of Civil Engineering in the University for the facts concerning the position of the Station and to Mr. Yamagawa, Adjunct Prof. of Physics, who has rendered much valuable aid during the passage of the volume through the press.

The Charts are lettered and numbered so as to serve for both this and a Japanese Edition which will be issued.

T. C. M.

Tokio, March 1880.

CONTENTS.

	PAGE.
Preface	iii
The Station and Instruments ..	1
The Observations.	2
Barometrical Observations ..	3
Barometric Tables.	4 to 7
Barometric Charts	
Temperature..	9
Thermometric Tables.	10 to 17
Thermometric Charts.	
The Wind	19
Tables Concerning the Wind	22 to 32
Wind Charts.	
Rain	33
Tables of Rainfall and Humidity.	35 to 39
Rain Charts..	
Conclusion	41

REPORT ON THE METEOROLOGY OF TOKIO

FOR THE YEAR 2539 (1879)

T. C. MENDENHALL.

THE STATION AND INSTRUMENTS.

The Meteorological Station, at which the following observations were made, is in the West wing of the small observatory belonging to the University of Tokio and is situated in Hongo Moto-Fujimicho, Tokio. The building was completed in the latter part of the year 2538 (1878) and the task of arranging the instruments and undertaking a regular series of meteorological observations was assigned to me at that time. The instruments were such as happened to be already in the possession of the University and their arrangement was completed sometime before the first of January 2539 (1879), the Directors of the University at the same time appointing Mr. Wuyeno as observer. The observations taken before that date, however, were in some degree irregular and the present report includes only those made during the year 2539 (1879). They have been continuous throughout the entire year, with a few exceptions in the case of two or three of the instruments which suffered from accidents preventing their use during a short time.

The instruments are, at present, all mounted in the small room constituting the second story of the West wing of the observatory and on the roof of the same. The approximate latitude of the station is $35°\ 43'$ and the longitude is approximately $139°\ 46'$. The height of the stone foundation of the building above the Sea level is 66.7 feet. The situation of the station is, all things considered, a very desirable one. It occupies an elevated position and is in a clear open space so that there can be no local disturbances of wind, rain, &c.

Concerning its instrumental equipment, it may be said to be the simplest which is compatible with the attempt to record the greater fluctuations in the principal meteorological elements. Although much information can be gained, and I believe has been, by a careful and continuous use of the few instruments now mounted yet there are several important additions which it would seem desirable to make as soon as possible, to which, however, a more extended reference will be found in a subsequent portion of this report.

The following list comprises the instruments now in use:—
One mercurial barometer
One standard thermometer
One maximum   „
One minimum   „
One hygrometer (wet and dry bulb)
One Beckley's recording Anemograph
One Robinson's Anemometer
One Rain gauge (Glaisher's pattern)

All of these are from Negretti and Zambra, London, except the Robinson's Anemometer which is French and registers in kilometres. Most of these instruments are found to be satisfactory in their performance.

The thermometers and hygrometer are mounted in, or rather from, the North window of the second floor. They are protected from undue exposure in the ordinary manner and are separated from the observing room by glass doors which are opened for observation. The maximum thermometer is Negretti and Zambra's model and the minimum is Rutherford's. The barometer is mounted upon the wall of the room above mentioned, the mercury in its cistern being at an elevation of 84 feet above the level of the sea. In this room is also the clockwork and recording apparatus belonging to the anemograph which is mounted upon the roof immediately above. The anemometer is also mounted upon the roof at a distance of about ten or twelve feet from the anemograph. The anemometer is not self recording.

The rain gauge is planted in the ground about 30 feet from the building, its upper edge being about four or five inches above the level of the ground.

THE OBSERVATIONS.

The observations, thus far, have been made at the hours of 7 A.M. 2 P.M. and 10 P.M. local time. This last hour is almost identical with the time of the "international" observation 7-35 A.M. Washington mean time. It will doubtless be desirable to increase the number of these observations to at least five or six during the day as soon as more complete arrangements are made. It is also intended to undertake a series of hourly observations during some months of the present year for the purpose of determining as nearly as possible the corrections necessary for the "daily means." The Directors of the University have recently appointed Mr. Namba as observer. Mr. Wuyeno remaining, and this addition to the force will make several improvements possible.

The observations are all recorded, as made, upon suitably prepared blanks, and all reductions and corrections are made afterwards. From these records the following tables have been compiled and the accompanying charts are based upon these tables or upon other similar ones. The tables give accurately the results of the observations, but the charts exhibit the various meteorological relations and fluctuations in a much more striking manner.

BAROMETRICAL OBSERVATIONS.

The barometer in use is Fortin's model as made by Negretti and Zambra. The internal diameter of the tube is approximately one quarter of an inch. It is graduated in inches and read by vernier to thousandths. I find no record of any reliable comparison of it with a standard. As before stated, it is mounted with the level of the mercury in its cistern at a height of 84 feet above the sea level. In the annexed tables the readings are reduced to the freezing point and to the level of the sea.

Table A gives the readings thus reduced for the entire year. The most interesting results in connection with the barometrical fluctuations are to be found in table B which is obtained by a reduction of the results in table A. In this table will be found the means for each month of the records at 7 A.M. 2 P.M. and 10 P.M. and also the annual mean of the same. A comparison of these means points clearly to the existence of diurnal maxima and minima, the mean heights for the year being respectively 29.977 inches at 7 A.M., 29.948 inches at 2 P.M., and 29.962 inches at 10 P.M. It will also be observed that this same relation exists in each set of monthly means, with two exceptions. It is hoped that a series of frequent observations, to be undertaken in the future, will indicate accurately the times of maxima and minima and determine the extent of the diurnal oscillation. Table B also contains the general mean for each month and for the year, as well as the maximum and minimum heights and the range for each month. The greatest range during any month was in February, the amount being 1.318 inches. The least fluctuation during any month was in July, the amount being .389 inches. The greatest barometrical height for the year was 30.515 inches which was recorded at 10 P. M. on April 21. The lowest point reached was 29.087 inches at 7 A.M. Feb. 23., the range for the year being 1.426 inches. The fluctuations of the barometer during the entire year are shown on the six pages of Chart No. 1. The first diagram of Chart No 2 shows the fluctuations of the monthly barometric mean, and the second exhibits the maximum, minimum, and range for each month of the year. On comparing these barometric Charts with others which follow, representing various meteorological phenomena, one is tempted to enter into various speculations which, however, it is wisdom to defer until a series covering a more extended period than one year can be obtained.

TABLE A. SHOWING READINGS OF THE BAROMETER THROUGHOUT THE YEAR.

Day.	January			February			March			April		
	7	2	10	7	2	10	7	2	10	7	2	10
1	29.904	29.970	30.082	30.235	30.254	30.357	30.055	29.964	29.934	30.023	29.959	29.958
2	30.123	30.070	30.100	30.325	30.181	30.166	30.014	30.033	30.236	29.813	29.672	29.633
3	30.196	30.139	30.181	30.113	30.014	30.117	30.294	30.206	30.214	29.792	29.752	29.912
4	30.058	29.800	29.733	30.137	30.685	30.130	30.089	30.011	30.012	30.125	30.136	30.165
5	29.906	29.984	30.140	30.220	30.276	20.353	29.926	29.734	29.775	30.125	30.045	30.068
6	30.200	30.148	30.190	30.328	30.351	30.350	29.742	29.821	29.881	30.004	29.858	29.847
7	30.225	30.154	30.161	30.305	30.102	30.020	29.987	29.937	29.988	29.775	29.645	29.669
8	30.085	29.984	29.865	29.983	29.821	30.061	30.201	30.174	30.264	30.015	30.103	30.222
9	29.800	29.767	29.970	30.137	30.116	30.155	30.189	30.030	30.033	30.259	30.130	30.031
10	30.174	30.155	30.257	30.225	30.142	30.171	29.988	29.825	29.821	29.765	29.727	29.865
11	30.283	30.255	30.242	30.142	30.071	30.170	29.996	29.976	30.036	30.048	30.052	30.220
12	30.145	30.084	30.101	30.138	30.105	30.076	30.085	29.985	30.057	30.373	30.356	30.459
13	30.158	30.004	30.072	30.085	30.024	30.005	29.889	29.737	29.669	30.413	30.252	30.188
14	30.112	30.128	30.207	30.171	30.071	30.146	29.483	29.421	29.766	30.198	30.139	30.127
15	30.137	29.882	30.125	30.172	30.131	30.123	29.837	29.759	29.777	30.068	29.887	30.439
16	29.555	29.592	29.685	30.091	30.013	30.125	30.129	30.114	30.222	29.567	29.714	30.021
17	29.832	29.822	29.968	30.151	30.066	30.064	30.213	30.081	30.089	30.020	30.161	30.123
18	30.678	30.060	30.188	29.968	29.877	29.862	29.901	29.888	29.905	30.254	30.169	30.233
19	30.240	30.177	30.254	29.870	29.836	29.901	29.846	29.086	29.653	30.262	30.194	30.141
20	30.150	30.163	30.305	29.912	29.963	29.902	29.606	29.472	29.655	30.003	30.379	30.091
21	30.411	30.415	30.490	30.026	30.067	29.845	29.793	29.755	29.915	30.085	30.223	30.513
22	30.400	30.238	30.145	29.885	29.803	29.754	29.965	29.764	29.928	30.200	30.201	30.257
23	29.971	29.656	29.929	29.087	29.159	29.028	29.965	29.764	29.928	30.347	30.287	30.286
24	30.091	30.023	30.126	29.850	29.977	30.081	30.161	30.176	30.318	30.208	30.068	29.997
25	30.165	30.068	30.018	30.022	30.063	30.088	30.355	30.269	30.231	29.814	29.684	29.713
26	30.265	30.236	30.334	30.135	30.129	30.236	30.159	29.978	29.877	29.832	29.879	30.088
27	30.356	30.251	30.157	30.165	30.232	30.308	29.884	29.881	30.075	30.222	30.155	30.212
28	29.985	29.979	30.125	30.313	30.251	30.191	30.209	30.074	30.073	30.172	30.122	30.007
29	30.031	30.012	30.172	......	......	......	30.083	29.891	29.886	30.006	29.997	30.021
30	30.427	30.062	29.823				29.582	29.739	29.863	30.077	30.056	30.134
31	30.221	29.763	30.057	......	......	......	29.912	29.832	29.880	......	......	......

TABLE A. SHOWING READINGS OF THE BAROMETER
THROUGHOUT THE YEAR.

Day.	May			June			July			August		
	7	2	10	7	2	10	7	2	10	7	2	10
1	30.158	30.100	30.130	30.040	30.054	30.132	29.971	29.965	30.001	29.963	29.935	29.958
2	30.086	29.989	29.799	30.157	30.101	30.128	30.051	30.010	30.063	29.940	29.911	29.920
3	29.814	29.742	29.782	30.127	30.124	30.086	30.079	30.013	30.018	29.972	29.913	29.900
4	29.810	29.720	29.775	29.809	29.709	29.659	29.967	29.920	29.911	29.882	29.809	29.825
5	29.880	29.851	29.660	29.607	29.572	29.656	29.854	29.796	29.783	29.843	29.776	29.819
6	29.960	30.016	30.063	29.780	29.738	29.753	29.825	29.738	29.742	29.832	29.760	29.837
7	29.895	29.765	29.532	29.793	29.724	29.749	29.720	29.667	29.716	29.840	29.737	29.700
8	29.468	29.411	29.677	29.780	29.738	29.753	29.722	29.746	29.919	29.760	29.568	29.611
9	29.735	29.736	29.901	29.796	29.720	29.749	29.982	29.916	29.979	29.549	29.521	29.588
10	30.022	30.054	30.016	29.681	29.653	29.814	29.965	29.710	29.620	29.617	29.530	29.667
11	30.057	30.002	29.949	29.863	29.788	29.792	29.717	29.703	29.705	29.722	29.680	29.725
12	29.784	29.675	29.680	29.656	29.559	29.626	29.683	29.704	29.771	29.771	29.689	29.783
13	29.687	29.614	29.714	29.674	29.681	29.787	29.879	29.796	29.839	29.756	29.658	29.640
14	29.819	29.886	29.946	29.834	29.783	29.816	29.841	29.803	29.817	29.571	29.487	29.515
15	30.162	29.981	29.962	29.821	29.828	29.807	29.871	29.849	29.815	29.570	29.552	29.643
16	30.054	29.960	29.968	29.719	29.751	29.811	29.924	29.883	29.951	29.705	29.649	29.712
17	29.755	29.627	29.802	29.811	29.793	29.865	29.985	29.944	29.960	29.711	29.673	29.689
18	29.989	29.939	29.964	29.956	29.926	29.968	29.985	29.946	29.973	29.730	29.675	29.751
19	29.883	29.894	29.989	29.765	29.707	29.717	29.977	29.888	29.898	29.810	29.801	29.782
20	30.020	30.018	30.062	29.818	29.851	29.881	29.928	29.889	29.952	29.962	29.921	29.948
21	30.110	30.086	30.080	29.915	29.877	29.876	29.873	29.860	29.901	30.022	29.985	30.011
22	29.927	29.709	29.721	29.894	29.785	29.801	29.917	29.834	29.907	30.010	29.927	29.958
23	29.733	29.701	29.827	29.848	29.883	29.857	29.879	29.812	29.811	29.985	29.903	29.955
24	29.957	29.952	30.027	29.948	29.889	29.873	29.843	29.810	29.818	29.950	29.870	29.871
25	30.053	29.986	29.912	29.879	29.803	29.738	29.860	29.800	29.765	29.891	29.863	29.923
26	29.823	29.737	29.685	29.798	29.755	29.885	29.842	29.777	29.805	29.948	29.926	29.987
27	29.669	29.819	29.996	29.947	29.913	29.919	29.878	29.854	29.912	30.008	29.968	30.007
28	30.023	29.944	29.935	29.965	29.901	29.976	29.967	29.915	29.976	29.960	29.854	29.889
29	30.011	29.982	30.016	30.065	29.987	30.016	29.977	29.965	29.918	29.961	29.858	29.918
30	29.983	30.026	29.875	29.976	29.989	29.974	29.942	29.876	29.924	29.916	29.840	29.815
31	29.861	29.871	29.611	......	......	......	29.945	29.807	29.918	29.825	29.750	29.855

TABLE A. SHOWING READINGS OF THE BAROMETER THROUGHOUT THE YEAR.

Day.	September			October			November			December		
	7	2	10	7	2	10	7	2	10	7	2	10
1	29.806	29.671	29.711	29.855	29.795	29.849	30.118	30.035	30.090	29.966	29.884	29.750
2	29.728	29.672	29.715	29.926	29.901	30.035	30.062	29.855	29.905	29.812	29.779	29.889
3	29.715	29.687	29.789	30.158	30.182	30.327	29.988	29.816	29.920	30.008	29.988	30.071
4	29.780	29.701	29.618	30.452	30.400	30.504	30.002	29.989	30.001	29.908	29.885	29.905
5	29.626	29.635	29.762	30.471	30.370	30.311	30.187	30.005	30.114	29.969	30.014	30.143
6	29.813	29.872	29.984	30.088	29.895	29.829	30.167	30.102	30.275	30.060	29.894	29.865
7	30.027	30.022	30.030	30.054	30.088	30.037	30.382	30.311	30.319	29.650	29.489	29.570
8	30.020	29.974	29.915	29.159	30.003	30.007	30.179	29.944	29.958	29.703	29.851	29.724
9	29.802	29.691	29.079	30.055	29.964	30.053	29.949	29.852	29.803	29.886	29.889	30.025
10	29.742	29.848	29.807	30.194	30.119	30.204	29.505	29.462	29.524	30.057	29.973	30.002
11	29.858	29.877	29.944	30.292	30.217	30.225	29.720	29.856	30.025	30.183	30.079	30.164
12	29.946	29.905	29.920	30.253	30.136	30.175	30.078	30.032	30.161	30.183	30.105	30.189
13	29.766	29.607	29.508	30.185	30.099	30.047	30.203	30.092	30.106	30.222	30.081	30.094
14	29.407	29.582	29.776	29.905	29.761	29.821	29.826	29.756	30.017	30.067	29.988	30.040
15	29.854	29.915	29.930	29.823	29.768	29.770	30.150	30.099	30.166	30.034	30.009	30.074
16	29.966	29.908	29.901	29.874	29.879	30.071	30.259	30.181	30.186	30.029	29.806	29.695
17	29.902	29.875	29.955	30.263	30.214	30.363	30.168	30.035	30.073	29.884	29.953	30.110
18	30.048	30.014	30.084	30.461	30.342	30.353	30.108	30.013	30.091	30.182	30.081	30.103
19	30.002	30.033	30.055	30.291	30.175	30.085	30.180	30.119	30.140	30.135	29.994	29.946
20	29.946	29.869	29.851	29.789	29.628	29.782	29.900	29.812	29.695	29.880	29.761	29.718
21	29.866	29.791	29.878	30.025	30.039	30.198	29.756	29.814	30.022	29.671	29.585	29.682
22	29.883	29.806	29.839	30.269	30.186	30.222	30.107	29.989	30.033	29.649	29.568	29.658
23	29.855	29.922	30.011	30.211	30.137	30.153	30.056	29.911	29.920	29.731	29.764	29.875
24	30.014	29.987	29.919	30.145	30.012	29.965	30.001	29.984	30.074	29.909	29.846	29.904
25	29.895	29.807	29.873	29.962	29.900	30.024	30.087	29.954	29.972	29.916	29.713	29.532
26	29.969	29.921	30.020	30.137	30.091	30.061	29.960	29.855	29.881	29.729	29.898	30.092
27	30.065	30.029	30.081	29.758	29.532	29.707	29.860	29.836	30.000	30.216	30.153	30.201
28	30.150	30.108	30.185	29.758	29.736	29.876	30.187	30.146	30.165	30.164	30.033	29.970
29	30.250	30.188	30.178	29.964	29.921	30.044	30.155	30.027	29.936	29.650	29.522	29.430
30	30.169	29.923	29.890	30.116	30.056	30.105	29.922	29.880	29.937	29.210	29.211	29.315
31	......	......	......	30.103	30.003	30.088	......	......	......	29.349	29.390	29.641

TABLE B. SHOWING MONTHLY MEANS, MAXIMA, MINIMA AND RANGE OF THE BAROMETER FOR THE YEAR.

Month	Means of Each Reading.			General Means.	Max.	Min.	Range.
	7 a.m.	2 p.m.	10 p.m.				
January	30.126	30.041	30.112	30.098	30.490	29.555	.935
February	30.091	30.045	30.095	30.077	30.405	29.087	1.318
March	29.987	29.901	29.965	29.951	30.355	29.424	.931
April	30.068	30.031	30.059	30.052	30.513	29.439	1.074
May	29.914	29.886	29.884	29.895	30.162	29.411	.751
June	29.856	29.817	29.853	29.842	30.157	29.559	.598
July	29.869	29.814	29.877	29.863	30.079	29.690	.389
August	29.836	29.776	29.816	29.809	30.022	29.487	.535
September	29.900	29.881	29.895	29.892	30.250	29.407	.843
October	30.096	30.017	30.077	30.063	30.504	29.532	.972
November	30.050	29.962	30.023	30.012	30.382	29.402	.980
December	29.904	29.845	29.887	29.879	30.222	29.210	1.012
Year	29.977	29.918	29.962	29.952	30.513	29.087	1.426

Chart No. 1

Showing Fluctuations in the Barometer during the Year 2539 (1879).

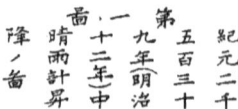

第一號

紀元二千五百三十九年明治十二年晴雨計中

降ノ昇

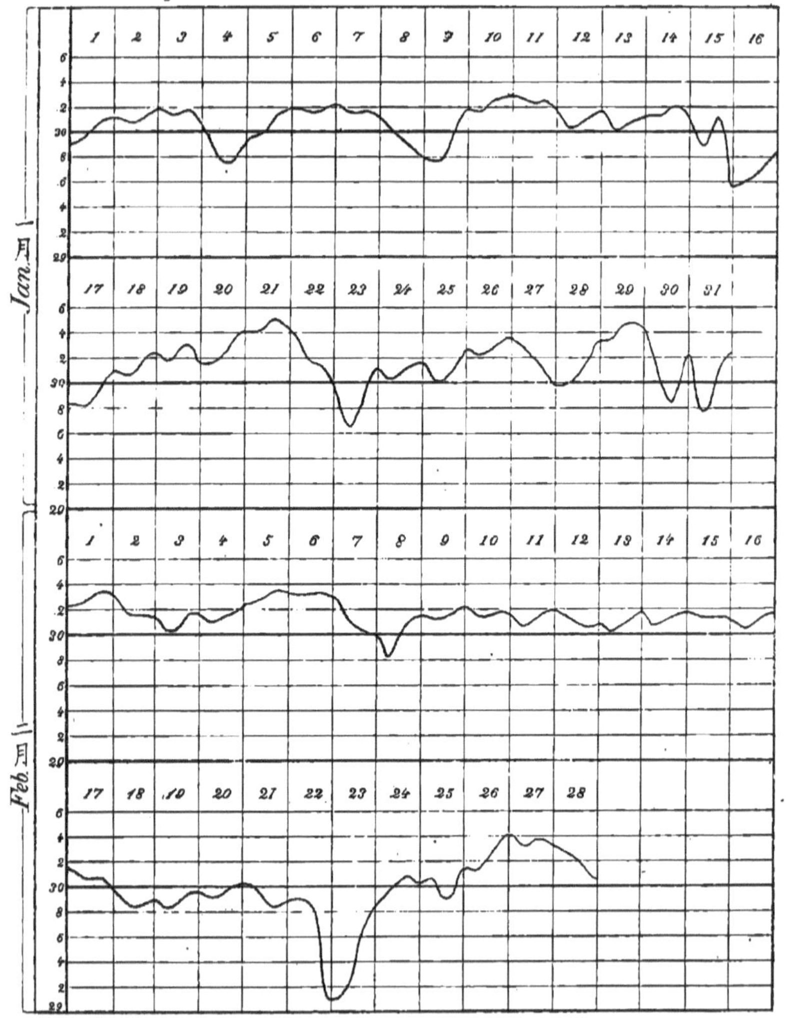

Chart Nº1

Showing Fluctuations in the Barometer during the Year 2539(1879).

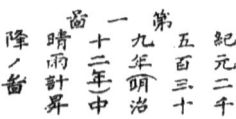

March 月三

April 月四

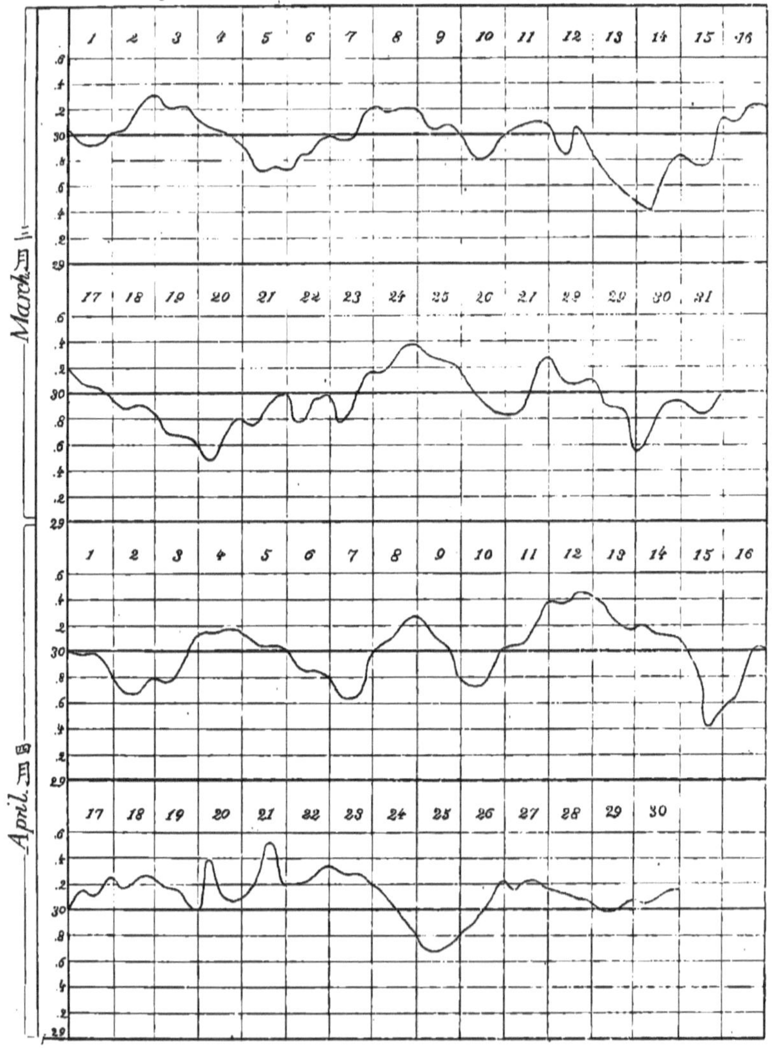

Chart No. 1

Showing Fluctuations in the Barometer during the Year 2539 (1879).

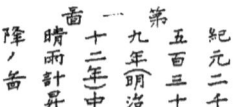

第一圖
紀元二千五百三十九年明治十二年中晴雨計昇降ノ表

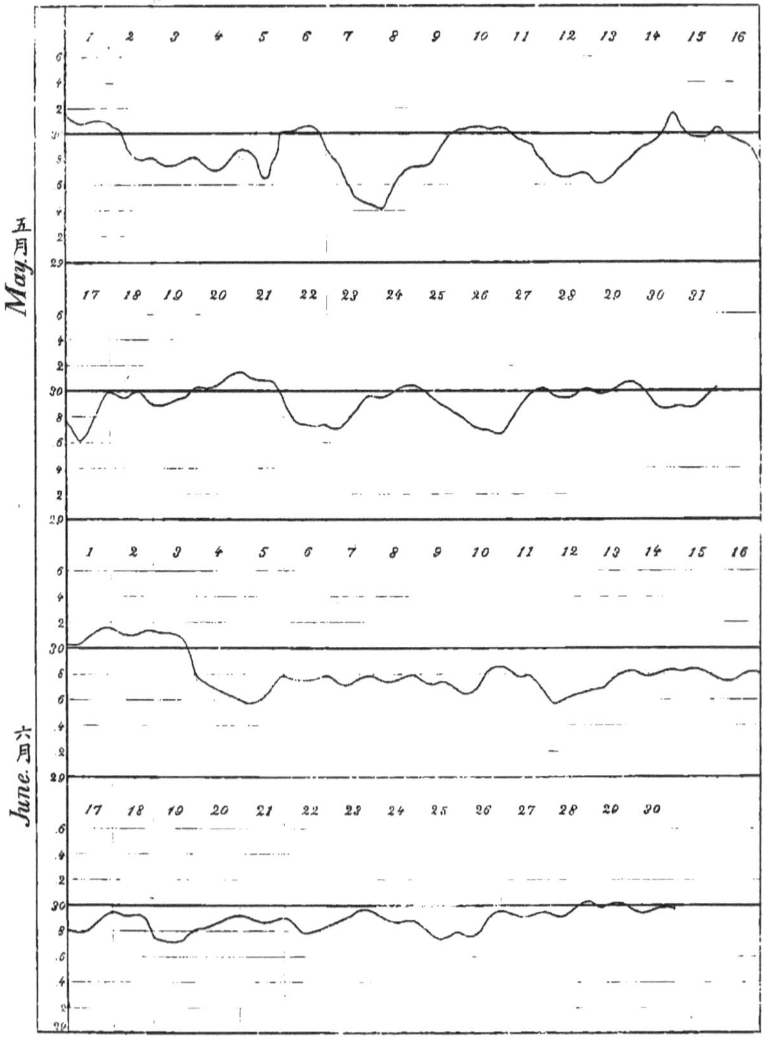

Chart No. 1

Showing Fluctuations in the Barometer during the Year 2539 (1879)

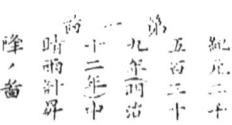

July 七月

Aug 八月

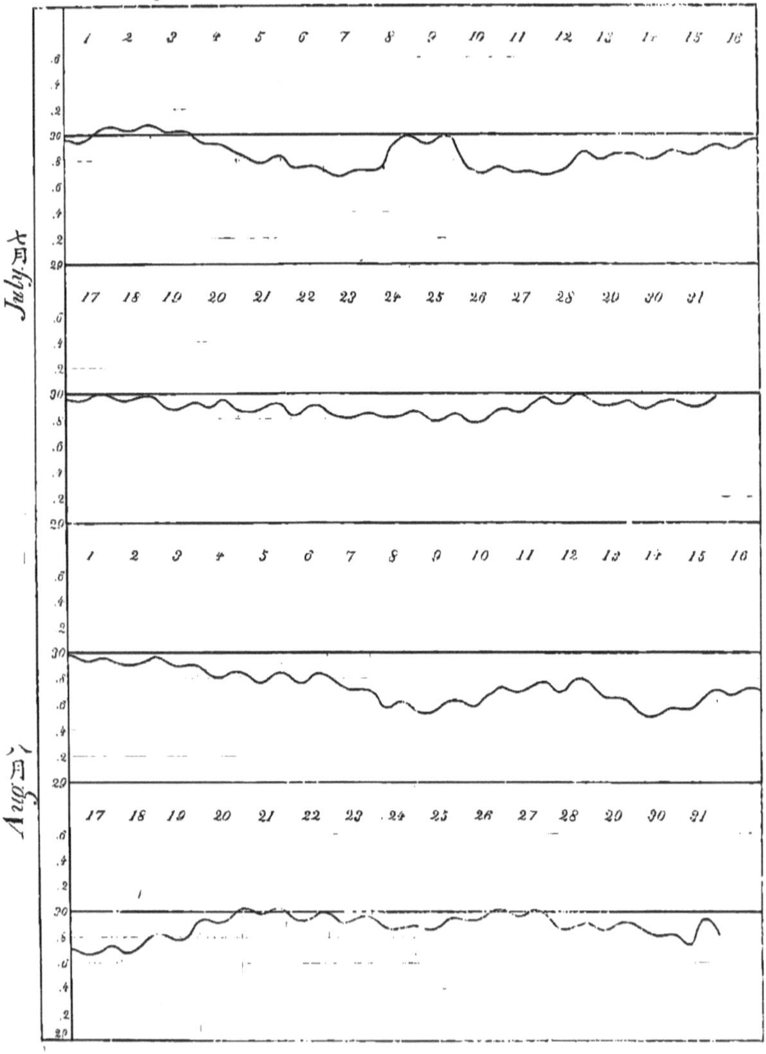

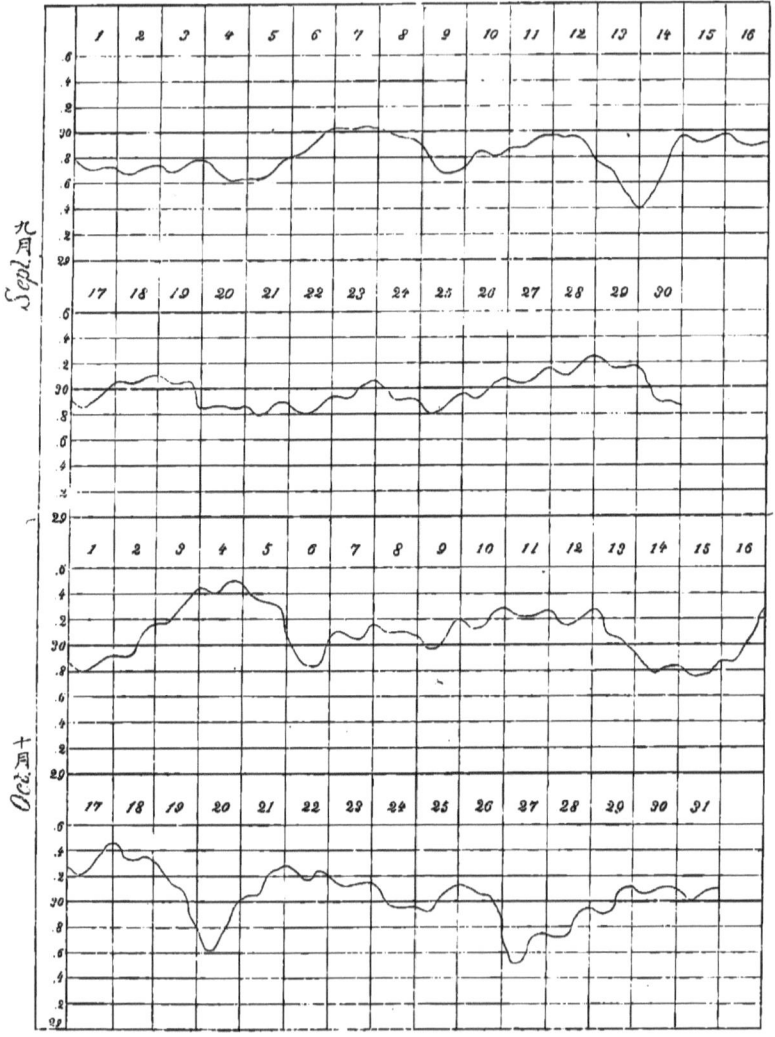

Chart No.1

Showing Fluctuations in the Barometer during the Year 2539(1879).

Chart No. 1

Showing Fluctuations in the Barometer during the Year 2539 (1879).

第一圖

紀元二千五百三十九年(明治十二年)中晴雨計昇降ノ圖

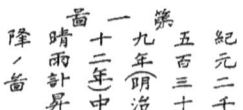

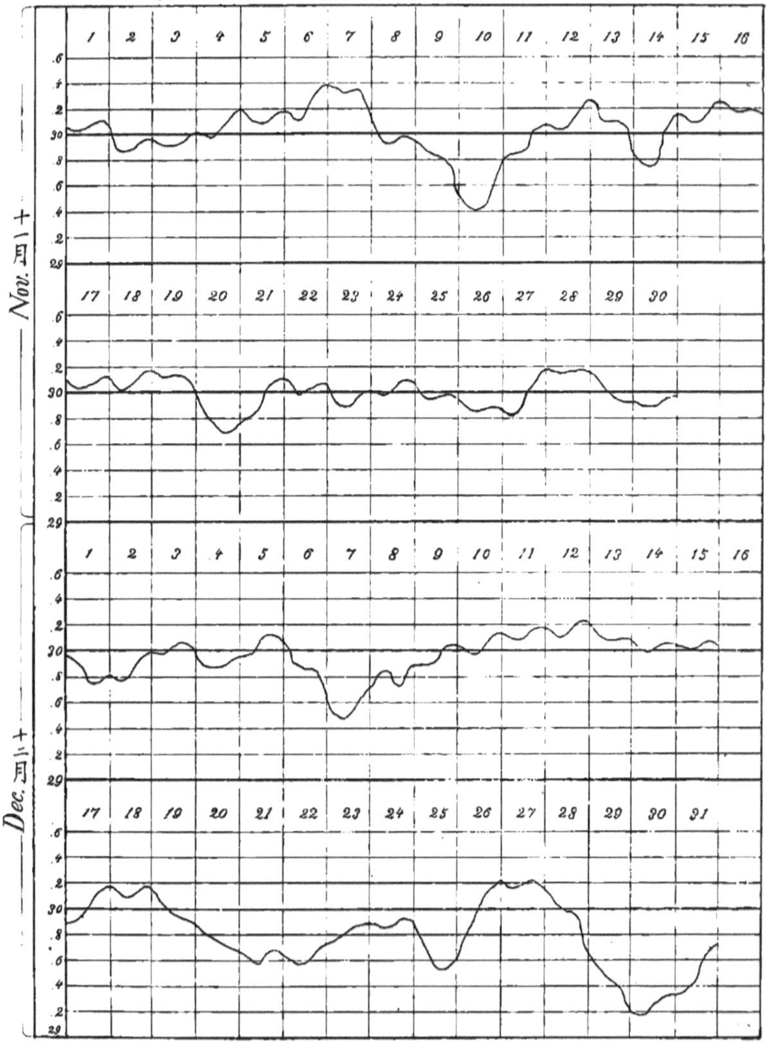

Chart No. 2.

Showing
1st Mean height of the Barometer for each month,
2nd Maximum, Minimum and Range for each month,

during the Year 2539 (1879).

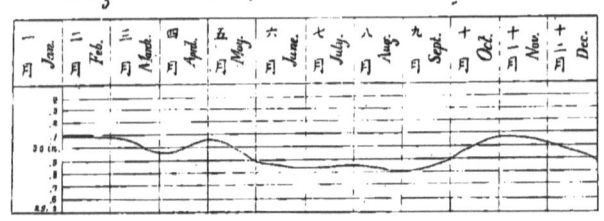

TEMPERATURE.

In the observations for temperature three thermometers have been made use of; a "standard," a maximum and a minimum, all by Negretti and Zambra and graduated in degrees F. The standard bears the number 16543 and is accompanied by a certificate of examination at the Kew Observatory. The errors of graduation within the range of our work are so small as to make a correction unnecessary. Most of the important results growing out of the temperature observations are exhibited in the following tables and charts. Table C contains all of the readings of the standard thermometer made during the year. This table is represented graphically in the six pages of Chart number 3, from an examination of which a good idea of the fluctuations in temperature throughout the year, will be obtained. Table D exhibits for every day of the year the maximum, minimum, and two mean temperatures, the first being the mean obtained from the observations made with the standard thermometer, and the second the mean from the observations of maxima and minima. It will be observed that these two means agree very closely with each other in many cases and do not differ widely in any.

A minimum temperature of 32 or under was observed as follows;

In January	on	27 days
,, February	,,	13 ,,
,, November	,,	1 ,,
,, December	,,	5 ,,
Total for the year		46 ,,

A maximum temperature of 90° or over was observed as follows;

In July	on	7 days
,, August	,,	5 ,,
Total for the year		12 ,,

Table E exhibits the range of temperature for every day of the year. Table F contains in a condensed form many of the most important facts found in the previous tables. It will be seen that the mean temperature for the whole year was $58°.5$; that the lowest monthly mean was $37°.7$ for January and the highest $80°.2$ for August. The lowest maximum temperature in any month was $60°.5$ in February and the highest, being the maximum temperature for the whole year, was $93°$ which was reached on August 15. The highest minimum temperature in any month was $69°.4$ in August and the lowest, being the minimum temperature for the whole year, was $24°.1$, which was reached on January 2 and also on January 7. Thus the entire range of temperature for the year was $68°.9$, the maximum daily range being $29°.8$ on March 23 and the minimum daily range $3°$ on March 6. This table is represented graphically in Chart number 4. The curve in the first diagram shows the fluctuations in the monthly means of temperature. The second diagram shows the maximum and minimum temperatures and range for each month and the third exhibits the maximum and minimum daily range for each month.

TABLE C. SHOWING READINGS OF STANDARD THERMOMETER.

Day.	January			February			March			April		
	7	2	10	7	2	10	7	2	10	7	2	10
1	27.8	44.3	33.8	32.8	40.5	32.0	52.2	57.5	56.5	54.4	67.8	59.2
2	25.6	47.0	35.1	29.0	38.5	39.0	52.5	50.3	44.8	62.8	70.8	62.4
3	28.7	50.5	40.0	33.0	50.5	39.8	39.8	43.5	42.5	50.5	42.5	41.1
4	28.5	49.1	48.5	34.3	49.0	38.5	42.5	49.9	50.5	41.2	44.6	43.0
5	36.1	45.2	31.2	33.0	45.6	36.0	49.4	54.1	46.8	44.6	56.5	52.9
6	26.0	43.6	35.7	31.7	42.5	38.8	41.6	40.0	39.7	44.8	66.1	58.7
7	27.0	48.0	36.2	33.0	40.0	40.0	37.9	45.5	37.5	53.5	68.0	61.2
8	31.8	48.7	39.1	38.0	44.0	32.5	37.6	44.9	38.1	45.8	57.5	51.5
9	34.0	47.0	35.0	29.1	40.5	32.7	35.7	48.5	42.0	41.0	43.5	39.5
10	32.0	44.0	34.0	29.0	43.5	35.5	38.0	43.0	39.9	42.0	50.2	46.5
11	33.0	41.8	31.7	33.0	36.5	33.8	41.2	52.1	43.5	45.0	47.0	41.4
12	31.5	38.7	32.0	26.0	42.8	34.5	37.7	51.6	45.9	37.5	51.5	42.7
13	25.5	44.7	35.0	30.7	51.7	38.5	42.0	57.0	50.7	42.0	45.3	46.0
14	34.5	47.7	36.2	36.5	53.0	40.1	48.7	56.6	39.8	51.0	62.4	55.2
15	32.5	47.6	41.1	36.7	37.0	33.2	39.0	47.0	33.3	49.8	56.7	51.9
16	44.7	50.7	42.0	33.5	48.4	40.0	37.2	49.2	37.5	55.2	58.8	44.7
17	35.5	45.7	33.5	37.3	51.0	44.8	32.7	50.5	42.5	44.4	59.0	55.1
18	30.7	44.8	35.1	33.1	57.4	49.0	39.5	47.1	43.4	47.0	64.9	57.4
19	30.1	37.0	32.5	41.3	40.5	37.8	38.5	41.5	40.6	57.0	68.0	61.1
20	32.0	44.5	37.0	34.8	51.2	42.4	38.2	52.5	44.5	62.5	64.1	60.0
21	26.1	45.3	36.4	34.2	50.7	50.6	39.0	54.5	42.0	58.0	62.5	46.4
22	30.0	40.6	38.3	37.9	46.0	39.1	35.5	50.7	38.5	48.0	62.2	55.7
23	35.7	46.0	41.5	48.5	49.5	43.9	33.0	51.2	42.8	52.0	69.5	60.4
24	35.5	41.0	36.6	38.7	52.8	45.4	39.0	49.4	42.8	61.7	70.4	63.0
25	31.8	43.3	35.6	43.8	53.0	48.8	34.9	55.7	52.5	63.5	67.8	58.2
26	29.0	40.6	31.7	42.5	59.8	49.1	55.3	59.5	48.3	50.0	54.1	50.2
27	30.5	36.7	32.5	46.7	59.0	49.8	47.0	55.8	41.4	52.0	66.1	60.0
28	34.5	42.3	32.5	46.0	59.8	44.1	41.0	56.0	51.7	58.1	67.4	59.8
29	33.5	44.8	36.5				43.7	66.8	58.8	58.0	69.9	61.2
30	33.5	36.5	37.0				62.0	71.0	57.5	60.8	71.2	61.7
31	45.5	49.9	38.5				52.5	67.4	57.4			

TABLE C. SHOWING READINGS OF STANDARD THERMOMETER.

Day.	May			June			July			August		
	7	2	10	7	2	10	7	2	10	7	2	10
1	60.0	70.3	63.5	62.5	69.8	64.8	77.2	86.3	76.4	79.4	87.7	79.0
2	63.3	70.2	64.0	59.0	64.0	61.5	80.4	85.5	66.9	75.8	88.8	80.2
3	60.6	68.8	62.3	60.0	65.4	59.9	81.5	86.0	77.4	78.2	85.5	78.3
4	60.5	71.0	63.5	62.6	66.6	66.3	80.2	87.0	78.8	80.2	89.5	80.8
5	58.0	59.0	58.5	68.6	75.0	67.5	77.5	83.5	80.2	77.5	91.6	81.8
6	56.1	58.8	55.5	67.0	76.8	69.7	78.5	86.0	79.2	78.0	88.6	78.6
7	54.0	60.0	62.0	69.8	80.5	70.2	80.4	91.0	80.3	76.6	85.7	76.4
8	62.0	74.7	63.8	69.0	82.1	71.0	84.0	88.5	76.0	74.8	81.5	75.0
9	64.0	74.4	63.2	70.6	72.0	62.0	71.0	78.6	71.5	73.0	80.5	73.7
10	60.4	72.0	62.8	67.0	73.5	66.0	71.0	82.8	78.8	75.7	84.8	76.7
11	57.2	73.1	68.0	61.5	74.0	70.0	75.5	82.8	78.0	76.0	81.5	74.7
12	63.0	66.8	64.7	69.0	72.7	69.5	75.5	82.5	73.0	75.0	86.7	77.3
13	64.5	64.3	56.5	65.2	74.8	70.0	70.2	80.2	73.3	76.9	84.4	79.2
14	57.4	70.5	64.0	68.5	77.2	71.4	70.0	79.4	71.7	77.7	90.3	81.4
15	63.8	71.2	64.7	72.0	73.2	69.8	70.7	77.0	70.0	80.0	92.0	80.7
16	64.0	74.8	66.8	68.5	77.7	72.0	74.0	82.0	76.7	76.2	89.5	81.0
17	57.7	62.2	61.0	72.5	79.7	74.0	80.0	85.2	77.7	76.3	88.7	81.2
18	58.4	66.0	60.0	69.6	77.5	72.3	79.8	85.2	79.2	77.0	88.8	78.8
19	60.3	63.7	62.9	73.7	79.9	75.7	82.5	86.6	80.0	76.0	84.3	78.0
20	63.4	73.7	65.7	73.8	80.4	71.8	83.0	87.2	78.7	74.7	86.3	78.8
21	66.6	75.0	67.0	71.0	77.7	74.5	79.9	89.0	80.2	73.3	84.8	77.7
22	65.3	67.8	67.3	70.2	75.5	71.5	81.5	89.6	75.0	76.5	84.6	77.7
23	69.5	73.7	67.4	68.8	73.5	69.2	77.0	88.5	79.2	76.6	83.8	71.8
24	66.7	80.0	68.7	70.8	78.7	72.5	78.2	87.7	81.4	71.7	81.4	75.8
25	71.0	74.8	69.8	74.5	84.0	78.0	76.5	89.7	81.8	74.3	84.7	78.2
26	74.0	81.9	75.3	76.0	82.0	71.2	82.5	90.0	79.5	74.8	83.7	77.7
27	67.7	60.7	57.9	71.5	74.6	69.2	79.5	80.4	78.7	74.7	85.4	78.0
28	58.4	61.2	57.7	70.5	77.2	71.0	76.5	83.6	76.8	77.0	85.5	79.7
29	58.0	70.8	62.7	71.3	78.0	72.5	75.2	83.3	76.8	75.5	88.8	79.4
30	59.0	65.5	57.7	74.4	81.6	74.5	74.8	85.2	85.3	77.0	85.8	79.7
31	59.2	66.8	62.8	......	......	......	75.2	87.2	79.5	79.4	86.4	80.8

TABLE C. SHOWING READINGS OF STANDARD THERMOMETER.

Day.	September			October			November			December		
	7	2	10	7	2	10	7	2	10	7	2	10
1	70.4	72.0	75.7	74.8	75.0	65.0	50.5	62.7	51.7	43.0	58.0	51.6
2	72.7	81.8	70.0	61.0	67.0	62.8	47.0	62.7	54.8	44.8	60.0	49.3
3	73.3	81.4	73.7	64.0	69.9	59.8	46.7	63.3	51.0	37.3	56.7	53.5
4	75.5	73.5	75.4	57.5	64.5	54.8	50.0	62.0	47.4	36.7	56.5	47.3
5	73.2	80.0	70.0	53.7	56.0	59.0	41.0	60.9	52.4	44.0	62.4	51.0
6	77.7	77.0	69.9	57.7	62.2	62.0	47.0	59.0	45.5	46.0	49.0	49.0
7	66.5	72.5	67.8	64.3	61.5	59.4	45.3	58.0	46.8	47.0	61.2	46.0
8	68.0	74.0	67.8	61.2	63.5	60.8	41.2	59.7	48.8	40.0	57.5	44.0
9	67.0	72.0	68.0	59.7	62.5	59.9	47.2	55.5	51.0	39.5	53.0	41.0
10	66.8	69.0	67.7	56.8	64.5	55.8	45.0	47.0	44.0	39.3	51.2	40.2
11	66.7	67.0	64.4	55.2	62.4	56.0	38.6	56.4	49.2	38.1	55.5	42.0
12	63.3	66.0	62.8	52.8	62.5	56.5	45.2	57.0	47.0	35.4	56.3	44.2
13	63.8	66.2	64.8	52.7	59.7	54.0	41.7	57.0	50.0	37.0	56.0	47.3
14	71.0	81.8	69.4	50.5	54.9	53.0	44.0	58.0	43.2	39.1	57.5	55.2
15	69.0	76.5	69.2	53.0	54.8	54.5	35.9	51.6	41.5	41.0	56.5	46.0
16	68.3	72.6	65.7	53.4	67.8	54.2	34.7	53.7	42.0	44.0	46.8	46.1
17	65.2	74.2	68.0	54.0	63.0	51.0	38.8	61.6	52.0	50.0	58.5	47.3
18	66.0	75.5	67.7	45.5	63.0	54.2	48.0	60.6	49.5	36.9	55.0	43.8
19	68.0	77.7	73.0	52.5	60.0	58.0	43.8	56.0	50.0	41.3	55.8	48.0
20	69.4	75.0	70.2	56.0	58.4	58.0	47.5	59.5	51.7	43.0	50.0	45.0
21	69.0	81.3	75.8	59.0	68.8	55.5	47.0	51.6	44.6	46.0	55.8	42.7
22	70.5	76.7	71.0	52.5	68.5	57.9	41.8	54.8	43.0	38.0	51.0	38.8
23	66.5	69.7	63.6	58.0	59.2	58.7	35.0	56.8	47.0	41.2	53.0	39.5
24	64.0	70.7	65.4	60.0	71.7	63.7	39.5	62.0	47.0	30.7	50.5	37.8
25	65.5	78.0	70.0	59.0	70.3	57.7	41.5	50.3	45.7	30.0	49.0	54.0
26	64.8	76.7	62.0	57.0	62.5	55.0	36.2	56.3	46.3	49.7	48.5	40.0
27	58.8	74.5	65.8	55.0	57.0	57.0	36.7	60.5	46.3	35.5	50.3	37.0
28	60.6	78.7	68.8	55.2	64.5	52.9	42.5	48.3	45.0	28.5	48.9	43.0
29	67.2	77.5	70.5	43.9	65.6	52.4	38.5	52.4	49.0	41.0	52.7	49.0
30	69.6	80.4	73.8	48.2	64.7	54.9	43.2	60.8	49.5	43.5	48.8	38.5
31	......	......	......	51.0	65.0	54.5	......	......	......	34.0	51.0	39.2

TABLE D. GIVING MAXIMA, MINIMA AND MEAN TEMPERATURES FOR THE YEAR.

Day.	January.				February.			March.				April.			
	Max.	Min.	M.	m.	Max.	Min.	M.	Max.	Min.	M.	m.	Max.	Min.	M.	m.
1	45.1	26.4	35.3	35.7	41.7	32.0	35.1	36.8	59.6	46.0	55.4	52.8	68.2	49.4	60.5	59.0
2	48.2	24.1	35.9	36.1	40.3	27.3	35.2	33.8	53.9	44.5	49.2	49.2	72.6	54.5	65.3	63.5
3	51.5	25.5	39.7	38.5	51.5	28.9	41.1	40.1	44.5	39.5	41.9	42.0	52.8	41.5	44.7	47.1
4	53.0	28.2	42.0	40.6	49.8	33.4	40.6	41.6	51.0	40.0	47.6	45.5	45.3	39.7	42.9	42.5
5	45.5	30.0	38.5	37.7	46.8	31.5	38.2	39.1	53.4	42.5	50.1	47.0	58.8	40.0	51.3	49.4
6	45.5	25.0	35.1	35.2	44.5	31.1	37.7	37.8	42.3	39.3	40.4	40.8	66.5	44.0	56.5	55.2
7	48.6	24.1	37.1	36.8	41.5	32.0	37.7	36.7	46.8	37.2	40.3	42.0	70.4	45.0	60.9	57.7
8	50.3	26.7	40.9	38.5	48.4	30.0	38.2	39.2	46.5	34.5	40.2	40.5	58.8	45.5	51.6	52.1
9	49.7	29.3	38.7	39.4	42.5	28.5	34.4	35.5	49.9	32.5	42.1	41.2	44.0	39.5	41.3	41.7
10	45.5	31.4	36.7	38.4	45.2	27.5	36.0	36.3	45.5	35.5	40.3	40.5	50.7	39.3	46.2	45.0
11	48.1	32.0	36.5	37.5	40.5	29.0	34.4	34.7	53.3	34.5	45.6	43.9	47.6	41.5	44.5	44.5
12	42.0	31.5	34.1	36.7	45.4	25.0	34.4	35.2	54.7	36.7	45.1	45.7	52.5	35.1	43.9	43.8
13	46.3	25.0	35.1	35.6	52.7	26.4	40.3	39.5	58.8	37.5	49.9	48.1	46.5	37.5	44.4	42.0
14	49.4	29.0	39.5	39.1	53.9	29.6	43.2	41.7	57.8	39.7	48.4	48.5	63.0	40.5	56.2	51.7
15	48.4	32.0	40.4	40.2	39.5	33.0	35.6	36.2	47.6	33.1	39.8	40.3	57.5	49.2	52.8	53.3
16	62.2	33.1	45.8	47.6	49.7	32.5	40.7	41.1	49.4	31.0	41.3	40.2	60.5	44.5	52.9	52.5
17	46.2	33.5	38.2	39.8	51.4	35.5	44.4	43.4	51.0	31.0	41.9	41.0	60.6	37.0	52.8	48.8
18	46.2	30.5	36.0	38.3	57.9	33.0	46.5	45.4	49.2	34.0	43.3	41.6	65.7	42.6	56.4	54.1
19	37.5	30.1	33.2	33.8	42.3	31.0	39.9	38.1	42.8	38.0	40.2	40.4	68.4	46.5	62.1	57.4
20	45.7	31.5	37.8	38.6	51.5	33.9	42.8	42.7	54.5	37.5	45.1	46.0	65.8	56.9	62.2	61.3
21	46.7	26.2	35.9	36.4	53.7	31.1	45.2	43.9	57.2	38.0	45.2	47.6	66.6	45.2	55.6	55.9
22	46.5	26.0	36.3	36.2	48.4	34.5	41.0	41.4	52.4	34.0	41.6	43.2	63.4	42.5	55.3	52.9
23	53.4	30.0	41.1	41.7	50.5	37.2	45.6	43.8	59.8	30.0	42.3	44.9	70.7	44.8	60.6	57.7
24	41.4	30.0	37.7	35.7	54.5	37.8	45.6	46.1	50.7	33.0	43.7	41.8	71.5	51.8	65.0	61.6
25	43.2	31.0	36.9	37.1	53.9	38.5	48.5	46.2	58.4	32.0	47.7	45.2	68.5	58.0	63.2	63.2
26	41.1	28.7	33.8	34.9	60.2	41.5	50.5	50.8	58.2	35.8	54.4	47.0	66.0	47.6	51.4	56.8
27	37.5	28.5	33.2	33.0	60.0	42.0	51.8	51.0	59.8	40.0	48.1	49.0	67.5	46.0	59.4	56.7
28	43.0	30.0	36.4	36.5	60.5	44.0	50.0	52.2	58.7	37.0	49.6	47.8	68.1	49.5	61.8	58.8
29	46.7	31.5	38.3	39.1	...	...	...	...	68.3	41.5	56.3	54.9	70.6	55.5	63.0	63.1
30	39.0	33.0	35.7	36.0	...	...		...	70.8	44.0	63.5	57.4	72.8	55.0	64.6	63.9
31	50.5	33.3	44.6	41.9	...	...	...	...	68.0	44.0	59.1	56.0	...	...	...	...

TABLE D. GIVING MAXIMA, MINIMA AND MEAN TEMPERATURES FOR THE YEAR.

Day	May Max.	Min.	M.	m.	June Max.	Min.	M.	m.	July Max.	Min.	M.	m.	August Max	Min.	M.	m.
1	70.8	54.8	64.6	62.8	70.4	58.9	65.7	64.6	86.6	71.0	79.9	78.8	89.3	74.0	82.0	81.6
2	72.6	59.0	65.9	65.8	65.3	57.0	61.5	61.1	87.0	71.5	77.6	79.2	89.4	73.8	81.6	81.3
3	70.2	60.0	63.9	65.1	65.2	57.3	61.8	61.2	86.8	72.0	81.6	79.4	88.8	75.0	80.7	81.9
4	71.8	58.5	65.0	65.1	68.0	59.3	65.2	63.6	87.4	77.4	82.0	82.4	92.5	75.4	83.5	83.9
5	62.5	54.7	58.5	58.6	76.5	61.3	70.5	68.9	83.8	76.4	80.4	80.1	92.4	76.3	83.6	84.3
6	59.8	55.0	56.8	57.4	77.8	59.8	71.2	68.8	86.4	75.0	81.2	80.7	88.9	74.8	81.7	81.8
7	64.2	52.9	58.7	58.5	81.8	65.2	73.5	73.5	91.6	74.4	83.9	83.0	84.9	72.0	78.9	78.4
8	77.5	55.0	66.8	66.2	82.8	63.4	74.0	73.1	90.9	75.4	82.8	85.1	84.6	72.9	77.9	78.7
9	75.2	58.0	67.2	66.6	73.3	61.5	68.1	67.7	74.6	69.1	72.0	71.8	83.3	71.8	75.7	77.6
10	73.7	54.4	65.1	64.0	77.4	59.5	68.8	68.4	85.6	69.4	77.5	77.5	85.6	69.4	79.1	77.5
11	73.0	54.8	66.1	63.9	76.0	57.7	68.5	66.8	85.6	70.4	78.8	78.0	84.4	72.5	77.4	78.9
12	69.2	56.0	64.8	62.6	75.0	61.0	70.4	68.0	85.8	71.5	77.0	78.6	87.5	70.8	77.7	78.7
13	68.3	55.5	61.8	61.9	75.7	64.5	70.0	70.1	86.0	69.9	74.6	74.9	85.4	73.3	80.2	79.3
14	72.5	55.0	64.0	63.7	77.7	64.7	72.4	71.2	80.2	66.6	73.7	73.4	90.4	75.0	83.1	82.7
15	73.5	55.4	66.5	64.4	73.8	67.4	71.7	70.6	77.7	68.0	72.6	72.8	93.0	79.9	84.2	86.4
16	75.4	56.3	68.5	65.8	79.7	66.5	72.7	73.1	82.8	64.4	77.6	73.6	89.9	74.7	82.2	82.3
17	63.8	55.0	60.8	59.4	82.2	67.7	75.4	74.9	86.8	73.5	80.9	80.1	88.8	73.7	82.1	81.2
18	66.1	55.5	61.5	60.8	78.4	68.0	73.1	73.2	87.3	75.5	87.4	81.4	90.0	75.4	81.5	82.7
19	65.2	57.8	62.3	61.5	80.5	69.0	76.1	74.7	90.1	76.4	83.7	83.2	85.8	72.0	79.4	78.9
20	71.2	59.2	67.6	66.7	80.8	71.0	75.2	75.9	88.7	74.0	82.9	81.3	87.0	72.0	79.9	79.5
21	75.5	61.5	69.5	68.5	78.3	68.5	74.4	73.4	90.8	72.4	83.0	81.6	85.6	72.2	78.6	78.9
22	72.8	62.8	66.8	67.8	76.3	69.9	72.4	73.1	90.0	74.7	82.0	82.6	85.6	72.9	79.6	79.2
23	73.8	64.4	69.5	69.1	75.2	67.9	70.5	71.5	89.8	73.5	81.6	81.6	84.2	73.0	77.4	78.6
24	81.1	60.0	71.8	70.5	79.7	66.5	74.0	78.1	89.8	74.5	82.4	82.1	81.8	69.5	76.3	75.7
25	75.7	67.0	71.9	71.3	84.4	68.7	78.8	76.5	92.0	74.4	82.6	83.1	86.5	71.0	79.1	78.2
26	84.6	69.1	77.1	76.8	84.2	70.4	76.4	77.3	91.4	74.8	84.0	83.1	85.3	72.4	78.7	82.3
27	78.4	57.9	62.1	68.1	76.9	68.4	71.8	72.6	88.8	74.8	79.5	81.8	86.7	72.4	79.6	79.5
28	62.2	57.5	59.1	59.8	77.5	66.8	72.9	72.1	84.8	71.5	78.9	79.6	85.7	74.0	80.7	79.8
29	71.3	54.8	63.8	63.0	78.8	65.8	73.9	72.3	83.8	73.7	78.4	73.7	89.4	74.5	81.2	81.9
30	68.8	54.8	60.7	61.8	83.6	68.4	76.8	76.0	85.3	73.3	81.7	79.3	86.0	74.4	80.8	80.2
31	68.4	56.5	62.9	62.4	...	...	...	...	88.6	73.0	80.6	80.8	87.8	74.8	82.2	81.3

15

TABLE D. GIVING MAXIMA, MINIMA AND MEAN TEMPERATURES FOR THE YEAR.

	September				October				November				December			
Day.	Max.	Min.	M.	m.	Max.	Min.	M.	m.	Max.	Min.	M.	m.	Max.	Min.	M.	m.
1	83.8	68.5	72.7	76.1	78.0	64.5	71.6	71.2	63.4	46.6	54.9	55.0	61.4	40.0	50.8	50.7
2	82.0	69.5	74.8	75.7	67.8	59.5	63.6	63.6	64.3	44.0	54.8	54.1	60.5	44.0	51.3	52.2
3	82.2	68.5	76.1	75.3	70.4	59.2	64.5	64.8	64.0	42.0	53.6	53.0	57.5	36.5	49.2	47.0
4	80.0	71.4	74.8	75.7	65.0	54.4	58.9	59.7	64.0	45.0	53.1	54.5	59.5	36.0	47.7	47.7
5	81.8	68.4	74.4	75.1	66.2	49.9	56.2	58.0	61.3	40.5	52.4	50.9	62.4	36.5	52.5	49.4
6	78.2	65.7	74.8	71.9	72.0	53.3	60.6	62.6	59.9	43.5	50.5	51.7	49.8	38.8	48.0	44.3
7	74.0	64.5	68.9	69.2	64.9	57.0	61.7	60.9	58.7	43.0	50.0	50.8	61.7	44.5	51.4	53.1
8	75.5	64.5	69.9	70.0	65.3	57.5	61.8	61.4	60.3	35.5	49.9	47.9	56.0	38.5	47.2	47.2
9	72.2	66.0	69.0	69.1	63.5	58.5	60.7	60.7	56.0	40.0	51.2	48.0	54.7	34.0	44.5	44.3
10	69.8	65.2	67.8	67.5	65.4	55.2	59.0	60.3	47.5	43.0	45.3	45.2	51.8	34.7	43.6	43.2
11	68.0	63.5	66.0	67.5	63.5	50.5	57.8	57.0	57.2	37.5	48.1	47.3	55.8	35.3	45.2	45.5
12	66.5	61.5	64.0	64.0	62.7	48.2	57.2	55.4	58.3	37.5	47.1	47.9	57.5	34.5	45.3	46.0
13	66.4	61.5	64.9	63.9	60.5	50.3	55.4	55.4	57.0	40.0	49.5	48.5	56.9	34.5	46.8	45.7
14	82.9	61.5	74.1	72.2	55.8	49.5	52.8	52.6	61.4	40.5	48.7	50.9	38.3	36.0	50.6	47.1
15	76.8	64.4	71.5	70.6	59.5	50.5	54.1	55.0	53.3	35.0	43.0	44.1	57.3	38.5	47.8	47.9
16	73.3	66.8	68.8	70.0	67.4	46.0	58.4	56.7	54.2	31.8	43.4	43.0	50.2	40.0	45.6	45.1
17	75.3	63.0	69.1	69.1	64.6	50.0	56.0	57.3	62.8	34.0	51.0	48.4	58.8	43.4	51.9	51.1
18	77.5	63.5	69.7	70.5	63.2	41.8	54.2	52.5	61.0	38.0	52.7	49.5	55.5	36.0	45.2	45.7
19	79.5	59.9	72.9	69.7	61.2	44.5	56.8	52.8	56.5	40.9	49.9	48.7	56.5	36.0	48.4	46.2
20	75.3	64.9	71.5	70.1	59.0	52.0	57.4	55.5	60.0	43.5	52.9	51.7	51.7	39.4	40.0	45.5
21	81.8	68.0	75.3	74.9	69.2	52.0	61.1	60.6	56.4	44.0	47.7	50.2	56.4	42.0	48.2	49.2
22	77.5	67.5	72.7	72.5	69.5	50.2	59.6	59.8	55.3	39.5	46.5	47.4	58.8	37.0	42.6	45.4
23	70.7	63.0	66.6	66.8	59.7	51.8	58.6	55.7	57.2	34.0	46.3	45.6	53.8	35.8	44.6	44.8
24	71.5	58.0	66.7	64.7	72.5	52.2	65.1	62.3	62.7	34.5	49.5	48.6	51.4	30.0	39.5	40.7
25	78.8	62.5	71.2	70.5	70.9	50.9	62.3	60.9	51.0	38.5	45.8	44.7	57.5	29.3	44.3	43.4
26	78.8	60.0	67.8	69.4	63.3	53.0	58.2	58.1	56.7	35.9	46.3	46.3	48.7	30.0	44.1	39.3
27	74.8	54.5	66.3	64.0	58.0	53.5	56.3	55.7	61.0	35.0	47.8	48.0	51.3	33.5	40.9	42.4
28	78.0	57.7	69.4	67.8	65.9	52.0	57.5	58.0	49.0	36.0	45.3	42.5	50.7	27.5	40.1	39.1
29	78.3	58.0	71.7	68.1	66.0	41.0	53.9	53.5	53.8	37.0	46.6	45.4	53.4	28.0	47.6	40.7
30	80.8	66.4	74.6	73.6	65.3	43.0	55.9	54.1	61.5	37.5	51.2	49.5	49.5	37.5	43.6	43.5
31	...	...	...	...	65.6	47.5	56.8	56.5	...	...	...	...	51.5	33.3	41.4	42.4

TABLE E. SHOWING THERMOMETRIC RANGE FOR EVERY DAY IN THE YEAR.

Day	January	February	March	April	May	June	July	August	September	October	November	December
1	18.7	9.7	13.6	18.4	16.0	11.5	15.6	15.3	15.8	13.5	16.8	21.4
3	24.1	13.0	9.4	18.1	13.6	8.3	15.5	16.1	12.5	8.3	20.3	16.5
2	26.0	22.0	5.0	11.3	10.2	7.9	14.8	13.8	13.7	11.2	22.0	21.0
4	24.8	16.4	11.0	5.6	13.3	8.7	10.0	17.1	8.6	10.6	19.0	23.5
5	15.5	15.3	10.9	18.8	7.8	15.2	7.4	10.1	13.4	16.3	20.8	25.9
6	20.5	13.4	3.0	22.5	4.8	18.0	11.4	14.1	12.5	18.7	16.4	11.0
7	24.5	9.5	9.6	25.4	11.3	16.6	17.2	12.9	9.5	7.9	15.7	17.2
8	23.6	18.4	12.0	13.3	22.5	19.4	15.5	11.7	11.0	7.8	24.8	17.5
9	20.4	14.0	17.4	4.5	17.2	11.8	5.5	11.5	6.2	5.0	16.0	20.7
10	14.1	17.7	10.0	11.4	19.3	17.9	16.2	16.2	4.6	10.2	4.5	17.1
11	11.1	11.5	18.8	6.1	18.2	18.3	15.2	11.9	4.5	13.0	19.7	20.5
12	10.5	20.4	18.0	17.4	13.2	14.0	14.3	10.7	5.0	14.5	20.8	23.0
13	21.3	26.3	21.3	9.0	12.8	11.2	10.1	12.1	4.8	10.2	17.0	22.3
14	20.1	24.3	17.6	22.5	17.5	13.0	13.6	15.4	21.4	6.3	20.9	22.3
15	16.4	6.5	14.5	8.2	18.1	6.4	9.7	13.1	12.4	9.0	18.3	18.8
16	29.1	17.2	18.4	16.0	19.1	13.2	18.4	15.2	6.5	21.4	22.4	10.2
17	12.7	15.9	20.0	23.6	8.8	14.5	13.3	15.1	12.3	14.6	28.8	15.4
18	15.7	24.9	15.2	23.1	10.6	10.4	11.8	11.6	14.0	21.5	23.0	19.5
19	7.4	8.3	4.8	21.9	7.4	11.5	13.7	13.8	19.0	16.7	15.6	20.5
20	14.2	17.6	17.0	8.9	15.0	9.8	14.7	15.0	10.4	7.0	18.5	12.3
21	20.5	19.6	19.2	21.4	14.0	9.8	18.4	13.4	13.8	17.2	12.4	14.4
22	20.5	13.9	18.4	20.9	10.0	6.4	15.3	12.7	10.0	19.3	15.8	16.8
23	23.4	13.3	29.8	25.9	8.4	7.3	16.3	11.2	7.7	7.9	23.2	18.0
24	11.4	10.7	17.7	19.7	21.1	13.2	15.3	12.3	13.5	20.3	28.2	21.4
25	12.2	15.4	26.4	10.5	8.7	15.7	17.6	15.5	16.3	20.0	12.5	28.2
26	12.4	18.7	22.4	18.4	15.5	13.8	16.6	12.9	18.8	10.3	20.8	18.7
27	9.0	18.0	19.8	21.5	20.5	8.5	14.0	14.3	20.3	4.5	26.0	17.8
28	13.0	16.5	21.7	18.6	4.7	10.7	10.3	11.7	20.3	13.9	13.0	23.2
29	15.2		26.8	15.1	16.5	13.0	10.1	11.9	20.3	25.0	16.8	25.4
30	6.0		26.8	17.8	14.0	15.2	12.0	11.6	14.4	22.3	24.0	12.0
31	17.2	......	24.0	......	11.9	......	15.6	13.0	......	18.1	......	18.2

TABLE F. SHOWING MONTHLY MEANS, MAXIMA MINIMA AND RANGE OF THE THERMOMETER.

	Jan.	Feb.	March	April	May	June	July	August	Sept.	October	Nov.	Decem.	Year
Means from Sd. Ther.	37.7	41.6	46.4	55.0	64.9	71.6	79.9	80.2	70.6	58.8	49.2	46.3	58.5
Means from Max. & Min.	37.8	41.1	45.6	55.8	64.5	70.9	79.5	80.4	70.1	58.3	48.6	45.7	58.0
Max.	62.2	60.5	70.8	72.8	84.6	81.4	92.0	93.0	82.8	78.0	64.3	62.4	93.0
Min	24.1	25.0	39.0	35.1	52.9	57.0	64.4	62.4	54.5	41.0	31.8	27.5	24.1
Max. Range	29.1	26.3	29.8	25.9	22.5	19.4	18.7	17.1	21.4	25.0	28.8	28.2	29.8
Min. Range	6.0	6.5	3.0	4.5	4.7	6.4	5.5	11.2	4.5	4.5	4.5	10.2	3.0

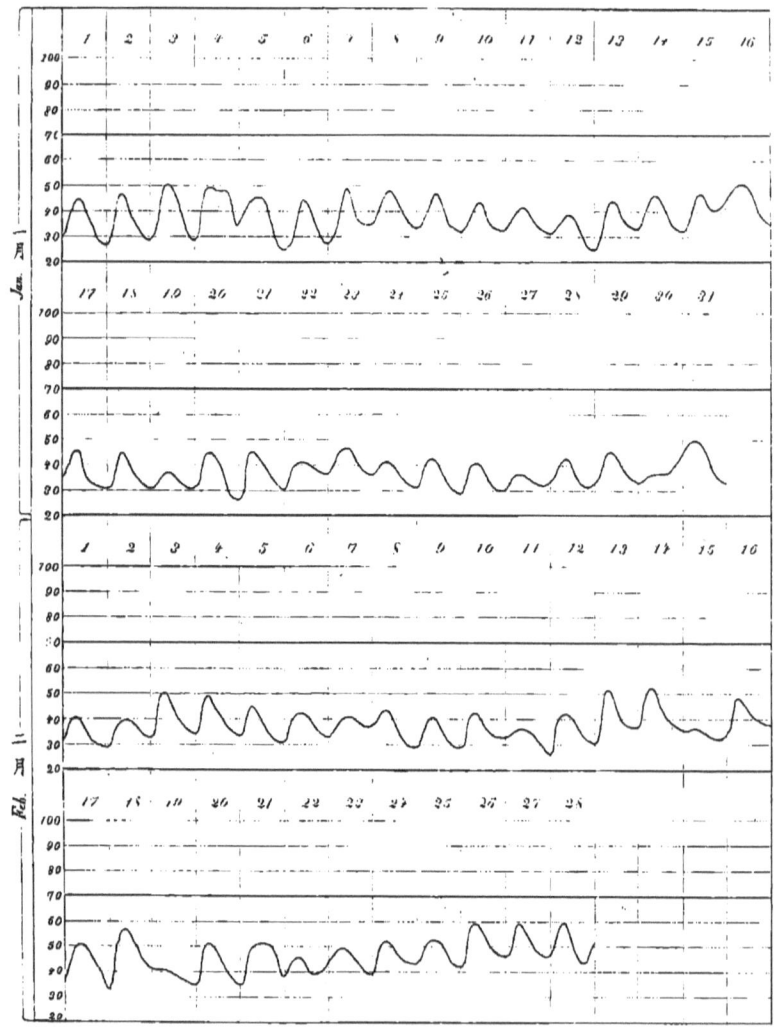

Chart No 3
Showing the readings of standard thermometers during the year 1879

Chart N°3
Showing the readings of standard
Barometer during the year 2532
(1879)

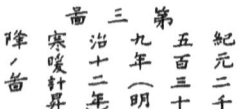

March.

April.

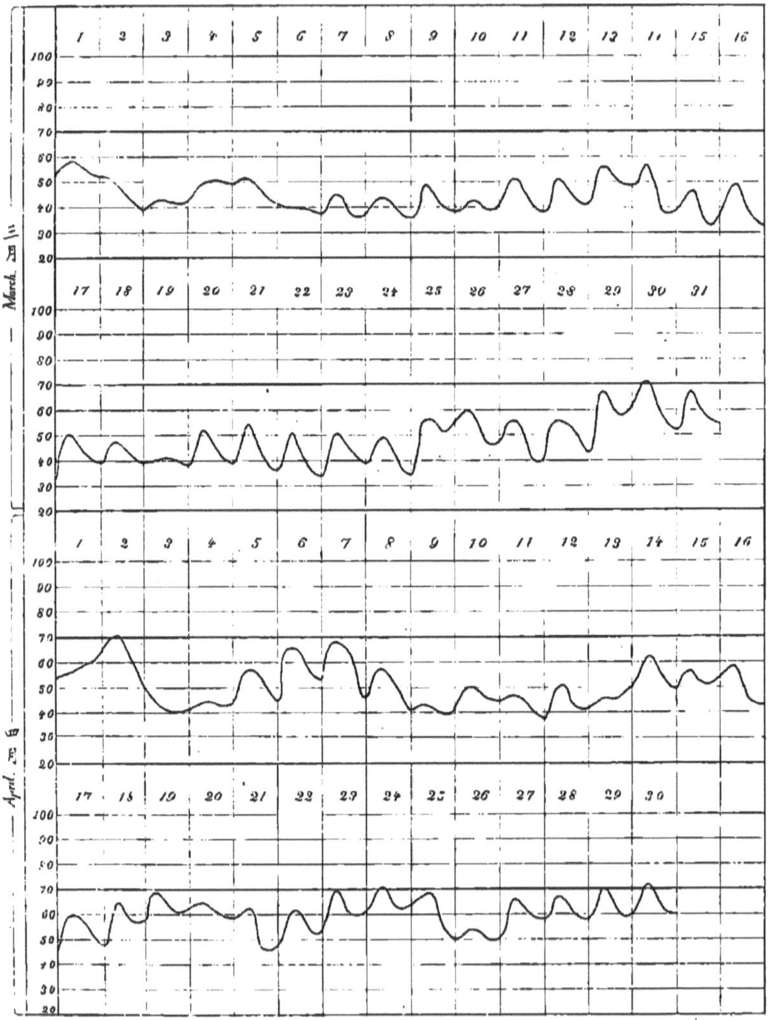

Chart N? 3
Showing the readings of standard
thermometer during the year 2533
(1879)

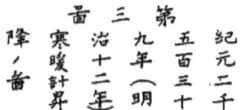

四月 May

六月 June.

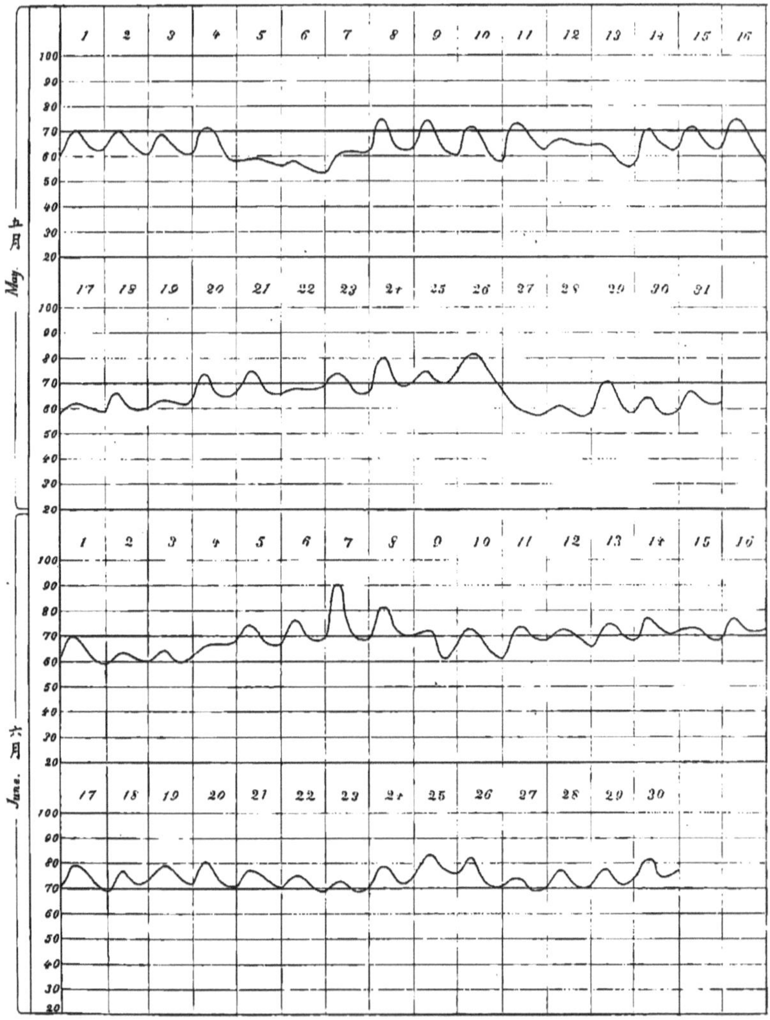

Chart No. 3

Showing the readings of standard thermometer during the year 2539 (1879)

第三圖

紀元二千五百三十九年（明治十二年）寒暖計昇降ノ圖

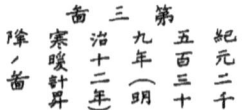

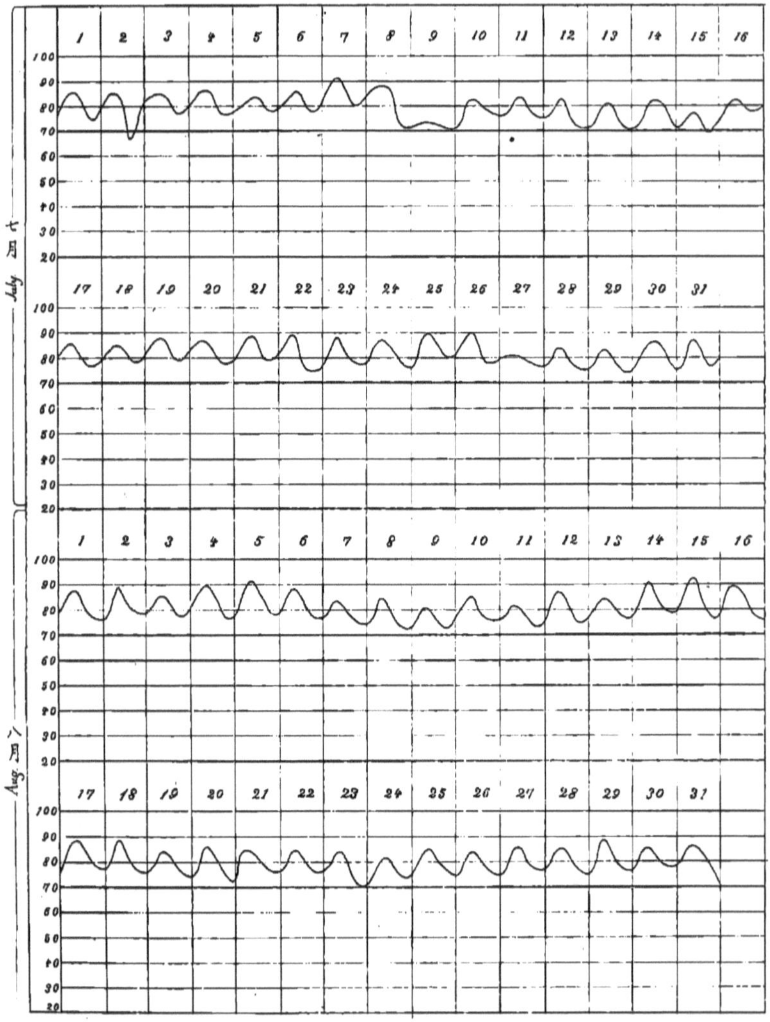

Chart No. 3

Showing the readings of standard thermometer during the year 2539 (1879)

第三圖

紀元二千五百三十九年（明治十二年）寒暖計昇降ノ圖

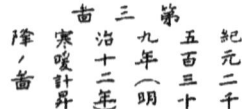

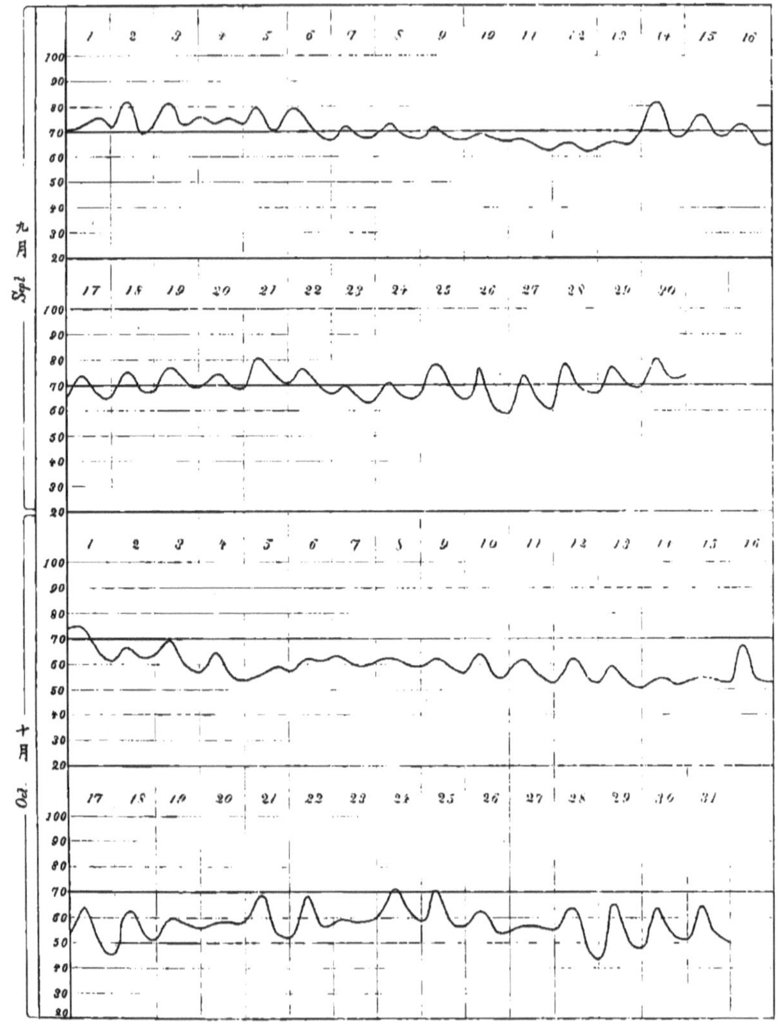

Chart No 3.
Showing the readings of standard
thermometer during the year 2539
(1879)

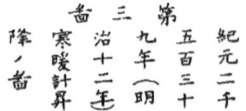
第三圖
紀元二千五百三十九年(明治十二年)寒暖計昇降ノ畫

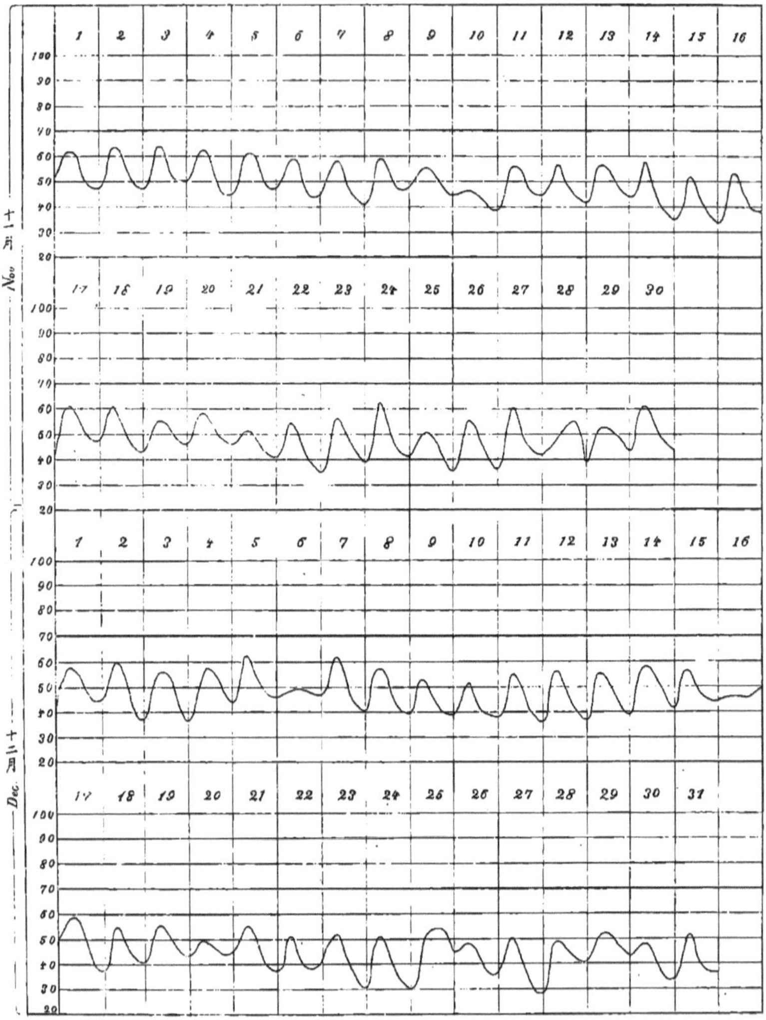

Chart N.º 4

Showing 1st. monthly means of standard thermometer,
2nd. max. min. and range for each month,
3rd. max. and min. daily range for each month.

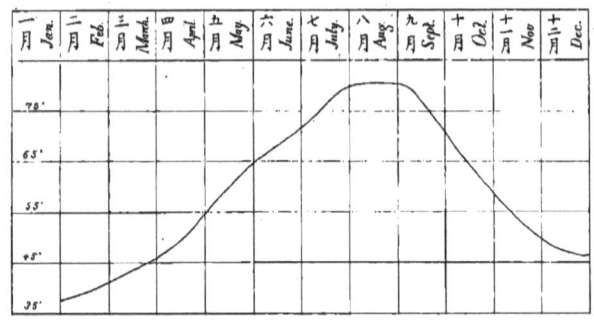

THE WIND.

Observations on the movements of the atmosphere have been made by means of two instruments; the Beckley's Anemograph and the Robinson's Anemometer. A slight interruption has occured in the use of both but fortunately at no one time have both been disabled. Two different Anemometers have been used during the year, one having been blown down and injured beyond repair by the high wind of Feb. 23. As soon as possible another was mounted in its stead. At another time the record of the Anemograph was interrupted on account of needed repairs the interruption lasting, however, only a few days. In the accompanying tables and charts the results as to the velocity of the wind are made up, as far as possible, from the records of the Anemometer rather than the Anemograph. The moving mass in the former being so much smaller than in the latter it has proved to be by far the most sensitive, often being in motion when the Anemograph is absolutely at rest. It has also been found upon a comparison of the two that while the Anemometer will record a wind of low velocity to which the Anemograph will not respond, in high wind the record of the latter is in excess of that of the former.

The direction of the wind has, however, been taken from the record sheets of the Anemograph which are certainly correct in this respect within the limits laid down in the charts and tables.

Table G gives the actual number of miles of movement of the atmosphere *since the last observation* at each of the three observations for every day in the year, with totals. From this it will be seen that the total movement during the year in all directions was 49380.6 miles being at the average rate of 135.3 miles per day or about 5.6 miles per hour.

In table H will be found the direction of the wind at the time of each observation recorded in table G. When there is no perceptible motion of the air at the time of making the observation the direction given is that of the last observed movement. Table I exhibits the total motion of the atmosphere for every day of the year with the prevailing direction of the wind during the day and the maximum and minimum movements for each month. Even with the direction of the wind for every hour of the day correctly recorded it is difficult to determine the *prevailing direction* in every instance with entire satisfaction. It is here made to depend upon both time and velocity of wind as far as possible but it will doubtless be found that when comparison is made between this and other tables there will be apparent inconsistencies.

The maximum movement of the atmosphere in a single period of 24 hours occurred on December 26, the total number of miles being 597.5 or a trifle less than an average of 25 miles per hour for the entire 24 hours. On this day occurred, in the city of Tokio the most extensive and disastrous conflagration which has visited it for several years, the rapid and distructive spread of which was due to the excessive velocity of the wind. In fact the maximum velocity for the year was reached during the afternoon of that day, being about 47 miles per hour. The wind came on that day from the North and Northwest, the record showing North in the morning, Northwest in the middle of the day and North again at night. The high wind of February 23 was North in the morning, Northwest at 2 P.M. and West at night. There have been no extremely high winds, such as are here known as "typhoons" during the year, although some have been reported off the Southern and South-eastern Coast of Japan.

The least motion of the Air for any day of the year was 24.5 miles on May 31.

Tables K, L and M show the winds classified as to time and direction. Table K shows the number of times the wind was recorded as blowing from various directions at the hours 7 P.M. 2 P.M. and 10 P.M. for each month and for the year. Table L shows the number of times the wind registered a velocity of 20 miles per hour and over from various directions, for each month and for the year. Table M shows the total miles of wind in each month from various directions. Table L is interesting as indicating the prevailing direction of high winds, by far the greater number coming from the North and Northwest. There are 30 records from those points against 10 from all others combined. The number of such winds in the first six months of the year exceeds that of the remainder of the year in exactly the same ratio.

These facts, as well as others of interest are strikingly exhibited in the charts which illustrate the direction and velocity of the wind. Chart No. 5 shows the prevailing direction of the wind during each of the months of the year. It is based upon table K and represents the relative number of times the wind has been recorded from each of the eight points, without regard to its velocity. The great preponderance of winds from the North and Northwest during the first three months of the year is distinctly shown, and also the fact that during April, May and June the winds seem to shift around to the South through the East. South winds are largely in excess during July and August, but in September a sudden change to the North occurs, ending in December with a diagram closely resembling that of January.

Chart No. 6 is constructed in precisely the same manner, except that in it the actual number of miles travelled by the wind in various directions is considered. While the general forms of the diagrams are similar to those of the preceding chart a comparison of the two will show distinctly the excess of high winds from the North and North-west. It will be observed on this chart that in the months in which the wind is generally in the South considerably smaller areas are included than in the others, which is due, of course, to the much less absolute movement of the air. Charts No. 7 and No. 8 exhibit the same results for the whole year. An examination of these two charts establishes beyond question two conclusions; that the wind blows more frequently from the North and Northwest than from any other directions; and that these are especially the directions from which winds of high velocity come. This last statement is strongly verified and illustrated by Chart No. 9 which exhibits, relatively, the number of days on which the velocity of the wind reached 20 miles per hour or over, from various directions. The first diagram of Chart No. 10 shows the general course of the movement of the atmosphere for the year, and is constructed as follows. Beginning at A a line is drawn representing in length and direction the sum of all of the winds from the northwest; from the end of this line another is drawn representing in the same manner the winds from the west and so on, finally terminating at B. The dotted line from A to B may be said to represent in direction and amount the resultant of the years movement. It indicates a total distance of 11000 miles, or an average velocity of almost exactly 30 miles per day from a point 27° West of North. The second diagram represents the total number of miles of wind during each month of the year, without regard to direction.

While it would be useless to generalize to any extent upon the results of a single year's observations of the movements of the atmosphere, yet these tables and charts so unmistakably lead to the conclusions given above in regard to the prevailing directions of the wind that it does not seem rash to venture the prediction that future observations will only serve to verify them.

TABLE G. SHOWING MILES OF WIND RECORDED AT EACH OBSERVATION IN THE YEAR.

Day.	January			February			March			April		
	7	2	10	7	2	10	7	2	10	7	2	10
1	18.0	27.7	35.0	104.8	58.6	25.0	57.0	9.0	27.0	15.0	53.0	88.0
2	24.6	20.0	37.5	58.4	45.3	39.8	59.0	88.0	103.5	86.5	119.0	70.0
3	39.1	24.5	27.3	67.5	35.4	23.6	93.0	105.7	63.5	73.5	99.5	62.0
4	26.1	17.0	80.6	44.8	70.0	58.2	42.0	35.0	38.0	29.5	45.0	11.5
5	89.3	104.4	56.4	38.4	55.6	68.3	32.0	34.0	87.2	16.0	25.5	66.5
6	31.4	29.4	27.5	33.7	35.5	30.1	67.3	86.5	75.2	26.0	31.0	60.0
7	36.3	15.7	17.7	63.8	13.4	15.8	13.0	17.3	61.8	10.5	31.0	69.0
8	43.1	42.2	8.5	29.1	125.0	181.0	107.5	93.0	22.0	15.9	82.0	79.0
9	46.1	66.6	142.8	104.2	36.9	31.3	33.5	54.6	21.4	59.0	50.0	103.0
10	130.6	59.9	46.0	65.2	50.3	35.3	22.9	7.0	10.4	61.0	21.0	22.0
11	86.4	67.1	19.5	50.2	50.7	30.8	91.3	99.0	27.7	47.0	147.0	30.0
12	52.2	38.6	30.6	45.1	35.8	37.0	16.5	15.2	27.0	18.0	35.0	73.0
13	29.0	25.3	19.9	35.8	75.1	34.8	18.6	36.0	12.5	15.5	45.0	23.0
14	77.8	48.4	16.5	69.3	77.8	35.9	31.0	32.2	95.0	28.0	34.0	47.5
15	50.5	10.8	27.2	56.3	61.8	75.2	86.8	49.7	131.5	7.0	20.0	47.5
16	59.8	41.5	42.3	111.4	87.1	45.4	139.0	111.3	32.0	88.0	149.0	17.6
17	45.0	73.9	76.5	30.5	38.3	48.0	41.4	30.1	14.0	42.5	30.5	59.0
18	102.6	73.6	118.2	24.5	26.7	32.8	35.5	50.4	57.6	16.0	32.0	72.0
19	76.6	29.0	43.5	58.9	77.0	64.1	21.0	24.5	23.7	10.0	71.0	95.5
20	66.6	65.2	26.4	36.2	29.7	37.0	57.0	35.0	52.5	53.5	74.0	66.0
21	23.2	31.6	18.2	67.2	31.7	58.6	31.0	25.0	142.5	44.0	129.0	113.5
22	24.6	28.6	10.9	39.0	44.3	73.7	100.0	53.0	53.5	92.5	24.0	56.0
23	48.9	44.2	108.8	115.6	107.0	288.0	29.0	66.5	87.5	7.5	36.0	60.0
24	26.1	25.5	17.0	132.0	93.0	15.7	163.0	134.5	42.0	13.0	108.5	145.5
25	55.7	13.1	3.7	86.3	39.0	8.5	19.0	32.5	122.0	124.0	86.0	87.0
26	74.2	22.3	17.2	28.5	42.5	53.5	81.0	60.0	39.0	124.0	84.5	44.0
27	38.2	28.8	32.3	30.5	28.0	37.0	18.5	92.5	188.0	26.5	38.0	46.2
28	59.1	12.9	9.1	17.0	26.1	69.7	50.0	61.0	91.5	22.6	60.5	77.0
29	63.9	61.8	19.1				7.5	79.5	166.5	56.0	57.4	24.8
30	46.8	35.4	26.7				179.5	80.0	61.0	12.6	17.0	40.0
31	48.6	87.9	116.7				20.0	30.0	65.0			
Sums	1640.4	1272.9	1279.1	1671.5	1497.9	1557.7	1861.8	1728.0	2045.0	1244.1	1835.4	1856.1
Total	4192.4			4727.1			5634.8			4932.6		

TABLE G. SHOWING MILES OF WIND RECORDED AT EACH OBSERVATION IN THE YEAR.

Day.	May			June			July			August		
	7	2	10	7	2	10	7	2	10	7	2	10
1	17.0	50.3	32.8	1.5	12.0	12.5	26.0	81.5	89.5	36.7	21.7	38.0
2	9.0	29.5	37.6	73.0	46.7	18.4	39.0	61.0	89.0	15.9	26.1	30.4
3	50.0	7.7	79.0	4.0	18.0	40.0	26.5	76.0	113.0	24.7	42.9	43.2
4	16.5	49.0	48.0	91.8	96.5	19.2	85.0	65.0	26.0	13.2	28.8	43.2
5	44.8	46.3	61.4	55.0	86.5	86.0	45.0	21.0	25.0	26.6	32.9	47.3
6	42.0	33.9	58.5	15.3	31.5	53.0	14.5	27.7	27.5	30.8	17.4	21.6
7	18.0	39.0	30.8	26.0	34.0	60.5	19.3	18.6	104.8	27.2	16.8	23.4
8	46.4	23.7	27.0	20.0	34.0	60.5	68.6	79.8	51.6	35.4	31.3	25.8
9	58.0	57.0	53.4	17.0	24.3	70.5	41.2	30.3	27.0	39.9	70.2	40.0
10	33.0	28.5	65.0	66.5	32.0	87.0	9.0	19.8	21.0	35.9	32.1	46.7
11	18.0	36.0	36.8	15.0	53.5	88.0	25.0	26.7	30.5	25.6	30.3	46.1
12	46.4	23.7	27.0	49.0	25.0	23.5	28.4	27.6	80.4	27.9	23.8	38.0
13	58.0	57.0	65.0	17.5	18.5	64.0	23.9	43.4	52.0	16.2	49.4	59.1
14	75.0	12.7	22.4	17.0	38.0	22.0	24.6	31.0	38.3	19.3	26.9	30.8
15	60.0	57.4	73.8	5.0	29.0	80.0	14.4	41.4	60.1	25.4	24.2	4.8
16	22.5	47.7	61.0	21.0	18.5	31.0	28.9	1.0	99.4	75.7	48.1	21.5
17	56.0	29.0	53.4	13.0	11.0	18.5	33.2	69.7	81.2	23.4	15.9	21.7
18	35.0	28.5	36.0	33.5	36.5	78.0	64.0	65.4	75.7	19.8	30.2	31.1
19	26.8	13.5	4.5	71.0	98.5	60.0	29.0	54.0	23.0	40.6	41.7	61.2
20	8.7	23.5	18.0	15.0	54.0	60.0	24.3	71.8	59.2	18.8	30.5	30.8
21	51.5	58.0	53.0	32.0	11.3	25.5	23.8	37.8	39.5	32.3	56.1	86.2
22	13.2	14.5	39.8	3.0	9.5	34.0	16.7	35.0	45.6	31.3	50.1	43.2
23	15.4	14.8	36.0	10.0	47.5	47.0	17.8	20.2	30.3	21.2	42.0	80.8
24	10.0	47.0	73.8	34.5	24.0	24.0	10.2	22.1	33.5	33.7	19.7	20.8
25	55.0	74.0	120.0	2.0	9.0	40.0	18.0	17.0	47.8	14.5	25.2	30.3
26	110.0	37.0	80.0	3.0	14.0	70.0	20.3	49.5	59.5	17.7	25.2	41.5
27	14.0	110.0	58.0	6.5	80.0	25.0	18.0	27.7	11.0	10.1	20.3	47.1
28	12.0	25.0	56.0	22.0	14.0	25.0	78.2	47.0	77.4	27.5	63.7	66.8
29	18.0	18.0	58.0	13.5	25.5	42.0	28.1	25.6	65.1	23.9	29.8	22.1
30	52.0	30.0	28.5	3.5	28.0	76.0	21.1	24.8	31.4	29.8	55.1	83.2
31	2.5	12.0	10.0	......	......	......	20.2	20.2	5.1	20.8	19.8	103.2
Sums	1092.7	1111.2	1513.5	749.1	1005.8	1459.1	946.2	1240.2	1620.4	850.8	1042.2	1338.9
Total		3717.4			3214.0			3806.8			3231.9	

TABLE G. SHOWING MILES OF WIND RECORDED AT EACH OBSERVATION IN THE YEAR.

Day.	September			October			November			December		
	7	2	10	7	2	10	7	2	10	7	2	10
1	44.6	25.4	21.0	146.2	236.1	74.6	40.1	31.9	19.4	17.5	20.4	18.1
2	26.9	59.3	46.6	80.6	39.3	42.5	27.3	33.9	17.6	28.8	47.4	21.1
3	31.2	28.8	48.5	27.8	55.9	51.5	20.2	29.4	15.8	36.4	19.1	15.1
4	81.1	40.5	74.4	51.0	30.2	29.6	163.7	257.3	42.5	22.5	16.8	24.2
5	45.7	18.6	77.4	52.8	36.9	53.6	38.9	31.1	16.6	24.1	46.2	73.0
6	22.7	37.8	48.2	31.1	22.9	82.7	38.1	78.0	106.0	97.0	95.3	82.4
7	49.3	46.5	29.8	38.6	55.1	83.5	27.2	13.4	17.8	6.5	54.8	85.6
8	55.7	33.4	30.5	57.5	21.3	13.9	55.8	12.5	18.7	55.2	62.4	87.1
9	41.6	47.4	24.7	11.6	16.4	15.6	38.7	15.8	91.6	31.4	20.7	33.9
10	37.8	38.7	37.5	72.1	35.4	25.3	44.4	62.4	81.0	34.2	31.7	10.6
11	36.0	64.9	68.2	37.5	18.4	85.5	32.5	19.9	14.1	35.6	41.5	13.7
12	110.5	68.2	90.9	28.2	16.5	18.1	29.4	27.2	23.7	41.4	40.8	20.6
13	153.2	102.2	108.7	31.9	38.6	16.5	45.5	24.9	19.5	47.8	54.9	33.3
14	42.8	37.2	68.0	31.3	17.9	4.4	46.9	11.9	219.7	37.0	46.1	17.2
15	42.1	26.8	26.4	23.9	41.3	20.8	63.6	28.1	25.7	37.2	42.9	13.5
16	23.9	43.7	39.5	20.9	91.8	56.2	28.5	19.7	11.9	42.2	47.6	124.0
17	46.8	24.0	32.7	95.2	20.2	23.1	17.5	26.5	16.3	215.4	75.2	35.0
18	31.3	32.5	24.7	32.6	15.2	70.8	66.1	14.1	28.7	19.5	80.4	6.7
19	31.9	22.9	25.4	43.9	41.8	30.3	28.6	32.9	41.6	27.1	23.0	10.5
20	9.4	15.1	25.3	83.5	99.1	24.0	51.2	8.6	20.8	26.7	17.9	17.5
21	21.8	32.2	9.8	114.0	104.3	48.0	87.7	11.4	91.8	69.7	124.2	147.1
22	34.1	28.1	17.2	28.4	30.0	24.9	35.4	31.0	14.5	84.5	77.4	77.2
23	24.7	34.3	40.3	44.6	42.7	45.3	19.5	19.5	18.6	123.6	115.7	36.5
24	51.4	33.9	20.9	64.2	24.7	24.5	25.9	68.8	53.4	24.4	18.9	15.9
25	53.0	24.2	15.1	22.5	22.7	13.3	41.8	37.6	19.8	28.4	6.9	61.8
26	45.4	50.6	48.7	52.4	33.6	34.3	38.6	31.2	23.6	204.5	215.5	177.5
27	25.2	29.6	29.5	50.5	81.0	12.5	52.3	54.7	118.5	55.9	28.1	13.8
28	27.1	27.8	23.1	19.1	33.2	23.7	28.2	42.0	29.0	36.7	20.7	18.4
29	21.4	30.4	55.8	22.2	21.0	21.6	32.3	36.8	18.8	58.1	73.1	20.0
30	55.4	60.3	70.0	37.7	27.7	62.8	21.8	32.6	16.6	75.7	38.1	40.2
31	......	......	......	33.5	30.1	19.7	......	......	......	39.7	20.4	72.9
Sums	1274.0	1165.3	1287.8	1487.3	1350.8	1003.1	1202.7	1145.1	1253.8	1684.7	1583.4	1425.9
Total	3727.1			3841.2			3601.6			4693.7		

For the year..........49880.6

TABLE II. SHOWING DIRECTION OF THE WIND AT EACH OBSERVATION IN THE YEAR.

Day.	January			February			March			April		
	7	2	10	7	2	10	7	2	10	7	2	10
1	N	SE	W	N	NE	NW	SE	SE	S	N	SE	S
2	W	S	NW	NW	N	NW	N	NE	N	S	S	S
3	SW	SE	S	NW	E	NW	N	N	N	NE	NE	N
4	NW	NE	SW	N	N	N	N	N	N	NE	E	E
5	N	NW	NW	NE	N	NW	N	N	N	N	S	S
6	W	SE	NW	N	N	N	NE	N	NE	NW	S	S
7	NW	SE	NE	NW	N	NW	SE	NE	N	NW	S	NW
8	NW	NW	S	NW	NW	N	NW	NW	NW	N	N	NE
9	NW	N	N	NE	NE	NW	NW	E	NW	N	N	N
10	N	NW	NW	N	NE	E	NW	N	E	N	N	N
11	NW	N	N	N	NE	NW	NW	NW	S	NE	E	S
12	N	N	NW	NW	S	NW	N	W	W	NE	E	SE
13	NW	N	W	NW	N	W	N	NE	S	N	N	N
14	N	N	SE	NW	N	W	N	NW	N	N	S	S
15	NW	S	NW	N	N	N	N	E	N	NW	NW	N
16	W	N	W	N	N	NE	NW	W	NW	NW	NW	N
17	NW	N	N	N	S	S	N	SE	S	N	SE	S
18	N	N	NW	W	S	SW	N	E	E	N	SE	S
19	N	N	N	N	N	W	NW	W	NW	SW	S	S
20	N	NE	NE	NW	S	S	N	SE	S	S	S	S
21	W	N	E	NW	SE	S	NW	W	NW	N	N	N
22	NW	N	NW	N	N	N	NW	NW	NW	N	S	S
23	N	E	NE	N	NW	W	W	NW	NW	NW	S	S
24	NE	E	NW	NW	NW	NW	NW	N	NW	S	SE	S
25	N	NE	NW	NW	NE	SE	NW	SE	SE	S	S	N
26	N	NE	W	N	E	NE	S	S	NW	NE	NW	W
27	W	NE	N	NW	SE	SE	W	N	N	N	S	W
28	NW	E	W	NW	S	SE	NW	SE	S	W	S	S
29	NW	N	SE	—	—	—	NW	SW	S	S	S	S
30	NW	N	SE	—	—	—	S	SW	S	NW	SE	E
31	NW	N	N	—	—	—	SE	SE	SE	—	—	—

TABLE II. SHOWING DIRECTION OF THE WIND AT EACH OBSERVATION IN THE YEAR.

	May			June			July			August		
Day.	7	2	10	7	2	10	7	2	10	7	2	10
1	SE	S	SE	S	N	W	SW	S	S	S	SW	S
2	E	S	SE	N	N	NE	SW	S	S	W	E	E
3	S	S	NE	N	NE	N	SW	SW	S	E	E	SE
4	N	S	SE	NE	NW	SE	S	S	S	S	SE	S
5	NE	N	SE	S	S	SW	S	S	S	NW	S	S
6	NE	E	N	S	S	S	W	S	S	NW	NW	S
7	NW	NE	NE	NW	S	S	SW	S	S	W	S	E
8	NW	S	W	NW	SE	S	SW	W	E	NW	N	E
9	N	S	N	S	NE	NW	E	E	E	N	NE	NW
10	N	S	S	NW	NW	SW	E	S	S	NW	S	E
11	N	SE	SE	NW	S	S	S	SE	SW	N	E	NW
12	S	NE	NE	SW	N	S	N	N	E	N	SE	SE
13	SE	E	NE	W	S	S	NE	E	E	SE	S	S
14	E	SE	N	NE	NE	SE	E	SE	SE	SW	S	S
15	W	S	SW	SE	SE	W	W	NE	N	NW	S	S
16	NW	S	S	S	SE	S	N	S	S	N	N	S
17	NW	N	NE	S	SE	SW	S	S	S	S	S	S
18	NW	NE	E	NE	SE	SE	S	S	S	S	S	SW
19	SE	NE	N	S	S	S	SW	S	SE	NW	NW	SE
20	NE	E	SE	NW	SE	E	SW	S	NE	SW	SW	SW
21	NE	E	S	NE	SE	S	W	S	S	S	S	S
22	S	NW	N	S	S	E	S	S	SE	S	S	S
23	NE	N	E	SE	E	E	N	NE	NW	SE	E	E
24	NW	S	S	E	S	NW	NW	SE	S	NE	NW	NW
25	S	S	S	NW	S	W	S	S	S	NW	E	S
26	S	S	SW	W	SE	E	W	SE	N	SE	NE	SE
27	S	NE	E	E	NE	E	N	SE	E	SE	S	S
28	NW	N	N	N	SE	E	N	SE	E	S	S	S
29	N	SE	S	E	S	SW	E	E	SE	NW	NE	E
30	S	SE	NW	SW	S	S	SE	N	SW	NE	S	S
31	NW	S	S	—	—	—	SW	SE	S	S	S	S

TABLE II. SHOWING DIRECTION OF THE WIND AT EACH OBSERVATION IN THE YEAR.

Day.	September			October			November			December		
	7	2	10	7	2	10	7	2	10	7	2	10
1	NE	SE	S	S	SE	NE	N	SE	E	NE	SE	SW
2	S	NW	NE	N	NE	NE	NW	NE	E	NW	N	NW
3	N	E	S	N	N	N	SW	N	W	W	NE	SE
4	SE	S	SE	N	NE	E	N	NW	NW	W	NE	NW
5	NW	SE	NE	N	N	N	N	SE	NE	NW	NE	N
6	N	E	E	N	N	N	N	NW	N	N	N	NW
7	N	NE	E	N	E	N	N	E	SW	NW	S	S
8	N	N	N	N	N	N	NW	S	W	S	S	NW
9	N	N	N	N	N	N	E	N	E	W	SE	NW
10	N	N	NE	N	N	N	N	N	N	N	NW	NW
11	N	N	N	N	SE	SE	SW	E	E	NW	NE	NW
12	N	N	NW	N	N	E	W	NE	W	NW	N	NW
13	N	NW	N	N	N	N	N	E	N	NW	N	NW
14	SW	S	N	N	N	N	W	W	W	NW	NE	NW
15	N	NE	E	E	N	N	W	NE	NW	NW	N	N
16	NE	N	NE	N	N	N	W	NE	NW	N	NW	NW
17	N	E	E	N	N	N	NW	NE	N	N	N	NE
18	N	N	NE	N	N	N	N	E	NE	NW	NE	NE
19	N	NE	NE	N	N	N	NW	E	N	NW	E	E
20	SE	N	SE	N	N	W	W	S	N	W	N	NW
21	N	SE	SE	NW	N	NW	N	N	N	N	NW	NW
22	N	N	W	N	SE	E	N	SE	SE	NW	NW	N
23	NE	E	NE	W	N	N	W	S	NW	W	NW	NW
24	N	N	N	N	N	W	W	NW	NW	NW	NE	SW
25	NE	NE	W	W	SE	SE	NW	N	NW	W	SE	S
26	NW	N	NW	N	NE	N	NW	NE	NW	N	NW	N
27	W	S	SE	N	NW	NW	W	N	N	N	N	E
28	N	S	SE	W	SW	NW	N	NE	N	N	N	NE
29	E	S	S	W	S	NW	NW	NE	N	N	NW	NE
30	S	S	S	NW	SE	NE	N	E	S	W	NW	SE
31	·			NW	NE	N	--	—	--	SW	NW	N

TABLE I. SHOWING MILES OF WIND AND PREVAILING DIRECTION FOR EVERY DAY IN THE YEAR.

Day.	January		February		March		April	
	Miles	P. D.	Miles	P. D.	Miles	P. D.	Miles	P. D.
1	80.7	S	188.4	NE	93.0	SE	156.0	S
2	82.1	SW	143.5	N	250.5	N	275.5	S
3	90.9	SW	120.5	NE	262.2	N	235.0	NE
4	123.7	W	173.0	N	115.0	N	86.0	NE
5	250.1	NW	162.3	N	153.2	N	108.0	E
6	88.3	NE	99.3	NE	229.0	N	117.0	SW
7	69.7	S	93.0	NW	92.1	E	110.5	SW
8	93.8	W	338.4	NW	222.5	NW	176.9	NE
9	255.5	NW	172.4	NW	109.5	W	212.0	SW
10	236.5	NW	150.8	NE	40.3	N	104.0	N
11	173.0	N	131.7	N	218.0	W	224.0	NW
12	121.4	N	115.9	W	58.7	W	126.0	E
13	74.2	N	145.7	W	67.1	W	83.5	W
14	142.7	NE	183.0	NW	158.2	NW	109.5	NW
15	88.5	NE	196.3	NW	208.0	N	74.5	W
16	143.6	NE	243.9	N	282.3	NW	413.0	NW
17	195.4	NW	126.4	NE	85.5	W	132.0	E
18	294.4	NW	81.0	NE	148.5	N	120.0	S
19	149.1	N	200.0	N	69.2	W	176.5	S
20	158.2	N	102.9	SW	144.5	W	193.5	S
21	73.0	N	127.5	W	198.5	W	286.5	NW
22	64.1	N	157.0	N	206.5	W	172.5	E
23	201.9	NW	540.6	NW	183.0	W	103.5	S
24	68.6	NE	260.7	NE	339.5	NW	267.0	S
25	72.5	NE	133.8	NE	173.5	S	297.0	S
26	113.7	N	121.5	NE	183.0	SW	252.5	S
27	99.3	NW	95.5	E	294.0	W	110.7	SW
28	81.1	NE	113.1	S	205.5	W	160.1	S
29	144.8	N			253.5	SW	138.0	S
30	108.9	NW			320.5	N	69.6	SE
31	252.7	N	......	......	115.0	SE	......	......
Max.	294.4	NW	540.6	NW	339.5	NW	413.0	NW
Mini.	64.1	N	81.0	NE	40.3	N	69.6	SE

TABLE I. SHOWING MILES OF WIND AND PREVAILING DIRECTION FOR EVERY DAY IN THE YEAR.

Day.	May		June		July		August	
	Miles	P. D.	Miles	P. D.	Miles	P. D.	Miles	P. D.
1	100.1	SE	26.0	W	197.0	S	96.4	SE
2	76.1	SE	138.1	N	186.9	S	72.4	N
3	136.7	SE	62.0	N	215.5	S	110.8	NE
4	113.5	SE	207.5	NE	176.0	S	85.2	S
5	155.5	NE	227.5	N	91.0	SW	106.8	N
6	131.4	NE	99.8	S	69.7	SW	69.8	NE
7	90.8	N	114.5	NE	142.7	SW	67.4	SW
8	97.1	NW	114.5	N	200.0	W	92.5	NE
9	108.4	E	111.8	SW	98.5	E	150.1	NW
10	126.5	S	185.5	NW	49.8	E	114.7	E
11	60.8	SW	154.5	SW	82.2	S	102.0	SE
12	97.1	E	97.5	SW	131.4	E	89.7	SE
13	180.0	NE	100.0	S	119.3	E	115.7	S
14	110.1	E	77.0	E	93.9	E	77.0	SW
15	191.2	SW	114.0	N	115.9	N	54.4	SW
16	131.2	S	70.5	NW	129.3	SE	140.3	SW
17	138.4	NW	42.5	E	184.1	S	61.0	N
18	97.5	N	148.0	SE	205.1	S	81.1	E
19	44.8	E	233.5	S	106.0	SW	143.5	NE
20	50.2	E	138.0	N	155.5	S	89.1	S
21	142.5	SE	68.8	SE	101.1	SW	174.6	S
22	67.5	W	46.5	SE	97.9	S	124.6	S
23	66.2	N	104.5	E	68.3	W	144.0	SE
24	130.8	SW	82.5	S	65.8	W	73.2	N
25	249.0	S	51.0	SW	82.8	S	70.0	NE
26	227.0	S	87.0	NW	135.3	S	84.4	E
27	182.0	SE	61.5	S	56.7	NE	77.5	S
28	93.0	NW	61.0	E	202.6	NE	158.0	S
29	94.0	E	81.0	E	118.8	E	75.8	NE
30	110.5	SE	107.5	S	80.3	SE	168.1	SE
31	24.5	W	......	......	45.5	NW	152.8	S
Max.	249.0	W	233.5	S	215.5	S	174.6	S
Mani.	24.5	S	26.0	W	45.5	NW	54.4	SW

TABLE I. SHOWING MILES OF WIND AND PREVAILING DIRECTION FOR EVERY DAY IN THE YEAR.

Day.	September		October		November		December	
	Miles	P. D.	Miles	P. D.	Miles	P. D.	Miles	P. D.
1	91.0	E	386.9	S	91.4	NE	56.0	SW
2	132.8	E	102.4	NE	78.8	NW	97.3	N
3	108.5	NE	135.2	NE	65.4	N	70.6	SW
4	146.0	S	110.8	NE	463.3	NW	63.5	NE
5	141.7	NE	143.3	N	86.6	NE	143.3	N
6	108.7	NE	86.7	NW	126.7	N	274.7	N
7	125.6	NE	127.2	N	58.4	N	146.9	W
8	119.6	NE	92.7	N	77.0	N	204.7	SW
9	113.7	N	43.6	N	146.1	N	86.0	SW
10	114.0	N	133.8	N	187.8	N	76.5	N
11	169.1	SE	91.4	NE	66.5	N	90.8	N
12	269.6	NE	62.8	NE	80.3	N	102.8	N
13	364.1	N	87.0	N	92.9	NE	136.0	N
14	148.0	SE	53.6	N	278.5	NW	100.3	N
15	95.5	NE	86.0	N	117.4	NW	93.6	N
16	107.1	NE	108.4	N	55.1	NW	213.8	NW
17	103.5	NE	138.5	N	60.3	W	325.6	N
18	88.5	NE	118.6	N	108.9	NE	56.6	N
19	80.2	NE	116.0	N	103.1	N	60.6	N
20	49.8	NE	206.6	N	80.6	W	62.1	N
21	63.8	E	266.3	NW	190.9	N	341.0	NW
22	79.4	N	83.3	NE	80.9	NE	239.1	NW
23	99.3	NE	132.6	NW	57.6	SW	275.8	NW
24	115.2	N	113.4	NW	148.1	NW	59.2	SW
25	92.3	NE	58.5	S	99.2	NW	96.6	SW
26	144.7	NW	120.3	NE	93.4	N	597.5	NW
27	84.3	NE	91.0	NW	98.8	N	99.8	NE
28	78.0	SW	76.0	W	99.8	N	75.8	N
29	107.6	S	64.8	SW	87.1	N	151.2	W
30	185.7	S	108.2	NE	70.4	SW	154.0	SW
31	......		85.3	N		......	142.0	W
Max.	364.1	N	386.9	S	463.3	NW	597.5	NW
Min.	49.8	NE	43.6	N	55.1	NW	56.0	SW

TABLE K. SHOWING THE NUMBER OF TIMES THE WIND WAS RECORDED IN VARIOUS DIRECTIONS IN EACH MONTH, AT THE HOURS 7 A.M. 2 P.M. AND 10 P.M.

	N			NE			E			SE			S			SW			W			NW		
	7	2	10	7	2	10	7	2	10	7	2	10	7	2	10	7	2	10	7	2	10	7	2	10
January	11	14	6	1	5	3	0	3	1	0	4	3	0	2	2	1	0	1	5	0	5	13	8	10
February	12	11	5	2	5	2	0	2	1	0	2	3	0	5	3	0	0	1	1	0	4	13	3	9
March	11	7	8	1	3	1	0	3	2	3	6	2	2	1	8	0	2	0	2	4	1	12	5	9
April	12	5	8	5	1	1	0	3	2	0	5	1	5	13	15	1	0	0	1	0	2	6	3	1
May	5	4	6	5	4	5	2	4	2	3	4	6	7	13	7	0	0	2	1	0	1	8	1	1
June	3	3	1	4	2	1	3	1	6	8	9	3	8	11	10	2	1	4	2	0	3	6	2	2
July	5	2	2	2	3	1	4	3	6	7	7	4	7	15	15	8	2	2	4	0	2	1	0	1
August	4	2	6	4	5	0	1	5	6	2	2	4	8	14	16	2	0	2	1	0	2	8	3	3
September	17	11	7	2	4	3	1	4	4	2	3	5	1	0	4	1	0	0	4	1	2	2	1	2
October	22	18	17	0	8	2	1	0	3	0	5	1	0	1	0	0	1	0	4	0	2	3	1	4
November	12	6	10	0	7	3	1	6	4	0	3	2	0	3	1	2	0	1	8	1	4	3	3	7
December	9	9	5	1	7	4	0	1	2	0	3	2	1	2	2	1	0	2	7	6	0	12	9	14
Year	123	92	74	26	52	30	13	36	40	15	53	36	41	96	83	18	6	15	38	6	24	91	34	63
Totals	289			108			89			104			210			39			68			188		

TABLE L. THE NUMBER OF TIMES THE WIND REGISTERED A VELOCITY OF 20 MILES PER HOUR OR OVER FROM VARIOUS DIRECTIONS.

Month	N	NE	E	SE	S	SW	W	NW	TOTAL
January	3	...	...	...	...	...	...	1	4
February	...	...	...	...	...	...	...	3	3
March	4	...	...	...	3	...	...	4	11
April	2	1	...		1	...		2	6
May	...	...	...		2	...	...	1	3
June	...	...				1	1	1	3
July	...	...	...		...			...	0
August	...	...			1			...	1
September	2	...			...			...	2
October	1	...						1	2
November	1	...						...	1
December	...	...	...	...	...	...	...	4	4
Total	13	1	0	0	7	1	1	17	40

TABLE M. SHOWING TOTAL MILES OF WIND IN EACH MONTH FROM VARIOUS DIRECTIONS.

Month	N	NE	E	SE	S	SW	W	NW
January	1980.4	235.7	73.5	126.2	114.4	98.6	214.8	1348.8
February	1782.9	278.6	159.2	127.0	302.8	......	91.7	1984.9
March	1512.4	457.1	146.3	210.3	932.8	406.1	664.0	1305.8
April	615.1	426.5	53.5	595.5	2067.4	290.7	327.0	543.9
May	284.8	650.4	455.2	331.9	1461.5	246.5	194.3	92.8
June	173.0	292.9	394.8	373.3	1066.5	339.5	266.0	308.0
July	177.8	328.7	289.4	419.1	1856.6	635.7	65.5	34.0
August	413.1	175.9	311.0	407.0	1352.7	163.9	146.1	262.2
September	1756.3	728.5	198.6	319.0	140.7	81.1	170.7	332.2
October	1507.8	556.6	251.4	13.3	33.2	121.1	616.3	741.5
November	1555.1	248.2	156.2	67.2	64.7	19.5	179.6	1371.1
December	808.3	114.7	44.7	188.0	58.1	477.3	120.2	2882.4
Total	12567.0	4493.8	2533.8	3177.8	9451.4	2880.0	3066.2	11210.6

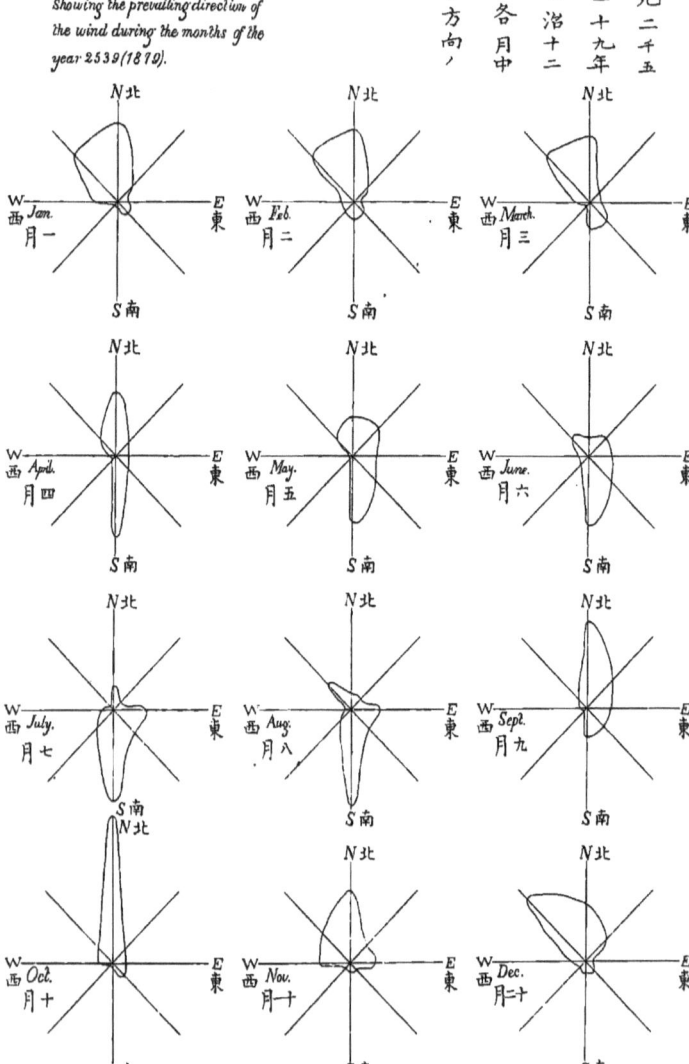

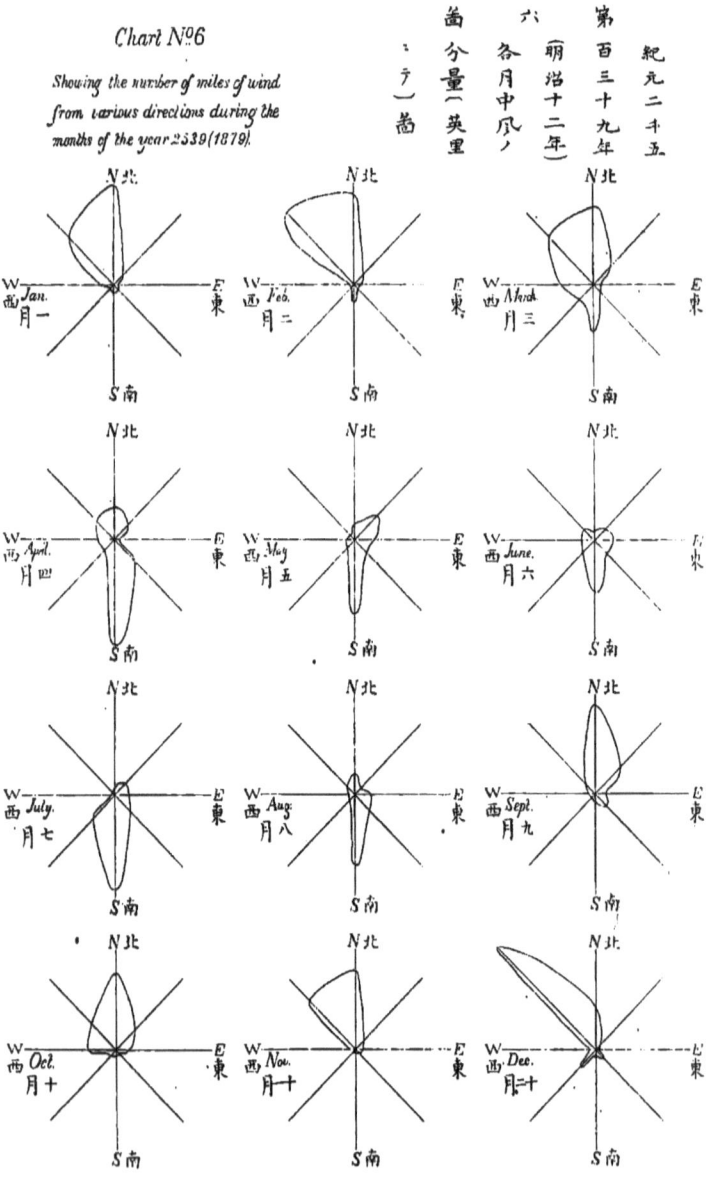

Chart Nº 6

Showing the number of miles of wind from various directions during the months of the year 2539 (1879).

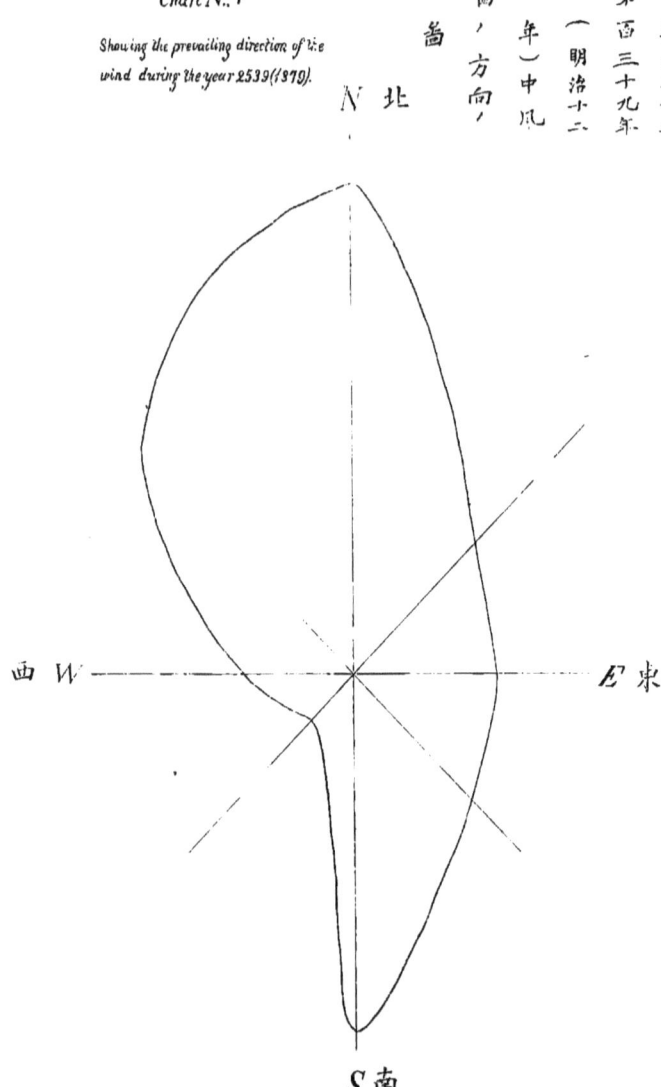

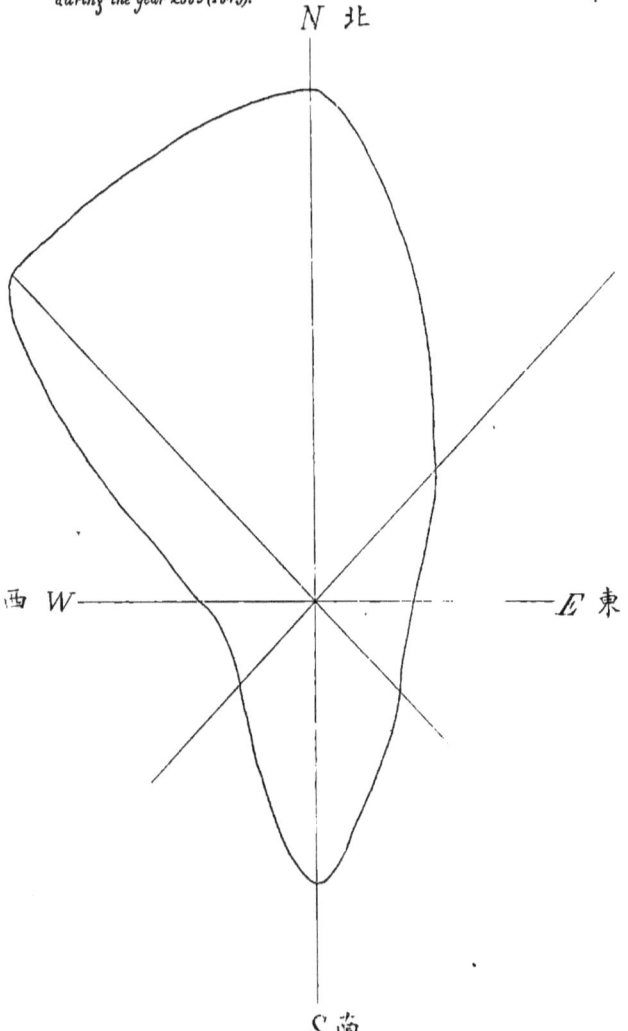

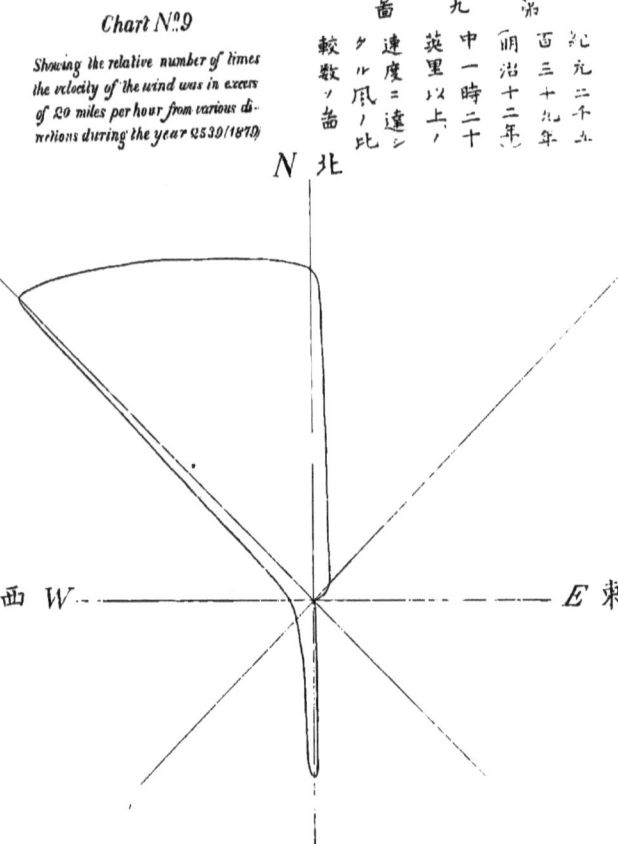

Chart No 10

Showing 1st the general course of the wind during the year 2539 (1879),
2nd the number of miles of wind during the months of the year.

第一紀元二千五百三十九年(明治十二年)中凡ノ惣方向ノ蓋第二同年各月中凡ノ分量(一次里ニテノ蓋

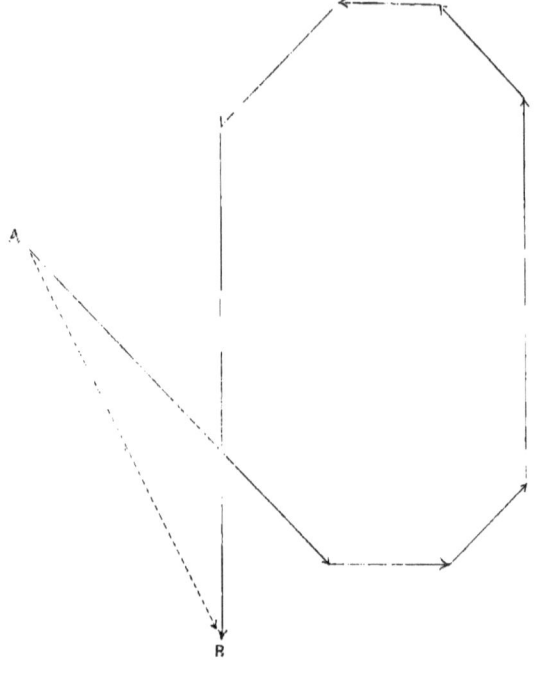

RAIN.

Table N exhibits the rainfall in inches for every day of the year. A graphical representation will be found on the two pages of Chart No. 11, where the horizontal lines are drawn equal in length in inches to the rainfall for each day. Table O contains the rainfall by months, classified according to the prevailing direction of the wind during the fall. In each vertical column will be found the number of days on which the rain fell, the wind being in a given direction and also the total amount of rain in inches. Both of the results are shown in a more striking manner in Charts No. 12 and No. 13. The first shows, relatively, the number of times the rain has come from different directions and the second the actual inches of rain from various directions for each month of the year. A comparison of these curves with those already given of a similar character representing wind alone, indicates some interesting relations and when a longer series of observations shall have been completed important deductions can doubtless be made. Charts No. 14 and No. 15 exhibit the same facts for the year, being constructed from the totals of table O. A comparison of these points clearly to a conclusion similar to that reached in regard to the wind ; that is that not only have by far the greater number of rainstorms come from the North and North-west but that it is particularly from the North-west that the heavy rains have come. In table P will be found the total fall of rain with the number of days on which rain fell and the number of clear days for each month and for the year. By a clear day is meant one during which not more than one fifth of the sky is covered with clouds at any one time. Of the total 58.975 inches of rain for the entire year, the greatest amount for any one month was 9.606 inches for June. In May and June rain fell on 33 days, the total amount being 18.409 inches. Less rain fell in November than in any other month, although the amount is only a trifle less than that for January. The greatest amount of rain on any one day was 3.96 inches on June 4. The maximum number of days in succession on which rain fell was 11,—from May 25 to June 4. The maximum number in succession on which rain did not fall was 14,—from January 1 to January 14. The maximum number of clear days in succession was 10,—from January 1 to January 10.

Snow fell on four days, as follows ;

January	27	.125 inches (melted)	
,,	28	.440	,, ,,
February	7	.058	,, ,,
,,	11	trace.	
	Total amount	.623	,, ,,

Chart No. 16 exhibits in the first diagram the proportion of clear, cloudy and rainy days in each month, the open space representing clear days, that crossed by one set of lines cloudy, and that by two sets of lines the days on which rain fell. The second diagram shows the total inches of rain in each month of the year.

Tables R and S exhibit percentages of humidity as computed from the observations of the wet and dry bulb thermometers. It will be observed that a very high degree of humidity exists throughout the whole year. The minimum percentage is 40 which was observed in December. I am inclined to the opinion, however, that the results obtained from these hygrometrical observations are not entirely trustworthy and during the present year the observations will be checked by those made with other instruments. The tables are inserted here, however, for comparison with those of future reports.

TABLE N. SHOWING RAINFALL IN INCHES FOR EVERY DAY OF THE YEAR.

Day	January	February	March	April	May	June	July	August	September	October	November	December
1	0	0	.125	0	0	40.8	0	0	.005	.470	0	0
2	0	trace	.710	0	0	30.0	0	0	0	.383	0	0
3	0	0	.618	.790	.052	.322	0	0	0	0	0	0
4	0	0	.300	0	trace	3.960	0	0	.700	0	0	0
5	0	0	.490	trace	0	0	.160	0	.050	0	0	trace
6	0	.040	.735	0	trace	0	trace	.110	.195	.340	0	1.272
7	0	.058 .174	.030	trace	1.910	0	0	.168	.010	.060	0	trace
8	0	.035	0	0	0	0	.002	.530	.005	trace	0	0
9	0	0	0	.550	0	1.243	.0012	.424	.300	trace	trace	0
10	0	0	0	.073	0	trace	trace	0	.300	0	1.200	0
11	0	trace	0	.050	.070	0	.002	.177	.730	0	.028	0
12	0	0	0	0	.340	.050	.855	0	1.230	0	0	0
13	0	0	0	.206	.408	0	.005	0	1.660	trace	0	0
14	0	0	.050	.050	.001	0	trace	0	0	.350	trace	0
15	.272	.216	0	1.207	0	.342	1.250	0	0	.260	0	0
16	.687	.227	0	0	0	.285	0	0	.220	0	0	.920
17	0	0	trace	0	1.530	0	0	0	.202	0	0	.520
18	0	0	trace	0	0	trace	0	0	0	0	0	0
19	0	.402	0	0	.060	.117	0	0	0	trace	trace	0
20	0	0	.400	.665	.168	trace	0	0	.410	1.560	.170	0
21	0	0	trace	.205	0	0	0	0	.040	0	.640	0
22	.010	.060	trace	0	.108	.550	trace	0	.028	0	0	0
23	.310	2.570	0	0	.001	.250	trace	1.780	.065	.310	0	0
24	0	0	0	0	0	trace	trace	trace	trace	.240	0	0
25	0	.130	0	.390	trace	0	0	0	trace	0	0	0
26	0	.060	.190	.200	.040	.110	0	0	0	.480	0	0
27	.125	0	0	0	.684	1.220	.120	0	0	2.180	0	0
28	.440	0	0	0	2.005	.495	.001	0	0	0	0	0
29	0	......	0	0	.005	0	.100	0	0	0	0	1.030
30	.315	......	1.350	0	1.100	0	trace	0	0	0	0	trace
31	.545	......	0	......	.208	......	trace	0	......	0	......	0

TABLE 6 SHOWING THE NUMBER OF TIMES RAIN FELL AND THE TOTAL AMOUNT OF RAIN IN INCHES WITH THE WIND IN VARIOUS DIRECTIONS FOR EACH MONTH AND FOR THE YEAR.

	N		NE		E		SE		S		SW		W		NW	
	No.	Amt.	No.	Amt.	No.	Amt.	No.	Amt.	No.	Amt.	No.	Amt.	No.	Amt.	No.	Amt.
January	2	.750	1	.010	0	0	1	.272	0	0	0	0	0	0	4	1.025
February	5	1.218	1	.010	0	0	2	.130	0	0	0	0	0	0	6	3.246
March	5	2.144	2	.510	1	.001	1	.125	1	.001	1	.001	2	.500	2	1.400
April	3	.324	2	1.050	0	0	1	.050	3	1.056	0	0	3	2.132	2	.203
May	2	.173	5	1.484	2	1.876	1	.052	5	1.480	5	.108	1	1.550	2	2.006
June	0	0	2	.817	2	.666	2	.351	1	1.220	2	1.103	3	4.011	3	1.544
July	1	.005	2	.002	2	.224	3	.004	3	.162	2	.002	3	2.105	1	.001
August	1	.421	2	.178	2	2.330	1	.140	1	.168	0	0	0	0	0	0
September	9	3.264	3	.555	0	0	2	1.530	0	0	1	.410	0	0	3	.143
October	8	1.666	2	.255	1	.260	0	0	0	0	0	0	0	0	4	4.051
November	2	1.591	0	0	1	.001	1	0	0	0	0	0	1	.028	3	.811
December	0	0	0	0	0	0	0	.001	0	0	0	0	0	0	5	3.744
Year	38	10.906	22	5.460	12	5.426	14	2.855	11	4.087	10	1.624	21	10.416	35	18.875

TABLE P. SHOWING THE NUMBER OF DAYS ON WHICH RAIN FELL, THE TOTAL AMOUNT OF RAIN AND THE NUMBER OF CLEAR DAYS FOR EACH MONTH FOR THE YEAR.

Month	Amount	No. of days on which Rain fell	No. of Clear days
January	2,089	6	15
February	4,575	11	15
March	5,002	15	16
April	1,638	13	13
May	8,803	20	7
June	9,606	18	6
July	2,507	18	7
August	3,220	7	10
September	6,102	19	8
October	6,647	15	7
November	2,041	7	18
December	3,745	7	21
Total	58,975	156	143

TABLE B. GIVING THE MEAN PERCENTAGE OF HUMIDITY FOR EVERY DAY OF THE YEAR.

Day	January	February	March	April	May	June	July	August	September	October	November	December
1	72	73	100	79	91	100	83	80	92	98	85	93
2	76	71	100	81	97	97	86	87	90	92	87	89
3	77	63	99	96	94	100	88	84	76	87	79	89
4	68	67	98	79	93	100	85	83	91	88	74	91
5	91	65	100	82	93	89	93	83	94	85	82	91
6	98	81	93	92	89	84	96	89	98	100	76	100
7	88	98	89	88	98	88	88	95	95	98	81	86
8	76	76	66	73	87	91	85	91	95	94	81	76
9	66	77	65	100	75	100	94	97	98	94	84	67
10	58	71	82	94	82	87	95	86	100	80	100	89
11	71	81	67	65	92	91	96	90	100	81	86	87
12	86	76	87	73	100	91	92	88	100	91	89	89
13	78	77	85	96	90	97	84	92	98	85	91	89
14	72	72	68	85	93	92	87	82	83	96	86	93
15	84	94	68	99	87	100	97	85	82	94	76	90
16	64	85	74	77	85	94	88	87	95	71	81	99
17	69	81	80	75	100	97	83	91	90	81	83	88
18	69	86	91	89	98	95	80	86	87	88	90	96
19	79	90	94	88	98	95	80	80	87	92	92	79
20	87	86	94	98	93	96	84	80	98	99	93	98
21	76	76	88	66	85	94	80	86	93	84	71	80
22	83	95	71	78	100	100	83	88	91	83	84	81
23	82	79	65	89	96	98	83	93	90	98	88	79
24	71	68	58	89	85	96	83	94	88	94	86	91
25	63	88	68	100	96	94	86	96	90	90	85	92
26	69	84	71	79	91	96	75	86	71	82	81	76
27	82	82	68	79	97	98	86	91	83	98	79	81
28	83	89	74	87	98	95	92	96	95	81	84	93
29	67		77	88	91	88	89	98	85	80	85	98
30	95		73	93	100	88	91	94	87	82	91	84
31	67	......	88	......	97	......	91	94	......	88	......	57

TABLE 8. GIVING THE MEAN, MAXIMUM AND
MINIMUM PERCENTAGES OF HUMIDITY
FOR EACH MONTH.

Month	Means	Maximum	Minimum
January	76	100	49
February	80	100	42
March	81	100	50
April	85	100	56
May	93	100	63
June	94	100	74
July	87	100	68
August	89	100	66
September	87	100	51
October	89	100	59
November	82	100	60
December	87	100	40

Chart No. 11

Showing the rainfall in inches for every day of the year 2539 (1879)

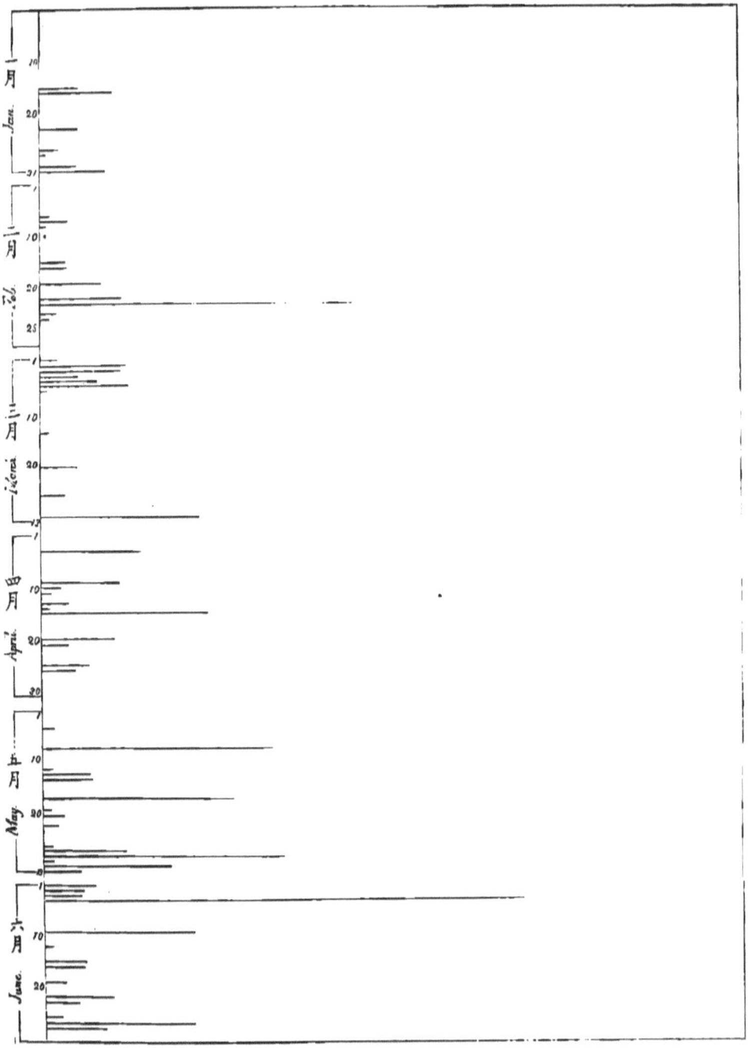

紀元二千五第百三十九年（明治十二年）一各日雨ノ分箇量（英寸ニテ）ノ箇

第十一圖

紀元二千五百三十九年(明治十二年)各日雨ノ分量(英寸、ミ)ノ圖

Chart No. 11

Showing the rainfall in inches for every day of the year 2539 (1879).

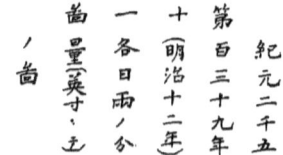

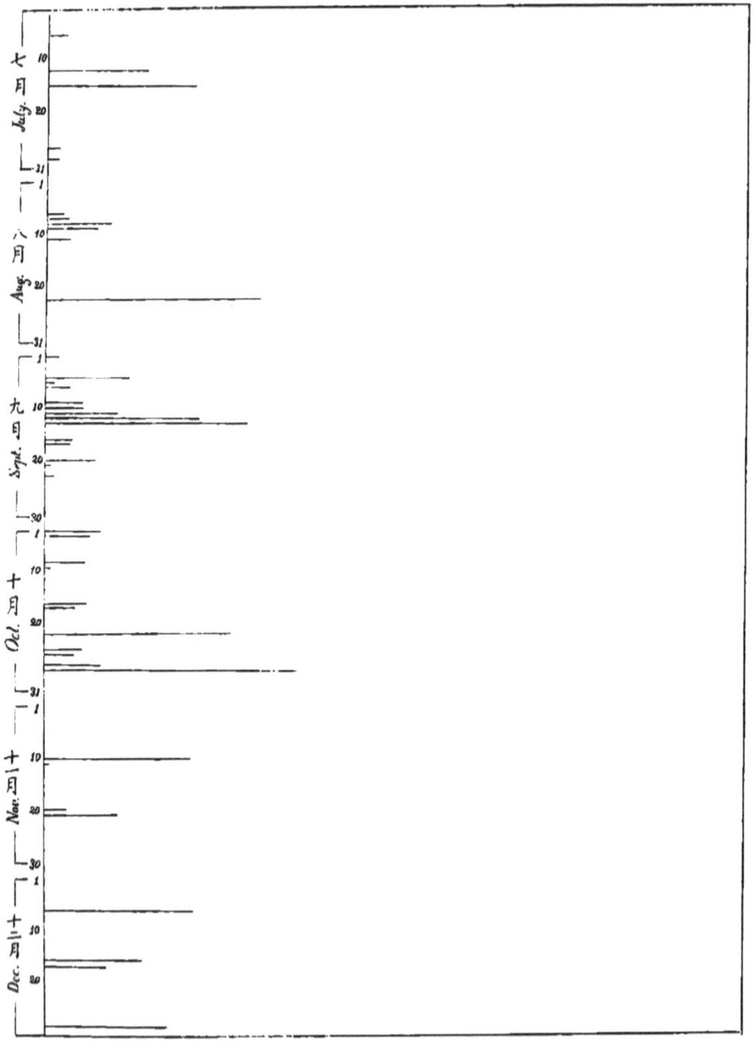

5

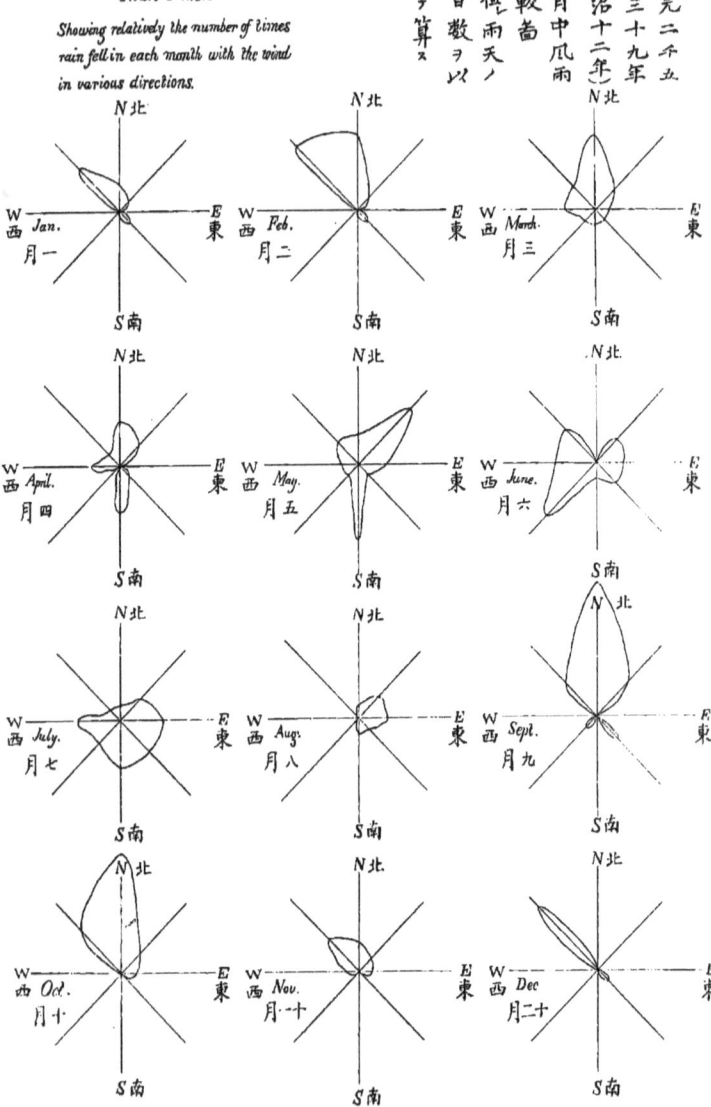

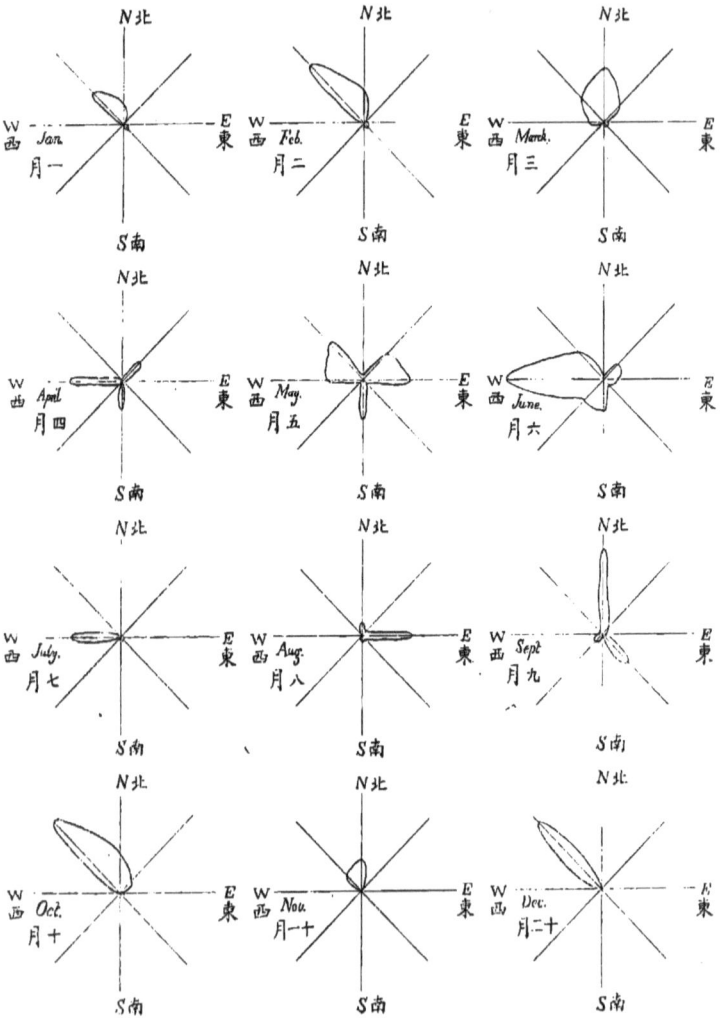

Chart No. 14.

Showing relatively the number of times
rain fell during the year with the wind
in various directions

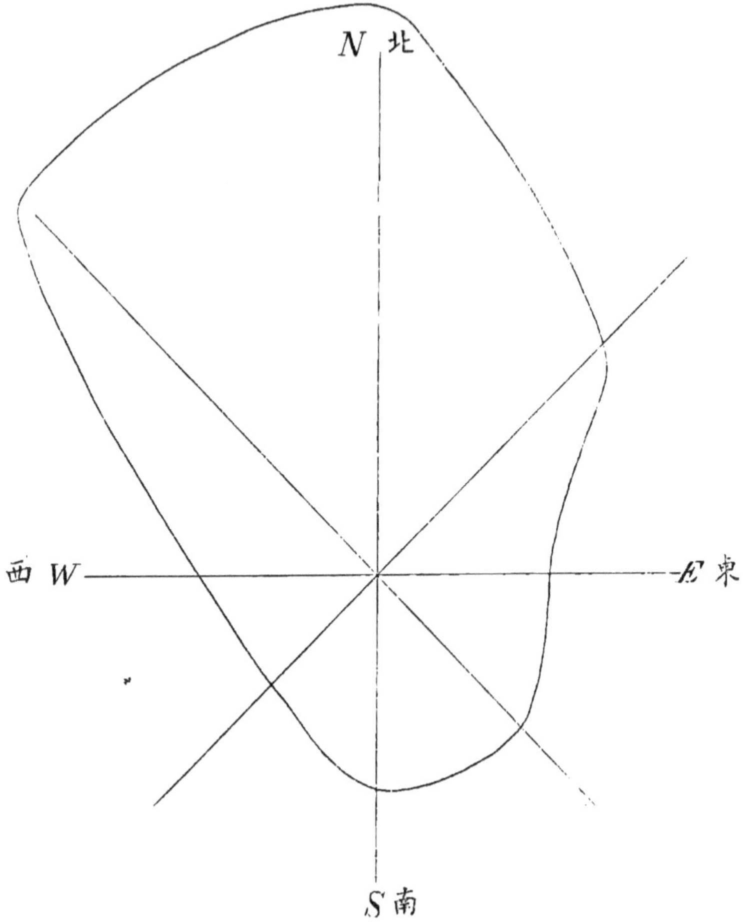

第 十 四 圖
(明治十二年)
圖中風雨比較
紀元二千五百三十九年
但雨天ノ日數ヲ以テ算ス

N 北
W 西 ——————— 東 E
S 南

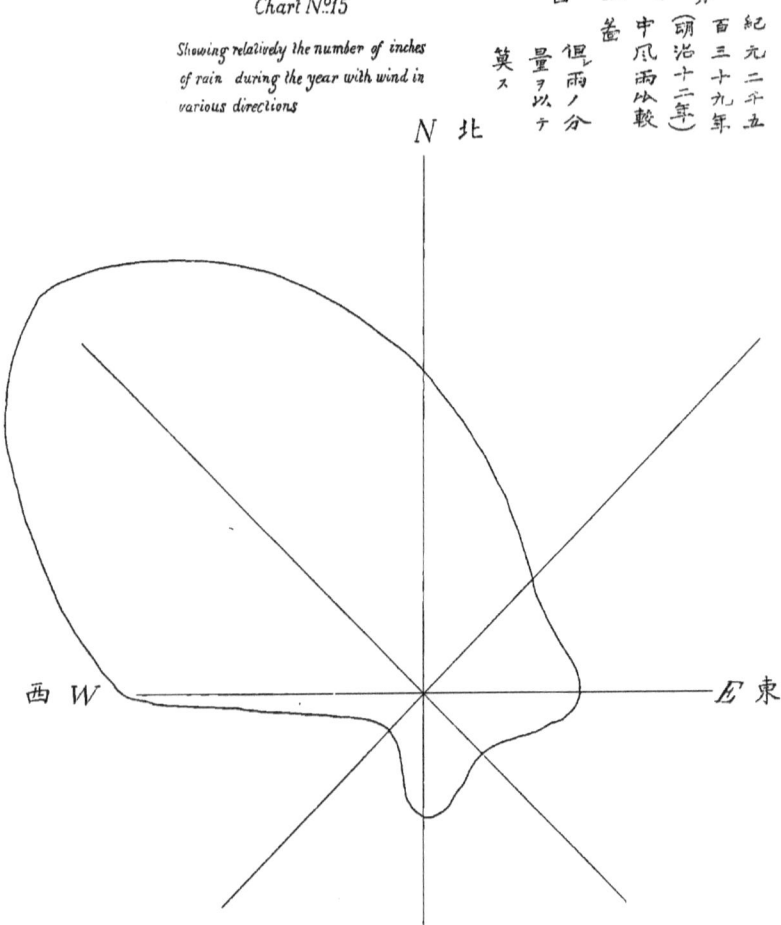

Chart N°16

Showing 1st the relative number of rainy, cloudy and clear days in each month and the total rainfall in inches for each month

第十六冊

第一紀元二千五百三十九年（明治十二年）中晴天、曇天、雨天ノ日數比較竝ニ第二回各月中降雨ノ全量（英尺）ヲ備ス

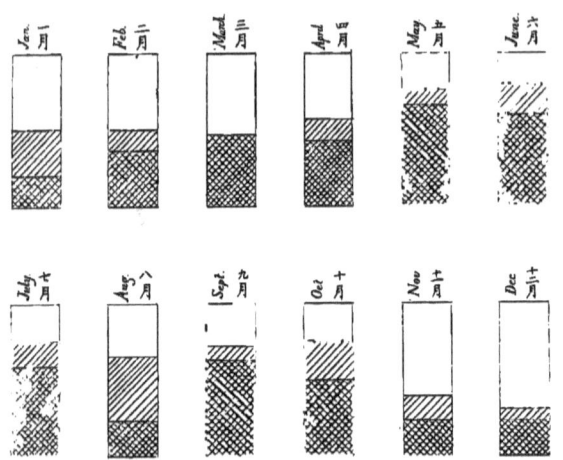

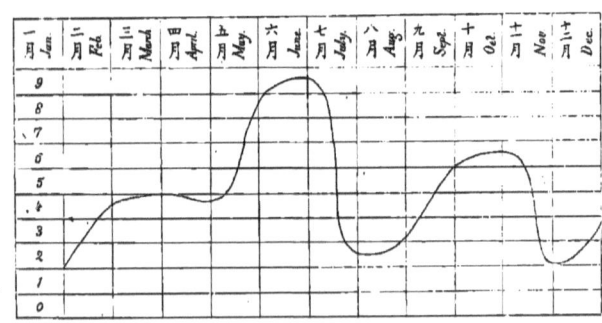

CONCLUSION.

It will be remembered that the foregoing tables and charts represent the results of only a single year's observations. To enter upon any extensive discussion of these results would be useless. Before attempting any important generalizations concerning the local meteorology it will be necessary to wait for a further accummulation of facts. Some general principles seem to be so clearly indicated by these results that I have ventured in a few instances, to call attention to them. Most of the important results of the year's work are here collected and classified for convenience of future comparison and it is believed that each year will add to their value. It is hoped that the efficiency and value of the work may be increased during the next year by carrying out some improvements already proposed and by making a few additions to the equipment which I will here suggest.

During the past year the necessity of duplicating several of the most important instruments has been shown. It is to be expected that now and then an instrument will become disabled by accident or otherwise and this may sometimes cause serious interruption to the work. The value of meteorological observations depends on their regularity and continuity. Situated as we are, so far from ordinary sources of supply for such material, the only way of preventing such interruptions seems to be by keeping duplicates of the principal instruments on hand at all times as far as possible. There is a double advantage in this, for results obtained from the observation of two or more similar instruments are much more reliable than those from a single one. I would therefore recommend that a supply of thermometers and an extra barometer be obtained as soon as possible. A wind vane is also much needed, to make us independant of the records of the anemograph, which, owing to its great inertia is believed to be neither sensitive nor extremely accurate. Without great expense an ordinary light vane may be made self recording which would add greatly to its value. As the wind is one the most interesting and important meteorological phenomena of this locality it would be extremely desirable to erect a self-registering anemometer, such, for instance, as is in use in the meteorological stations of the United States Signal Service. If desired, a registering apparatus can be easily added to the anemometer now in use.

It is intended during the present year to begin a series of observations upon Earth-temperatures. The temperature at and immediately below the surface of the earth will be ascertained by means of thermometers and for greater depths, down, perhaps, to a depth of 40 feet it is proposed to use the thermo-electric method. Some preliminary experiments upon this method are now in progress in the physical labomtory of the University with results that give fair promise of success in its use. Early in the present year a telegraph line connecting the Observatory with the physical laboratory was completed which will without doubt prove to be a great convenience. One of the special considerations which led to its construction was the desirability of taking advantage of the exceptionally favorable conditions for the study of the velocity of sound. At 12 M. of each day a time gun is fired which can be distinctly heard at both the Observatory and the University. Although the location of the gun is not precisely in the prolongation of the line joining these two points, the deviation is not great and the necessary reduction can be made with ease. Observations upon the direction and velocity of the wind, the temperature and the humidity of the atmosphere will be made at the time at both stations and the time of the arrival of the sound at each will be recorded on a chronograph. It is expected that in this way a large number of observations upon the transmission of sound under widely varying meteorological conditions will in time be secured, which may contribute somewhat to the solution of a problem of very considerable importance. Although not a question pertaining strictly to meteorology it is one of great interest and it is hoped that a considerable series of results may be ready for the next annual report.

There is another phenomenon which, although not strictly meteorological, is of such interest and importance to all residents of Tokio, and indeed of Japan, as to demand attention and investigation whenever and wherever possible. Much attention has already been given in this country to the study of the phenomena of earthquakes and a great variety of seismographs have been constructed and used in their observation. Some of these are very complex, being designed to register several of the elements of the phenomenon, while others are more simple in their construction. It is, perhaps, not too much to say that in spite of the efforts already made our knowledge of earthquake phenomena is still very indefinite and uncertain. While I would not recommend the construction or purchase of any complex registering apparatus for use in the meteorological observatory, I regard it as highly desirable to erect some simple indicator, which may not be liable to get out of order and which, in connection with some of the time cylinders in use, or to be used in the observatory, may indicate the time of the shock, certainly, or with the smallest chance of failure. If we shall succeed in this one determination with unfailing certainty the result will be a contribution of no small value and well worth the trouble and expense which will be rendered necessary.

www.ingramcontent.com/pod-product-compliance
Lightning Source LLC
Chambersburg PA
CBHW051736300426
44115CB00007B/593